MW01644668

OD·DOMESTIC OD·EXPEDITED OD·PEOPLE OD·GLOBAL OD·TECHNOLOGY

HELPING THE WORLD KEEP PROMISES™

OLD DOMINION FREIGHT LINE
OLD DOMINION FREIGHT LINE, INC.
2442148
MC-8571

OD·DOMESTIC OD·EXPEDITED OD·PEOPLE OD·GLOBAL OD·TECHNOLOGY

HELPING THE WORLD KEEP PROMISES™

Jeffrey L. Rodengen

Edited by Elizabeth Fernandez
Design and layout by Sandy Cruz and Danielle Taylor

Write Stuff Enterprises, LLC
1001 South Andrews Avenue
Fort Lauderdale, FL 33316
1-800-900-Book (1-800-900-2665)
(954) 462-6657
www.writestuffbooks.com

Publisher's Cataloging-In-Publication Data
(Prepared by The Donohue Group, Inc.)

Rodengen, Jeffrey L.

Old Dominion Freight Line : helping the world keep promises / Jeffrey L. Rodengen ; edited by Elizabeth Fernandez ; design and layout by Sandy Cruz and Danielle Taylor ; [foreword by Steve Forbes].

p. ; cm.

Includes index.
ISBN: 978-1-932022-55-1

1. Old Dominion Freight Line—History. 2. Freight and freightage—United States—History. I. Fernandez, Elizabeth. II. Cruz, Sandy. III. Taylor, Danielle. IV. Forbes, Steve, 1947- V. Title. VI. Title: Helping the world keep promises

HE199.U5 R63 2011
388.044/06573 2011938050

Completely produced in the United States of America
10 9 8 7 6 5 4 3 2 1

Also by Jeffrey L. Rodengen

The Legend of Chris-Craft
IRON FIST: The Lives of Carl Kiekhaefer
Evinrude-Johnson and The Legend of OMC
Serving the Silent Service: The Legend of Electric Boat
The Legend of Dr Pepper/Seven-Up
The Legend of Honeywell
The Legend of Briggs & Stratton
The Legend of Ingersoll-Rand
The Legend of Stanley: 150 Years of The Stanley Works
The MicroAge Way
The Legend of Halliburton
The Legend of York International
The Legend of Nucor Corporation
The Legend of Goodyear: The First 100 Years
The Legend of AMP
The Legend of Cessna
The Legend of VF Corporation
The Spirit of AMD
The Legend of Rowan
New Horizons: The Story of Ashland Inc.
The History of American Standard
The Legend of Mercury Marine
The Legend of Federal-Mogul
Against the Odds: Inter-Tel—The First 30 Years
The Legend of Pfizer
State of the Heart: The Practical Guide to Your Heart and Heart Surgery with Larry W. Stephenson, M.D.
The Legend of Worthington Industries
The Legend of IBP
The Legend of Trinity Industries, Inc.
The Legend of Cornelius Vanderbilt Whitney
The Legend of Amdahl
The Legend of Litton Industries
The Legend of Gulfstream
The Legend of Bertram with David A. Patten
The Legend of Ritchie Bros. Auctioneers
The Legend of ALLTEL with David A. Patten
The Yes, you can of Invacare Corporation with Anthony L. Wall
The Ship in the Balloon: The Story of Boston Scientific and the Development of Less-Invasive Medicine
The Legend of Day & Zimmermann
The Legend of Noble Drilling
Fifty Years of Innovation: Kulicke & Soffa
Biomet—From Warsaw to the World with Richard F. Hubbard
NRA: An American Legend
The Heritage and Values of RPM, Inc.
The Marmon Group: The First Fifty Years
The Legend of Grainger
The Legend of The Titan Corporation with Richard F. Hubbard
The Legend of Discount Tire Co. with Richard F. Hubbard
The Legend of Polaris with Richard F. Hubbard
The Legend of La-Z-Boy with Richard F. Hubbard
The Legend of McCarthy with Richard F. Hubbard
Intervoice: Twenty Years of Innovation with Richard F. Hubbard
Jefferson-Pilot Financial: A Century of Excellence with Richard F. Hubbard
The Legend of HCA
The Legend of Werner Enterprises with Richard F. Hubbard
The History of J. F. Shea Co. with Richard F. Hubbard
True to Our Vision: HNI Corporation with Richard F. Hubbard
The Legend of Albert Trostel & Sons with Richard F. Hubbard
The Legend of Sovereign Bancorp with Richard F. Hubbard
Innovation is the Best Medicine: The extraordinary story of Datascope with Richard F. Hubbard
The Legend of Guardian Industries
The Legend of Universal Forest Products
Changing the World: Polytechnic University—The First 150 Years
Nothing is Impossible: The Legend of Joe Hardy and 84 Lumber
In it for the Long Haul: The Story of CRST
The Story of Parsons Corporation
Cerner: From Vision to Value
New Horizons: The Story of Federated Investors
Office Depot: Taking Care of Business—The First 20 Years
The Legend of General Parts: Proudly Serving a World in Motion
Bard: Power of the Past, Force of the Future
Innovation & Integrity: The Story of Hub Group
Amica: A Century of Service 1907–2007
A Passion for Service: The Story of ARAMARK
The Legend of Con-way: A History of Service, Reliability, Innovation, and Growth
Commanding the Waterways: The Story of Sea Ray
Past, Present & Futures: Chicago Mercantile Exchange
The Legend of Leggett & Platt
The Road Well Traveled: The Story of Guy Bostick and Comcar Industries
The Legend of Brink's
Kiewit: An Uncommon Company: Celebrating the First 125 Years
The History of Embraer
Parker Hannifin Corporation: A Winning Heritage
AECOM: 20 Years and Counting
A Symphony of Soloists: The Story of Wakefern and ShopRite
JELD-WEN: Celebrating 50 Years
Innovation, Passion, Success: The EMC Story
Powering Business: 100 Years of Eaton Corporation

TABLE OF CONTENTS

FOREWORD

HELPING THE WORLD KEEP PROMISES™

BY

STEVE FORBES
EDITOR-IN-CHIEF
FORBES MEDIA

SERVING THE NEEDS AND WANTS of other people is the moral basis for capitalism. To be successful in a freely competitive environment, it is a fundamental requirement that an enterprise must provide a product or service which somebody else wants or needs. Of equal importance, the delivery of the goods or service must be efficient enough to be rewarding for the provider.

The transportation industry is just about as mature as an industry can be. Goods and cargos of every description have been transported for hire for thousands of years. Yet, even in a mature industry, times and circumstances change, requiring innovation and adaptation. Old Dominion Freight Line was started by Earl Congdon Sr. and his wife, Lillian, in 1934, smack in the pit of the Great Depression. The business endured the restrictions of World War, stifling federal regulation, economic cycles, labor unrest, bitter competition, and ultimately, deregulation. Through it all, a culture of service to the customer was firmly established, and it was this purpose, as the late Peter Drucker, author of *The Effective Executive*, would say, that would differentiate Old Dominion from its competitors.

Service is an often over-simplified concept. Service is provided by people, not companies. A company must embrace a culture of service so that its representatives—at every level and responsibility—provide service beyond the expectations of its customers, and beyond the level provided by its competitors. For Old Dominion, this culture grew within an atmosphere of family spirit and family values shared by the Congdon family, and ultimately throughout the entire organization. From Earl Congdon Sr. and Lillian, followed by many decades of leadership by North Carolina Transportation Hall of Fame inductee Earl Congdon Jr., and led today by Old Dominion CEO David Congdon, a sincere dedication to both employees and customers has been rewarded by the highest measures of loyalty in the industry. The Congdon family is quick to explain that it is the Old Dominion team—from drivers, dockworkers, service center managers, schedulers, IT staff, and maintenance personnel, to executives and everyone at every level—that has combined to make Old Dominion the premier LTL carrier in the nation today, and increasingly, throughout the world. Testament to this enduring prowess is the fact that

Old Dominion Freight Line is the only publically held LTL carrier still run by its founding family.

The timely and damage-free delivery of the supplies, products, and components of industry are at the heart of American manufacturing excellence. Every Old Dominion customer has made promises to its own customers, who in turn have made promises to others. A single break in this chain of trust can materially affect dozens of businesses, and scores of lives. Helping the World Keep Promises, as the title of this engaging chronicle suggests, is the full expression of this positive culture which has allowed Old Dominion to rise above its competitors in virtually every measure of success. Delivering on these promises extends not only to customers, but to employees, suppliers, Wall Street analysts, and shareholders alike.

Will circumstances and conditions arise again to challenge the trucking and transportation industries? Of course. Once you have finished reading how Old Dominion met the many challenges of expansion, recession, regulation, competition, and technology, I believe you will agree with me that Old Dominion is uniquely prepared to overcome any obstacles and take advantage of every opportunity. Whatever the future may hold, Old Dominion will continue helping the world keep promises.

Steve Forbes serves as chairman and editor-in-chief of Forbes Media. A two-time presidential candidate, Mr. Forbes has been an active supporter of business and industry for decades and is on the board of directors for many nonprofit organizations, including the Ronald Reagan Presidential Foundation, FreedomWorks, and the Heritage Foundation.

Acknowledgments

Many dedicated people assisted in the research, preparation, and publication of *Old Dominion Freight Line: Helping the World Keep Promises*™.

Research Assistant Torrey Kim conducted the principal archival research for the book, while Executive Editor Elizabeth Fernandez managed the editorial content. Senior Vice President/Creative Services Sandy Cruz and Graphic Designer Danielle Taylor brought the story to life.

Several key individuals associated with Old Dominion provided their assistance in development of the book from its outline to its finished product, including David Carter, Sandy McBride, Johnnie Morris, and Carrie Harrison. A special thank you goes to Steve Forbes for contributing the book's foreword.

All of the people interviewed—Old Dominion employees, retirees, and friends—were generous with their time and insights. Those who shared their memories and thoughts include: Mark Albright, Thom Albrecht, Doug Ball, Ernie Benge, Cornell Brenson, David Carter, L. B. Clayton, Harwood Cochrane, David Congdon, Earl Congdon, Jack Congdon, Bill Cranfill, Karen Dillman, Ken Erdner, Sam Faucett, Marty Freeman, Wes Frye, Greg Gantt, Wayne Goldston, Chris Harrell, Dave Heaton, Bob Hoover, Terry Hutchins, Rick Keeler, John Larkin, Buddy McBride, Joel McCarty, Joann McMillan, Matt Nowell, Chip Overbey, Mark Penley, Matt Penley, Greg Plemmons, Ed Richardson, Brian Stoddard, Leo Suggs, Mike Venegoni, Ed Wolfe, Mike Wood, Frank Wrenn, John Yowell, and Megan Yowell.

Finally, special thanks are extended to the staff at Write Stuff Enterprises, LLC: John Fakler and Christian Ramirez, senior editors; Elijah Meyer, graphic designer; Dennis Redman, on-press supervisor; Lynn C. Jones and D. Nicole Sirdoreus, proofreaders; Barbara Martin and Patti Dolbow, transcriptionists; Donna M. Drialo, indexer; Amy Major, executive assistant to Jeffrey L. Rodengen; Marianne Roberts, president, publisher, and chief financial officer; and Stanislava Alexandrova, marketing manager.

IN MEMORY

Earl Congdon Sr.
1906–1950

Lillian Congdon Crowder
1918–1993

John Yowell
1951–2010

THIS BOOK IS DEDICATED TO THE MEMORIES OF Earl Congdon Sr., Lillian Congdon Crowder, and John Yowell, longtime member of the Old Dominion family.

Earl Congdon Sr., a father, husband, and industry pioneer, founded Old Dominion Freight Line in 1934 with his wife Lillian, a woman far ahead of her time. She was a tough, savvy businesswoman, as well as a dedicated wife and mother, who used her life savings as seed money to launch the company.

After Earl Congdon Sr. suddenly passed away in 1950, Lillian assumed the presidency, running the company alongside her sons Earl Jr. and Jack. Even after she retired, she remained a strong presence within the company. She passed away in 1993 at the age of 84.

From 1983 until he sadly passed away unexpectedly in 2010, John Yowell served as the heart of the company. Originally hired to run the IT department, Yowell rose through the ranks to become executive vice president and chief operating officer. The John Yowell Family Spirit Award was established in his honor in 2011.

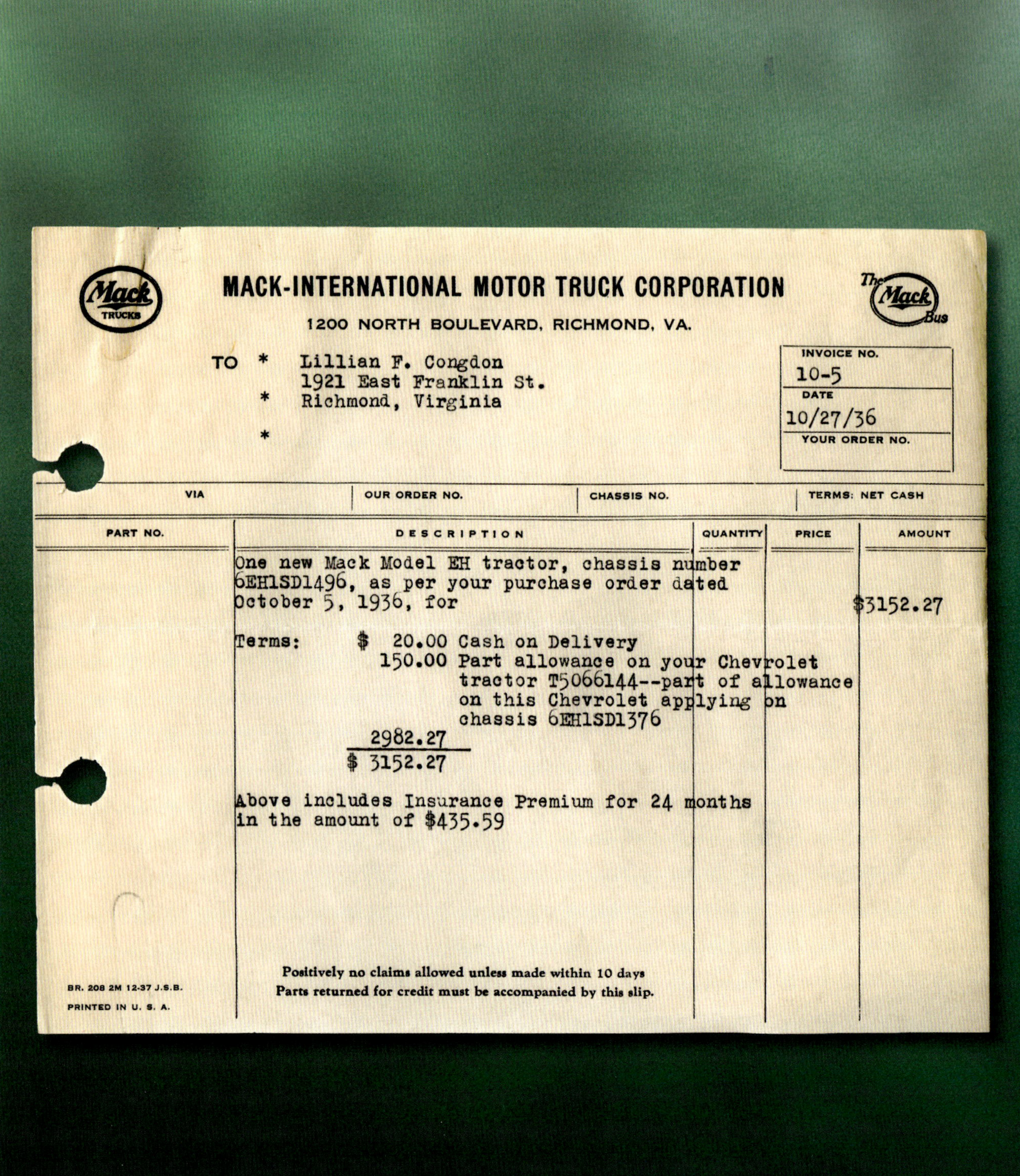

MACK-INTERNATIONAL MOTOR TRUCK CORPORATION

1200 NORTH BOULEVARD, RICHMOND, VA.

TO * Lillian F. Congdon
1921 East Franklin St.
* Richmond, Virginia
*

INVOICE NO. 10-5
DATE 10/27/36
YOUR ORDER NO.

VIA	OUR ORDER NO.	CHASSIS NO.	TERMS: NET CASH

PART NO.	DESCRIPTION	QUANTITY	PRICE	AMOUNT
	One new Mack Model EH tractor, chassis number 6EH1SD1496, as per your purchase order dated October 5, 1936, for			$3152.27
	Terms: $ 20.00 Cash on Delivery 150.00 Part allowance on your Chevrolet tractor T5066144--part of allowance on this Chevrolet applying on chassis 6EH1SD1376 2982.27 $ 3152.27			
	Above includes Insurance Premium for 24 months in the amount of $435.59			

Positively no claims allowed unless made within 10 days
Parts returned for credit must be accompanied by this slip.

BR. 208 2M 12-37 J.S.B.
PRINTED IN U. S. A.

This bill of sale is for a Mack Model EH tractor that Old Dominion bought in October 1936 for the steep price of $3,152. Old Dominion bought another identical tractor that year from Mack, but both ended up catching fire several years later.

CHAPTER ONE

A SINGLE TRUCK

1934–1939

Mother did the paperwork on her dining room table, and Dad drove the truck, and that's how Old Dominion got started—it was a case of preservation, of putting meat on the table. It was a job for Dad—he had no idea in this world of staying in the trucking business at that time.

—Earl Congdon Jr.[1]

WHEN LILLIAN HERBERT BEGAN her first job at a telephone company, she had not yet met Earl Congdon Sr., the enterprising motorcycle enthusiast and auto mechanic who would later become her husband and business partner. She could never have predicted that the money she saved during her time on that job would eventually serve as the seed money for what would become Old Dominion Freight Line, an international company with yearly revenues topping $1.9 billion.[2]

That eventual success did not come easily. The Congdon family and Old Dominion's employees would overcome countless challenges as the freight line expanded while shifting government regulations transformed the industry in the decades to follow. The loyal dedication of Old Dominion's staff grew a small family trucking business into an industry leader, employing more than 12,000 people while still maintaining its family atmosphere.

A Chance Meeting at a Church Luncheon

Earl Congdon Sr. was born on July 20, 1906, in Providence, Rhode Island, to Arthur and Ella Congdon. Earl Sr.'s father had inherited a portion of his family's $2 million estate and invested in the stock market. However, he became a victim of the 1929 market crash and lost most of it. With the remainder of his inheritance held in a trust, Arthur supported his family by selling pianos.[3]

Earl Sr. grew up with an eye for the mechanical side of things, repairing cars in the family driveway and racing motorcycles around his Rhode Island community. Deciding that college was not for him, Earl Sr. embarked on a cross-country motorcycle trip in 1927 with a friend, during which the 21-year-old stopped at a church luncheon in Richmond, Virginia, to get a bite to eat. There, he met Lillian Herbert, and it was love at first sight.[4]

Lillian Herbert was a native Virginian. Born on April 21, 1909, she grew up on a small farm outside the Richmond city limits.[5] Her father, a farmer who later worked as a streetcar operator, died of a head injury while on the job.[6] At the young age of 16, Lillian left school to help support her family and took a job as an operator at a telephone company. A standout at her job, Lillian became a supervisor and instructor before the age of 19.[7]

Earl Congdon Sr. had a lifelong passion for all things mechanical. He worked on cars, trucks, and motorcycles throughout his youth, which came in handy when he later became the sole driver and mechanic during Old Dominion's early days.

The Fascinating Background of Lillian Congdon Crowder

In 1936—just two years after Old Dominion hauled its first truckload of eggs under the watchful eye of Lillian Congdon—*Fortune*® magazine conducted a poll asking whether readers believed "married women should have a full-time job outside the home." The result? Only 15 percent of respondents approved of this concept, a revealing statistic at a time when only 11.7 percent of married women worked outside the home.[1]

It was during that period that happily married mother-of-two Lillian Congdon not only worked full time, but did so in the largely male-dominated trucking industry. She was a woman far ahead of her time.

Lillian started working at the age of 16 to help supplement the family's income following her father's death. She continued to demonstrate that same resolve throughout Old Dominion's early days. After using her savings to fund the company's first truck, she was instrumental in helping the business succeed during the company's early years, negotiating with customers, evaluating fleet purchases, and even driving the truck when Earl Sr. was sick.

Described by the *Richmond News Leader* as "a slip of a thing, only 100 pounds and little more than 5 feet tall,"[2] Lillian worked around the clock, helping to grow Old Dominion day by day. "The only time we got much sleep was on weekends," she told the newspaper reporter, who noted that as the owner of Old Dominion, "Mrs. Congdon took care of the boys and ran the one-truck operation at the same time."[3]

According to Harwood Cochrane, retired owner of Overnite Transportation, which once shared a terminal with Old Dominion in the early days, "She was pretty, she was nice, and she was tough as nails."

Despite the fact that *Fortune*® readers may not have supported married women who worked, Old Dominion's success is largely based on the fact that this woman did just that. According to Earl Congdon Jr., "If it wasn't for her, we wouldn't have anything."[4]

After Earl Sr. and Lillian had their chance meeting at the church luncheon, Earl Sr. made his way back to Rhode Island on his motorcycle. On the way home, however, tragedy struck. According to Earl Congdon Jr., "A 14-year-old kid swiped his parents' car, came out of his driveway, and panicked when he saw the motorcycle coming."

The underage driver crashed into the motorcycle with such force that Earl Sr.'s lower leg had to be amputated. Earl Sr. also suffered a concussion, several broken ribs, and two fractured arms. During Earl Sr.'s 10-month hospital stay, in the course of which he was fitted with a prosthetic leg, Lillian frequently came to visit. They married in January 29, 1928, a year after Earl Sr. was discharged from the hospital.[8]

Earl Sr.'s family gave the couple a new Chevrolet Roadster as a wedding present.[9] However, in the

CANNED FOODS

are best. They're picked fresh—packed fresh.

No. 10 TINS OUR SPECIALTY

LESLIE H. PHILLIPS, Pres. and Treas. W. T. LEWIS, Jr., Sec'y and Mgr.

Phone Dial 3-2769

PHILLIPS-LEWIS CO., INC.

WHOLESALE

INSTITUTION GROCERS

Office and Warehouse: 14th and Cary Streets

WE SELL U. S., STATE and MUNICIPAL INSTITUTIONS, COLLEGES, HOTELS and HOSPITALS.

RICHMOND, VA. AUG. 26TH 1935

AMERICAN-HAWAIIAN STEAMSHIP CO.,
NORFOLK, VA.

GENTLEMEN:-

WE ARE ENCLOSING ORIGINAL BILL-OF-LADING COVERING 655 CS PINEAPPLE, DUE TO ARRIVE ON S. S. "ALASKAN".

WHEN THESE GOODS ARRIVE, WE WOULD THANK YOU TO TURN SAME OVER TO THE OLD DOMINION FREIGHT LINE, 5 SO. 20TH ST., OF YOUR CITY.

YOURS VERY TRULY,
PHILLIPS-LEWIS CO. INC.,

SEC'Y & MANAGER.

WTL.RL

DEAR MR. CONDOR:-

WE ARE ENCLOSING ORDER ON THE AMERICAN-HAWAIIAN STEAMSHIP CO. FOR 655 CS PINEAPPLE, DUE TO ARRIVE ON S. S. "ALASKAN". WE UNDERSTAND THIS BOAT IS DUE TO ARRIVE ON SUNDAY, AUGUST 25TH, AND AS PER OUR CONVERSATION WHEN YOU WERE IN THE OFFICE SEVERAL DAYS AGO, YOU SAID YOU WOULD PICK THIS UP ON TUESDAY, AND MAKE DELIVERY WEDNESDAY MORNING.

PHILLIPS-LEWIS CO. INC.
W. T. Lewis Jr.

This is an example of an early order for Old Dominion's services. In 1935, the company was hired to haul 655 cans of pineapple from the SS *Alaskan* in Norfolk back to Richmond.

midst of the Depression, the couple needed viable income, so they traded their wedding gift for their first truck. "Dad was going to drive the truck until the Depression was over and he could get a decent job. So Dad became an owner/operator and drove that truck for several years," Earl Jr. explained.[10]

Earl Sr. and Lillian operated their modest trucking business from home. The couple supported themselves successfully until their growing business was sidelined following an unfortunate accident. While at the wheel of the truck in 1932, Earl Sr. fell asleep, crashing the truck into a bridge abutment in Maryland. The accident represented a total loss except for the $50 the couple was able to collect after selling the wrecked truck for scrap metal.[11]

During that time, the Congdon family continued to grow, with Earl Jr. born in 1930 and Jack born in 1933. But without a truck for their business, Earl Sr. took a job in Baltimore as a terminal manager with Virginia Motor Express in 1933. However, the company subsequently went out of business.[12]

Earl Sr. next took a job selling cars at a Packard dealership. The business policy among Packard's sales team was that salesmen would take turns greeting potential customers as they walked into the showroom.

"One day, a little old lady came in, and the salesman whose turn it was to greet the little old lady never budged, thinking she was not a good prospect," Earl Jr. said. "Dad approached the lady, sold her a car, and got fired" for greeting the customer when it was not his turn.[13]

At a loss for what to do next, Lillian and Earl Sr. put their heads together to secure a source of income until Lillian had what she described as "a wild idea." She told Earl Sr. that she had managed to save $1,700 and suggested that they go back to Richmond and start a daily trucking route from Richmond to Norfolk. With Lillian's seed money, they officially launched Old Dominion Freight Line. The company's first vehicle was a straight-body truck, with the cab and cargo area attached rather than separated as in a tractor-trailer rig. "He drove it while I took orders at home on the phone," Lillian recalled.[14]

The Congdons settled on Cliff Avenue in Richmond, where their house served as company headquarters and truck bay, along with home to the young family of four. Old Dominion's first truckload consisted of crated eggs delivered from Norfolk to Richmond in the summer of 1934.[15] "We 'gypsied' all over the country," Lillian recalled. "We took hauling jobs anywhere."[16]

Despite the fact that Lillian, having worked at the telephone company, had perfect business

Old Dominion's early advertising urged potential customers to "Phone Us For Rates." Callers did not know they were often reaching Lillian at home, juggling her roles as a wife and mother of two with her career at Old Dominion.

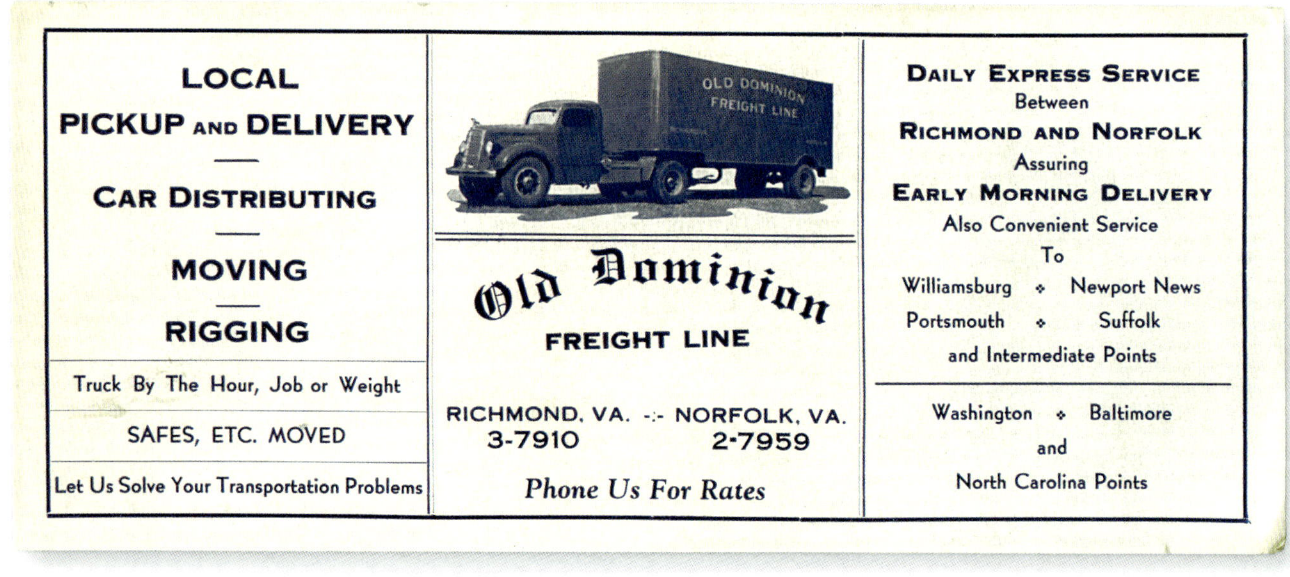

The Congdons' young sons, Earl Jr. and Jack, sit atop the hood of one of the two Mack Model EH tractors that Old Dominion bought in 1936.

etiquette on the phone when taking customers' orders, it was clear to some callers that Old Dominion was operating out of the family home. "I remember Mother telling me that a customer called her one day and wanted to bring some freight to her terminal," Earl Jr. said. "Mother hemmed and hawed, since she had no terminal, and the customer then laughed and said, 'That's all right, little lady. I know you don't have a terminal.'"[17]

When Lillian wasn't spending time with her family or taking orders for freight business, she also served as the company's alternate driver. In 1934, Earl Sr. came down with a kidney ailment, and Lillian drove the truck while he recuperated. "I'll never forget the first night I drove," she recalled. "I had a flat tire on the road. Fortunately, some sailors came along. They fixed the tire for me."[18]

Congress Regulates the Trucking Industry

The railroad industry, which had been losing business to trucking companies, was among the entities that lobbied Congress for increased regulation within the trucking industry.[19] As a result, Congress passed the Motor Carrier Act of 1935, which controlled prices charged by trucking companies and required them to acquire a Certificate of Public Convenience and Necessity (CPCN) from the Interstate Commerce Commission (ICC).

Any trucking company interested in acquiring a CPCN for a particular route had to prove that it had already been running that route prior to the act's passage. The ICC would then "grandfather" the company into keeping that route. Old Dominion applied for a CPCN and was granted one, but only between Richmond and Norfolk, Virginia.

"That was an interstate certificate, which meant that the freight we hauled had to originate or be destined to points beyond Virginia," Earl Jr. explained. "What we could do was haul export freight from Richmond to Norfolk that was leaving the country or bring import freight back from Norfolk into Richmond."[20]

Alternately, Old Dominion could handle interline freight, meaning that if another carrier had a CPCN from New York to Richmond but couldn't go to Norfolk, that company would hire Old Dominion to take the freight the rest of the way from Richmond to Norfolk.[21]

The Congdon family was frustrated that the ICC did not grant Old Dominion a broader CPCN, but Earl Sr. and Lillian did not have the appropriate documentation to prove that they had been operating broader routes than Richmond–Norfolk, which left the ICC to only grant them the Richmond to Norfolk route.[22] As Earl Congdon Jr. explained:

Mother said, "When the Interstate Commerce Commission man came in, Dad was rude to him and

The Impact of the Motor Carrier Act

In 1935, Congress passed the Motor Carrier Act, which regulated the trucking industry for the first time in US history. For a young company like Old Dominion, just getting started, the new regulations proved a difficult challenge. Because Old Dominion's main customers at the time required deliveries between Richmond and Norfolk, the company was relegated to continue that route—and only that route—until it could purchase or lease the operating authority of a company that owned Certificates of Public Convenience and Necessity (CPCNs) for other routes.

The Motor Carrier Act would have a vast impact on the entire trucking industry. Carriers were not only required to demonstrate the "public convenience and necessity" of their businesses to the Interstate Commerce Commission (ICC), they also had to standardize the rates that they charged.

The Motor Carrier Act "required motor carriers to file all rates—also called tariffs—with the ICC 30 days before they became effective," noted author Thomas Gale Moore in an analysis of the law. "Anyone, including a competitor, was allowed to inspect the filed tariffs. If the proposed tariffs were protested by another carrier (a trucker, a regulated water carrier, or a railroad), the ICC normally suspended the rates pending an investigation of their legality."[1]

What many government regulators may not have foreseen were the unexpected consequences of the Motor Carrier Act. One effect which had significant implications was that freight often took longer to arrive at its destination. Trucking companies were often required to travel miles out of their way to make deliveries due to the complicated rules on their CPCN.

For instance, if Old Dominion, which had a CPCN to travel between Richmond and Norfolk, bought another company that owned a CPCN between Richmond and Arlington, any freight traveling between Arlington and Norfolk would have to go through Richmond on its way to the destination. Even if the trucking company shortened its route considerably by traveling directly between Arlington and Norfolk over other highways, it first had to go to Richmond before proceeding on to its destination, according to the convoluted restrictions in the ICC rules.

The financial implications of the regulation had a direct affect on both trucking companies and customers. "Products exempt from regulation moved at [shipping] rates 20 percent to 40 percent below those for the same products subject to ICC controls," Moore wrote. "For example, regulated rates for carrying cooked poultry, compared to unregulated charges for fresh dressed poultry (a similar product), were nearly 50 percent higher."[2]

However, for Old Dominion and the other freight companies operating in the 1930s, there were only two choices: operate under regulation, or go out of business. Needless to say, it was a difficult way to operate a business.

An early Old Dominion truck rolls through the streets of Virginia in 1936.

felt that this was his private information, and what right did this fellow have to know all of this?"

Between not having any paper records and being perhaps a little impolite to the Interstate Commerce Commission fellow, Dad ended up with [just the] Richmond to [Norfolk route]. ... I heard Dad say many times, "Darn it, I was operating prior to 1935 from Providence, Rhode Island, to Atlanta, Georgia, and I ended up with a certificate from Richmond to Norfolk." He was not a happy camper over that.[23]

Moving Out of the House

After working out of their home for nearly a year, the Congdons decided to branch out and give Old Dominion's sole truck a proper terminal. The company leased space outside Pender's grocery store in Richmond. Without a loading dock, Earl Sr. had to physically lift freight from the ground to the truck bed.[24]

Eager for a more professional and easy-to-use terminal, the Congdons retained the company's first cartage agent in 1935, aligning with the Tiller Brothers in Richmond. As a child, Earl Jr. would often accompany his mother to the Tiller Brothers' office on the streetcar. "It was a ramshackle little building, and we went up some wooden stairs to the office, and there were old tires stacked about 10 high beside the stairs," he later recalled.[25]

However, seeing Lillian going in and out of the Old Dominion office at the cartage agent proved a distraction for some employees at Tiller Brothers, unaccustomed to seeing a woman around the terminal.

"Mother was quite attractive as a young lady, and my dad was a jealous fellow, so they discontinued the Tiller Brothers' arrangement and moved into our first real terminal in 1936," Earl Jr. noted.[26]

Old Dominion settled into its own small terminal, located at 20th and Franklin streets in Richmond, which featured two trucking bays.[27] Old Dominion used one bay, while the other was used by Overnite Transportation, which would later become a competitor.[28]

After about a year at the new location, the Congdons felt it time to treat themselves to a source of refreshment for their hard work—a water cooler.

"They paid $36 for it," Earl Jr. later recalled. "The only problem was they didn't have $36, so they had to finance it. Can you imagine having to finance a water cooler? But it was tough. They started a truck line with no money and no personnel but themselves, and they had some really hard times."[29]

The Congdons made a payment every month over an eight-month period until the water cooler was paid off.[30] By then, Old Dominion was not just a one-truck operation anymore, and it could no longer operate with a single driver, so the Congdons hired local driver Pop Townsend to help drive the route. He stayed with Old Dominion until he passed away in 1947.[31]

By the end of 1936, Old Dominion had six tractor-trailers and 12 straight-body trucks.[32] The Congdons knew Old Dominion was outgrowing the terminal it shared with Overnite Transportation, so they moved into a terminal in Richmond with seven truck bays to handle Old Dominion's growing fleet.[33] The Congdons considered the terminal a costly venture but one that was essential to helping the company grow.[34]

With a larger terminal came more employees, including Lillian's niece Phyllis Fletcher and Earl Sr.'s brother Howard Congdon. Howard worked for Old Dominion between 1935 and 1937, earning between $17 and $20 per week to help out wherever needed, including driving and loading freight. However, he left after two years to return to Providence, Rhode Island.

"I believe the work at a freight company in the mid-1930s was a pretty grim business, and Howard just didn't feel that amount of work was commensurate with the low pay at the time," Earl Jr. said. "He even told me once, 'Your dad was wallowing in the gutter down there, and our family was used to better things.' "[35]

Fletcher joined the company in 1938 and also remained for two years, working as the sole office clerk for $6 per week.[36] When she started with Old Dominion, the company employed just six drivers, each earning $17 weekly, and they finally brought a mechanic on the payroll, Bernard Aignew. The company hauled such commodities as dried fruit, burlap, coffee, canned goods, and paper.[37]

A Side Venture

To supplement the growing company's income, Earl Congdon Sr. made an agreement to lease six

By 1936, Old Dominion owned an impressive fleet, including 12 straight trucks and six tractor-trailers.

COMMONWEALTH OF VIRGINIA NO. 104
STATE CORPORATION COMMISSION

PERMIT

In Accordance with Chapter 129, of the Acts of the General Assembly of Virginia, 1936;

-- Lillian P. Congdon, t/a Old Dominion Freight Line, Richmond --

is authorized to transport property *by motor vehicles as a Contract Carrier, and has agreed to comply with the laws of the Commonwealth of Virginia and the rules and regulations of the State Corporation Commission lawfully applicable or made applicable to contract carriers.*

Dated at Richmond, this 18th *of* August 19 36

State Corporation Commission

H. Lester Hooker

Commissioner

In 1936, Lillian Congdon received her permit to operate as a contract carrier throughout Virginia.

trucks to the Manchester Board and Paper Co.[38] With Old Dominion's own freight hauling business serving as the source of funds for its employees' paychecks, the contract with Manchester Board and Paper became the mainstay of the Congdon family income and would continue as such for more than a decade.[39]

Initially, the ICC questioned the legality of the arrangement in which Old Dominion owned the trucking equipment and performed the maintenance on the trucks while Manchester was free to use the trucks for its own operation.[40] Earl Sr. wrote a letter to the ICC on December 21, 1937, letting the commission know that the ICC should deal directly with Manchester Board and Paper regarding the matter, and by 1939, Old Dominion received a written approval from the ICC to continue the contract carrier agreement between Manchester and Old Dominion.[41]

That year, Old Dominion underwent its first experience with unionization. Two Old Dominion drivers, working with Teamsters, attempted to organize the company in 1939. A three-month strike ensued, but Old Dominion continued to operate during the strike period, and the union failed to get a contract, leaving Old Dominion nonunion for the time being.[42]

Getting Accustomed to Regulation

Freight companies were just learning how to operate under the new regulatory environment by the end of the 1930s, and Old Dominion was no exception. In an attempt to grow the company's territory, Earl Sr. and Lillian decided to lease the operating authority of Carter Brothers Express Lines in May 1939. Under the two-year lease agreement, Old Dominion could operate between Richmond and Covington, Virginia, including the territory that includes most intermediate points.[43]

However, just a few months later, the ICC pointed out that although Old Dominion had legally leased the authority, Carter Brothers had never registered its intrastate authority with the ICC, making Old Dominion's interstate operations unauthorized.[44]

"In view of the fact that the Carter Express Lines has no application for registration before the Interstate Commerce Commission, you will not be authorized to conduct any interstate motor carrier activity over such leased intrastate rights," the ICC wrote to Lillian on July 28, 1939, thus putting an end to the arrangement.[45]

In 1939, Old Dominion bought more than $12,000 worth of equipment, including two International D-40 tractors with 24-gallon fuel tanks, and a 28-foot Trailmobile Model H-31 trailer.[46] "All the equipment purchased in the late 1930s was only financed for one year to one and a half years," Earl Jr. said. "I wonder how we were able to manage a cash flow, paying off trailers that soon."

However, Old Dominion's investments in equipment and employees had begun to pay off. By the end of the 1930s, Old Dominion had assets of $6,960.60, with no liabilities.[47] Profits in 1939 were $5,100.[48] The company's growing fleet would prove essential to its growth as the country entered World War II, offering new expansion opportunities for many American companies.

Old Dominion expanded its fleet throughout the 1940s.

CHAPTER TWO

ATTEMPTS AT EXPANSION

1940–1949

I spent that summer as a pickup and delivery driver. I would drive around Richmond hoping my friends would see me driving a tractor-trailer because no one else could do that!

—Earl Congdon Jr.[1]

BY 1940, OLD DOMINION HAD 45 EMployees and three service centers across Virginia in Richmond, Newport News, and Norfolk.[2] The company employed 12 drivers, each earning about $17 per week, and hauled various commodities ranging from fruit to burlap to coffee to paper.[3]

Earl Sr. and Lillian Congdon were fifty-fifty owners of Old Dominion by the time this photo was taken in 1948, each drawing about $4,800 a year from the company for their tireless work.

While Old Dominion expanded, the United States underwent a dramatic transformation throughout the 1940s as the country entered World War II. By October 1940, the draft registration of approximately 16 million American men began, marking the beginning of a wartime atmosphere throughout the country even before the US officially entered the war in 1941.[4] Old Dominion would see changes to its business structure throughout the decade as World War II affected companies across the nation.

Lean Business by Necessity

An Old Dominion balance sheet for 1940 indicates that the company had assets of $21,124, with liabilities of $14,539, totaling a net worth of $6,585.[5] Profits were driven not only by expansion and hard work, but also by Earl Congdon Sr.'s lean-business skills and his determined ingenuity.

The Congdons employed several methods to stretch their corporate dollars and ensure that Old Dominion could maximize its earnings. Like many other start-up organizations, Old Dominion plowed profits back into the company, investing in both equipment and employees to ensure growth. That strategy left little precious cash for miscellaneous expenses, and as a result, Old Dominion operated on a shoestring budget.

"Dad was always a bit strapped for money," Earl Jr. recalled, noting that a few simple shortcuts helped Old Dominion save cash in the early days.[6]

For example, Earl Sr. didn't keep any antifreeze in the trucks because the radiators tended to leak, "so each night during the winter, we would drain the water out of the trucks, and the next morning when it was time to go to work, we'd have to close the petcock and put water back in the trucks," Earl Jr. explained. "We didn't have any heaters in them either, so things were pretty lean."[7]

Commercial vehicles in the 1940s were required to have both front and rear license plates, but Earl Sr. tried to save money by separating the pair he received from the licensing office. He would put one plate on the front of one tractor and would then affix

Old Dominion traveled routes that covered all kinds of terrain in the 1940s.

its match to the front of a separate tractor, ensuring that both tractors had front plates—but not with unique numbers on them.

"One day, Dad got a call from the scales," Earl Jr. later recalled. "The trucks were being weighed, and the man at the scale said, 'Mr. Congdon, you don't have but one license on the front of tractor No. 54,' and Dad said, 'Well, the one on the back must have fallen off.' And the man said, 'I'm afraid not, it's on the front of tractor No. 55,' which was right behind. He was always trying to stretch a buck."[8]

Unions and Old Dominion

By the start of the 1940s, Jimmy Hoffa had begun to gain power within the International Brotherhood of Teamsters, which he would later run as the organization's president from 1957 to 1971.[9] The Teamsters union was established in 1903 and has continued to exist into the 21st century, with approximately 1.4 million members in 2011.[10] According to the *Encyclopedia of US Labor and Working Class History*, "In the 1940s, Hoffa drew on the union's strength in the upper Midwest to organize trucking operations in the South. Using the leapfrog organizing technique, Hoffa wielded the threat of secondary boycotts to force Southern nonunion trucking firms to sign collective bargaining agreements with the Teamsters."[11]

Like many trucking companies, Old Dominion worked as a nonunion operator during its early days, but that would change in 1940, when a major customer convinced Earl Sr. to help the Teamsters organize Old Dominion's drivers.[12]

The Congdons participated in Teamster activities, with Lillian Congdon receiving a Western Union telegram from Virginia Governor James H. Price's office on August 17, 1940, inviting her to a truck operators conference to discuss a labor dispute.[13]

OLD DOMINION'S EARLY BRANDING EFFORTS

Left: Old Dominion began using its distinctive green-and-white color scheme in the 1940s.

Below: These Old Dominion tractors and trailers display the company's signature look.

By the 1940s, Old Dominion Freight Line had begun to recognize the importance of creating an identifiable brand. Anyone on the road today can recognize Old Dominion's trucks from a great distance, as the company's distinctive green-and-white tractors crisscross the country. However, it took many efforts over many years before Old Dominion would achieve strong brand recognition.

When the Congdons started Old Dominion in the 1930s, they originally decided to paint the trucks navy blue with red wheels, red chassis, and red fuel tanks.[1] Then, the company purchased several tractors and trailers from International Harvester in the 1940s. Those vehicles arrived at Old Dominion painted dark green, so Old Dominion repainted some of its units dark green with a red stripe and black fenders, with the company's straight trucks painted dark green without the black fenders.[2] Old Dominion's name and logo would be emblazoned across the side of the trailer in an oval pattern.

These changes marked the beginning of what would become Old Dominion's brand identity.

Old Dominion would continue as a union operator for several more years thereafter, until the situation would come to a head later in the decade.

The War Effort

As a trucking company operating under government regulation, Old Dominion continued to face scrutiny from the Interstate Commerce Commission (ICC) in the 1940s.

In September 1941, an Old Dominion tractor-trailer was discovered transporting intrastate Virginia freight without Virginia license plates. The vehicle had a North Carolina tag, but the State Corporation Commission (SCC) threatened to take away Old Dominion's contract carrier permit due to the lack of Virginia tags. Since Old Dominion had no common carrier intrastate authority, such an SCC decision would have prohibited Old Dominion from hauling any Virginia intrastate freight.[14] This event, coupled with the fact that Old Dominion continued to operate its Norfolk-to-Richmond route over specific preassigned roads, served as the impetus for the company's decision to expand its territory.

In 1941, Earl Sr. was approached by Karl Lenker, a friend and German-born owner of local freight company Dixie Transfer.[15] Lenker, who had not yet become a US citizen, was concerned about the beginning of World War II.[16] "Earl, I've got to get rid of this truck line. I'm not sure whether they're going to throw me in prison or what they're going to do with me during the war, being a German," Lenker explained.[17]

Lenker's Dixie Transfer had a Certificate of Public Convenience and Necessity to run from Richmond to points within both North Carolina and South Carolina, routes which appealed to the Congdons. Earl Congdon Sr. offered to buy Dixie's trucks from Lenker. He then said to his friend, "Now as far as your operating authority—that Certificate of Public Convenience and Necessity—I will lease that certificate from you for one year, with the option to buy it at the end of the year for $10,000."[18]

The lease for the first year was $100 per month, to be applied toward the purchase price if Old Dominion subsequently chose to purchase it.[19] Lenker agreed to the deal on December 20, 1941, and New Dixie Lines, Inc. was incorporated.[20] Old

Old Dominion staffers pose in front of a truck circa 1940.

This Old Dominion tractor-trailer from 1940 advertises the company's impressive geographic reach, just six years after Earl Sr. and Lillian Congdon started the company.

Dominion finally had the opportunity to expand outside of Virginia.[21] Earl Sr. personally hauled the first load into the Carolinas, and the company continued to carry freight throughout New Dixie's former territory, with Old Dominion drivers typically unloading freight with cartage agents throughout the Carolinas.[22]

As Old Dominion expanded, the United States became completely engaged in World War II. The federal government, as well as state governments, began to make some minor concessions to trucking companies that were operating in a regulated environment, and Old Dominion was intent on obtaining additional routes. The company applied for, and was granted by the Commonwealth of Virginia, emergency authority to operate over US 60 from Richmond to Norfolk for the remainder of the war because heavy amounts of traffic were moving along that route to assist with the war effort.[23]

In addition, Old Dominion was able to use the routes that one of its competitors was already running. When Virginia intrastate commerce first underwent regulation, a company called Hampton Roads Transportation Company "was awarded a monopoly on three routes between Richmond and Norfolk, Virginia," Earl Jr. later recalled.[24]

The first route went from Williamsburg to Norfolk on US 60, the second route operated down US 1 to Petersburg, and then US 460 to Norfolk. The third route ran down US 301 to US 58 and US 58 to Norfolk.[25] Hampton Roads, which had been a major competitor to Old Dominion, sold its three routes to Wilson Trucking in 1942, and Wilson then sold the Route 60 certificate to Old Dominion for $8,000.[26] This expansion gave Old Dominion permanent authority to run intrastate routes in Virginia.

With the company expanding so quickly throughout 1941 and 1942, Old Dominion did not have the manpower to fully devote its resources to the business it was cultivating in the Carolinas, thanks to its lease with New Dixie. "Dad did not put any sales representatives in North and South Carolina and ended up with a one-way operation from Richmond to the Carolinas, which was not profitable," Earl Jr. later recalled.[27] "We were so busy at that time hauling military cargo between

Old Dominion continued to expand, opening new terminals across the region.

Richmond and Norfolk that the New Dixie trucks were utilized pretty much in that endeavor."[28]

Therefore, at the end of the one-year trial period in December 1942, Old Dominion let its lease with New Dixie lapse and decided that the timing was not yet right to expand into the Carolinas, keeping the company firmly planted in Virginia, with business booming due to the war freight haul.[29]

A Sprawling Terminal

In 1942, Earl Sr. and Lillian officially became fifty-fifty partners in Old Dominion and purchased a lumber mill to convert into a truck terminal.[30] The lumber mill, located at Graham and Catherine Streets in Richmond, dated back to the 1890s and offered space for the company's first maintenance shop and a sizable lot across the street for fleet parking.[31]

"We had probably seven or eight loading spots on this terminal, and Dad put an addition on it and rented it out to another carrier, so we had a little rental income coming in," recalled Earl Jr.[32]

The facility also featured an outdoor dock that could accommodate about 14 trucks, a main office, a dispatch office, and storage space.[33] With wood floors covering the non-air-conditioned second floor office and concrete floors on the first floor, "the building was a real fire trap, but was considered a fine terminal for its day," Earl Jr. noted.[34] There, the company settled into what would be its home for 20 years.

Although still involved in the company, Lillian gave up some of her responsibilities as more office staff were hired, allowing her to focus on other pursuits, such as spending time with her growing sons, tending her garden at home, and taking up golf.[35] At the time, Bill Jones, brother-in-law to Earl Sr. and Lillian, worked for the company as the Staunton terminal manager. The early staff of Old Dominion also included Fran Morris, the company's first secretary; Ed Coleman, who started as a driver and worked his way up to Norfolk terminal manager; Charlie Matthews, Richmond terminal manager and salesman; and J. H. Callahan, the company's first rate clerk.

Old Dominion also opened its own operations in Norfolk and Newport News in the mid-1940s, whereas the company had previously been using cartage agents for operations in those areas.[36]

Growing the Fleet

With a new terminal ready to accommodate additional vehicles, Old Dominion set about expanding its truck line. But in 1942, as World War II embroiled nearly every continent, government permission was required before a company could purchase additional trucks. Old Dominion filed for permission to buy a tractor and trailer in March 1942, hoping to get more trucks moving with freight.[37]

By 1944, Old Dominion's fleet consisted of 14 straight trucks, 18 tractors, and 25 trailers.[38] The company had assets of $124,768, with liabilities of about $54,000, totaling a net worth of approximately $70.768.[39] Old Dominion employed a staff of 74 that year, including three mechanics, 13 line-haul drivers, five terminal supervisors such as Norfolk terminal manager Tommy Cox, 13 local drivers, 16 platform employees, and five terminal clerks—but still no salespeople on staff.[40]

In 1944, Old Dominion's two partners, Earl Sr. and Lillian Congdon, drew $4,800 each in salary for the year.[41] Considering the size of the business and the fact that Old Dominion's vehicles traveled 587,736 miles in 1944 as a common carrier and another quarter-million as a contract carrier to deliver 64,000 shipments,[42] the Congdons' salaries were not astronomical, but still considerably higher than the average American salary of $2,600 at the time.[43]

On September 2, 1945, Japan signed a formal surrender to the United States and its allies, officially ending World War II.[44] Old Dominion would no longer require a permit to buy new equipment, but the company would also no longer benefit from war-related freight hauls.

Revenue in 1945 was $371,876, with income before taxes a sparse $202.[45] However, the company had assets worth nearly $152,000, most of which consisted of Old Dominion's fleet.[46]

That year, Old Dominion experienced its first fatal accident, losing 25-year-old driver Howard Sprague Jr. and two passengers that he had picked up. Sprague's truck was involved in a collision with a car driven by a sergeant stationed at Camp Lee, Virginia. During the accident, the tractor came loose from the trailer, fell into a ditch, and caught fire. The experience served as the impetus that would later lead to Old Dominion continuously earning one of the best safety records in the trucking industry. "The injured were pinned in the wreckage and burned when fire swept over the tractor," Earl Jr. later recalled. "I remember this incident, and naturally, my parents were very distressed."[47]

Union Strike Hits Old Dominion

In 1946, a union strike that lasted for more than 10 weeks created significant strife for Old Dominion, with unpaid bills piling up as drivers refused to work.[48] The strike had significant implications for Old Dominion, directly affecting the future of the company's interactions with unions.

The Teamsters union announced a strike in the spring of 1946, shutting down all unionized carriers from Richmond northward.[49] Old Dominion, which had unionized employees at all of its locations at the time, was affected by the notice and had to shut down while the drivers continued to strike for two and a half months. The strike stretched the company thin—without drivers, a trucking company was essentially dormant. Fortunately, before the strike reached the three-month mark, Old Dominion drivers wanted to throw in the towel.

"One night, after 11 weeks, when the family was having dinner, the telephone rang, and it was one of our line-haul drivers stating, 'We drivers are sick of this strike and sick of this union,'" Earl Jr. later wrote. "The driver said, 'We want to go back to work Monday morning. Will you open for us?' Dad, of course, agreed, and Old Dominion opened for operations as a nonunion carrier in the city of Richmond."[50]

The company's city drivers in Norfolk and Newport News remained with the union but came back to drive again around the same time, allowing the company to operate at nearly full capacity once again.[51] Unfortunately, the company had lost money during the strike, since it had not been able to run its routes. To secure additional capital, the Congdons were forced to sell the company's interstate operating authority between Richmond and Norfolk over US 1 and US 460 to Davidson Transfer and Storage for $10,000.[52]

During the strike, the Congdons found it necessary to lay off its office workers due to the abrupt loss of revenue. Lillian, who had been enjoying her semiretirement away from the office, came back to work while the company slowly rebuilt its staff.[53]

A New Employee

Fortunately for Old Dominion, short-staffed following the strike, the company welcomed a new up-and-coming driver in 1946: the Congdons' eldest son, Earl Jr.

At the age of 16, Earl Jr. learned to drive a ton-and-a-half 1945 International straight truck from veteran Old Dominion driver Walker Brooks. Earl Jr. worked for the company over the summer as a pickup and delivery driver for Old Dominion. By the following summer, at 17, Earl Jr. began driving regular runs at the wheel of a tractor-trailer.[54]

Brooks taught Earl Jr. the intricacies of driving a truck, accompanying him as a passenger, following behind him or driving side by side. During one instance when Brooks was following Earl Jr. from Richmond to Norfolk, Earl Jr. stopped at a red light on a hill, but when the light turned green, Earl Jr. accidentally had his tractor in reverse.[55] "When I engaged the clutch, my truck started backwards and of course scared the daylights out of Walker," Earl Jr. recalled. "He blew his horn, but of course the minute the truck started backwards, I realized my mistake and stopped. We did not have an accident, but Walker and I both still remembered this after nearly 50 years."[56]

An Offer to Sell

By the end of 1947, Old Dominion owned 16 straight trucks, 25 tractors, and 35 semitrailers. At that point, Old Dominion was acquiring straight trucks with 12-foot bodies, which cost about $2,500 each.[57] Pretax profit for 1947 was $9,293, and Earl Sr. and Lillian each continued to draw a salary of $4,800 a year.[58] That was in addition to the approximately $30,000 per year the family earned from its arrangement with the Manchester Board and Paper Company. Earl Sr. continued to lease five tractors and six trailers to Manchester, with Old Dominion absorbing the maintenance costs on the leased equipment. "Old Dominion even bought Manchester's blown-out tires for $20 each," Earl Jr. later recalled.[59]

With the company gaining profitability each year, it was inevitable that the Congdons would receive an offer to sell. In 1947, Earl Sr. and Lillian Congdon were offered $25,000 to sell Old Dominion. Earl Sr. seriously considered making the sale and moving the family to Florida, where he planned to buy a motel.[60]

Earl Jr. did not want to move because he was 16 years old and enjoying high school in Richmond at the time, but the offer for Old Dominion was turned down due to Lillian's insistence on staying the course.[61]

"Mother saved the company several times, and this was one of them," Earl Jr. recalled. "She said, 'Well, you can sell your half if you want to, but my half is not for sale!' "[62]

With that, Earl Sr. abandoned his idea of being a motel owner in Florida and went back to the business of operating a freight line.

Earl Jr. Goes Cross-Country

In 1948, Old Dominion began distributing airfreight as part of a collaboration with Globe Freight Airline, Inc., and the company was featured in a newspaper advertisement showing an Old Dominion straight truck backed up to a Globe Freight aircraft, offering Old Dominion wider exposure.[63]

It proved a record year, with assets of $203,906, liabilities of $91,939, and partnership capital of $109,345.[64] Pretax income in 1948 was $29,599, providing the company a much-needed boost after the losses it suffered during the strike just a few years earlier.[65] Revenue for the year was $418,400, with expenses of $386,642. "[It was] by far our best year," Earl Jr. recalled.

The Congdons' oldest son, Earl Jr., had taken on additional responsibilities with the company by that point. Earl Sr. tried to instill a work ethic in him by buying him a Buick convertible at age 18, but would not give him any gasoline, even though the Congdons had access to a company pump. "He wanted me to figure out that if I didn't work, I wouldn't be able to drive the Buick because I wouldn't have any gas," Earl Jr. explained.[66]

Earl Jr. worked hard at the company, learning every aspect of the business. "I drove a tractor-trailer over the road most of the summer of 1948," he noted. "Did I have a ball! It was a real fun summer for me. I remember that truck No. 69 had a terrible vibration. Dad said it had been wrecked. Years later, we discovered it had a bent driveshaft."[67]

The next year, Old Dominion had an opportunity to work with Wilson Freight Forwarding Company, which needed some freight hauled from Richmond to Cincinnati, Ohio, with a load to return back to Richmond. Earl Jr., eager to make his way across the open road, asked his father for an opportunity to take the job, but Earl Sr. told his son, "You have only had over-the-road experience between Richmond and Norfolk, where it's flat. You have to cross the mountains to Cincinnati, and I don't want you to do it alone. If you would like to go with Floyd Redmon, who has had experience driving in the mountains, that will be fine."[68]

Earl Jr. agreed and made the journey with Redmon, a veteran Old Dominion driver. He became infinitely grateful that his father had used the wisdom that he'd learned from driving outside of Virginia to send his son on the trip with an expert because he hadn't expected to face so many obstacles:

As we approached the mountains, I was driving, and Floyd was my coach. I made it to the top of the mountain without a problem, but as soon as I started down the other side, I kept applying my brakes, and every time I applied the brakes, I used part of the reserve air supply, which of course was needed to stop the truck since we had air brakes. When the air pressure got down to 35 pounds, Floyd looked over at me and he said, "If you don't pull over,

THE NAME "OLD DOMINION"

The term "Old Dominion" refers to the Commonwealth of Virginia, where Old Dominion was founded.

THE TERM "OLD DOMINION" IS FAMILIAR TO MANY people, partly because of their familiarity with the famous freight line. The true origins of this term stretch back centuries. The word "dominion" refers to the complete ownership of a territory. In the 1600s, King Charles II of England referred to Virginia as among his "dominions," along with England, Scotland, Ireland, and France, because he considered Virginia "the best of his distant children."[1] At the time, Virginia residents considered themselves the most loyal of King Charles' American settlements, so the commonwealth adopted the nickname "Old Dominion" to demonstrate solidarity with England following restoration of the monarchy in 1660.[2]

Old Dominion Freight Line was based in Virginia, Lillian Congdon's home state, where Earl Sr. and Lillian first met in the 1920s. The name represented the Congdon family's strong connection to the state. Since the company originally traveled routes only between Richmond and Norfolk, the name "Old Dominion" also described the freight line's territory.

Over the years, as Old Dominion moved into North Carolina, some publications referred to the company as "the North Carolina freight line with the Virginia name." Even as the company has spread across the country, it remains proud of its original Richmond roots, continuing its legacy as Old Dominion Freight Line.

This 1948 photograph is among the first professional pictures taken of an Old Dominion tractor-trailer.

stop the truck, and build up some air, I'm bailing out and will leave you to ride it down the mountain with no brakes." Had Floyd not been there, I might not be here now.[69]

The trip back was equally challenging, with Earl Jr. continuing to learn important lessons from the veteran driver. While climbing a steep hill in Charleston, West Virginia, Earl Jr. stopped at a traffic light. However, when the light turned green, the truck's heavy load and the slope of the hill made it impossible for Earl Jr. to get the truck moving. He tried repeatedly to get it to move, but it simply would not budge. He awakened Redmon, who had been sleeping in the passenger seat, and asked him for assistance.[70]

Redmon advised Earl Jr. to set the brake, after which the two men switched places so that Redmon was at the wheel. According to Earl Jr., with no one behind him, Redmon "backed the truck halfway down the hill, jackknifed it expertly, and snaked his way from side to side up the hill, timing the traffic light so that it would be green when he reached the top. Around the corner he went, through the green light, stopped the truck, and said 'Okay, you can drive now.' I was impressed and thanked the Lord that I had not gone to Cincinnati alone."[71]

By 1949, Earl Jr. was eager to learn more about the trucking business and took a Motor Carrier Safety course at the University of Virginia along with W. O. Malbone, one of Old Dominion's senior employees. "I have a picture of the graduating class, and believe me, I was a child among men," he said.[72]

Despite Earl Jr.'s hard work and genuine interest in the company, at 19, he was still learning the nuances of the business world. However, Earl Sr. realized that for his son to become a solid businessman, he would have to learn from his mistakes.

According to Earl Jr., when he and Malbone returned from the safety course, they presented Earl Sr. with "the harebrained scheme that we needed to put a vehicle on the road between Richmond and Norfolk and load it with spare tires and maybe a couple of cans of gasoline and some water and whatever else—maybe a safety kit," Earl Jr. later recalled.

The vehicle chosen was a Dodge Power Wagon that Earl Sr. had bought brand-new, a huge workhorse of a truck that was similar to military vehicles used in World War II.[73] Earl Jr. told his father that

Old Dominion would "have that Power Wagon flying back and forth between Richmond and Norfolk in case it might see an Old Dominion truck in trouble. It would be there to repair it."[74]

Old Dominion placed an advertisement describing the radio-equipped Power Wagon as a modern piece of equipment that carried emergency medical supplies, including a stretcher, and that the driver was thoroughly trained by the American Red Cross to render first aid. Not only was the driver able to help in medical emergencies, but he was also an able mechanic. The car carried gasoline, water, batteries, and other parts that would facilitate emergency roadside repair jobs.[75]

Unfortunately, the Power Wagon safety vehicle proved a massive drain on the company's finances. Between the cost of operating the Wagon and the driver's salary, "what we were going to do was wipe out Old Dominion's profit with this stupid thing," Earl Jr. later recalled. However, he appreciated the fact that his father had given him the freedom to make the decision and learn from it.[76]

Earl Jr. later recalled another character-building experience that he and his father shared, during which Earl Jr. was allowed some wiggle room to develop his decision-making skills:

One incident involved our driver, Keeton, who drove International tractor No. 106, which was our newest in 1949. Keeton had been fired for continually getting drunk and came to me, as the boss' son, asking me to intercede for him with Dad to get his job back. He promised faithfully that if I could resecure his job that he would never drink on the job again. I believed him and went to Dad to plead Keeton's case. Dad smiled and said, "I'm going to take him back based on his promise to you, but I don't believe that he will change, and I predict a problem."

Sure enough, no more than two weeks later, Dad called me in the office and said, "You'll have to go to Norfolk and bring back No. 106. Keeton's drunk." Needless to say, that was the end of Mr. Keeton.[77]

The End of a Decade

Old Dominion ended 1949 with considerably less earnings than the year before. Pretax income in 1949 came in at just $1,048, prompting Lillian and Earl Congdon Sr. to reduce their pay to $3,100 each.[78] The lowered earnings were due, in part, to spending more money on improvements. In 1949, the company had spent $25,000 to construct a terminal in Norfolk, built of corrugated metal, and featured 10 loading bays on each side of the dock.[79]

By the end of 1949, Earl Jr. had graduated high school and had begun to attend Smithdeal Massey Business College as a full-time student in the mornings. After school, he would work from 2:00 P.M. until 9:00 each night as Old Dominion's Richmond dock foreman.[80]

What Earl Jr. did not realize was that as the company entered the 1950s, his skills would be tested more than ever before, and he would be thrust into a new and unexpected role within the company.

This 1950 advertisement featured Old Dominion's "Road Patrol," a Dodge Power Wagon that Old Dominion had equipped with first aid supplies and mechanical equipment. Focusing on the company's safety record, the ad let readers know that Old Dominion had not experienced a single chargeable accident on the road in the past five years.

CHAPTER THREE

LOSS OF A PIONEER

1950–1958

She rolled up her sleeves and said, "Let's go to work." It was a very sad time for us.

—Earl Congdon Jr.
on his mother's perseverance following
the unexpected death of his father[1]

BY 1950, THE CONGDONS HAD BEEN immersed in the trucking industry for 20 years. Old Dominion had been launched 16 years earlier, growing from a one-truck operation to a full-fledged freight line. None of the company's success could have been possible without the hard work of Earl Sr. and Lillian Congdon, who had built the company from the ground up. Working side by side over the years, the couple knew each other's strengths and capitalized on them to help the business. However, in 1950, that successful partnership would be affected by a heartbreaking event that no one could have predicted.

On March 18, 1950, 43-year-old Earl Sr. was descending the basement stairs at a friend's house when he fell down the steps. He suffered a serious brain injury from the fall. Tragically, he passed away just four days later, on March 22, 1950.[2]

Earl Sr.'s accident may have been partly attributable to the injuries he had sustained decades earlier during his motorcycle accident at the age of 21. Despite his prosthetic lower right limb, Earl Sr. had been determined to continue driving, making his living operating trucks and hauling freight. However, losing part of his leg wasn't the only lingering effect of the accident. During the 1927 motorcycle accident, Earl Sr. had broken his arm, which had not healed properly.[3]

"That was part of what caused him to fall down the basement stairs," Earl Jr. explained. "The handrail was on the right-hand side, and it was his right arm that was broken, and we think he tried to reach across to grab the rail with his left hand, but it turned him around backward, and he went down the stairs headfirst, on his back. There was a steel I beam at the foot of the basement stairs that he hit his head on."[4]

Following Earl Sr.'s death, Lillian received offers from others who wanted to purchase Old Dominion, but she turned them down, determined that she and her sons would continue to run the company.[5] Lillian, who had stepped back from having a major role at Old Dominion a few years prior to Earl Sr.'s accident, returned to work and asked Earl Jr. to be her general manager at the age of 19.[6] He left Smithdeal Business College, which he had been attending full time, and enrolled in night school at the University of Richmond so that he could help out with the day-to-day operations at Old Dominion.[7]

On March 22, 1950, Earl Congdon Sr. passed away. A true pioneer in his industry, Earl Sr.'s vision would live on through the work and dedication of his wife and two sons.

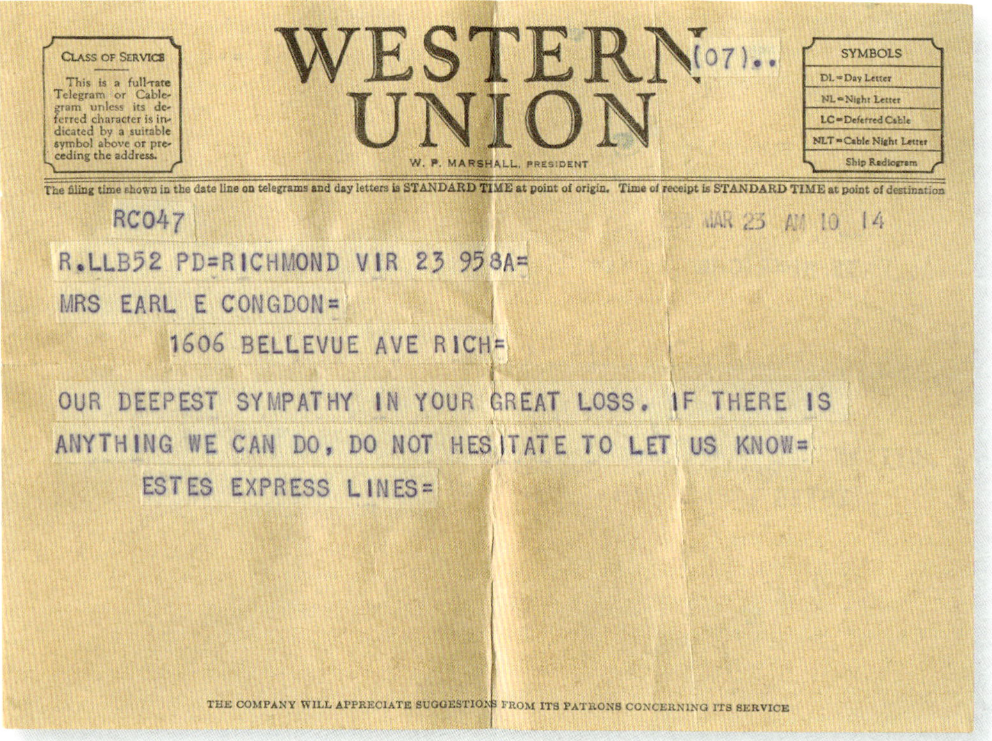
CLASS OF SERVICE
This is a full-rate Telegram or Cablegram unless its deferred character is indicated by a suitable symbol above or preceding the address.

WESTERN UNION (07)..

W. P. MARSHALL, PRESIDENT

SYMBOLS
DL=Day Letter
NL=Night Letter
LC=Deferred Cable
NLT=Cable Night Letter
Ship Radiogram

The filing time shown in the date line on telegrams and day letters is STANDARD TIME at point of origin. Time of receipt is STANDARD TIME at point of destination

RC047

MAR 23 AM 10 14

R.LLB52 PD=RICHMOND VIR 23 958A=

MRS EARL E CONGDON=

1606 BELLEVUE AVE RICH=

OUR DEEPEST SYMPATHY IN YOUR GREAT LOSS. IF THERE IS ANYTHING WE CAN DO, DO NOT HESITATE TO LET US KNOW=

ESTES EXPRESS LINES=

THE COMPANY WILL APPRECIATE SUGGESTIONS FROM ITS PATRONS CONCERNING ITS SERVICE

Estes Express, a local freight company that Old Dominion considered a competitor, sent Lillian Congdon this touching telegram to express sympathy after Earl Sr.'s tragic passing.

"We were fortunate to have 100 loyal employees, all of whom were very anxious to help Mother make a success of Old Dominion," Earl Jr. noted.[8] Early employees in the 1950s included Lawrence Sizer, director of maintenance; H. T. McNamara, sales manager and later Richmond terminal manager; Secretary-Treasurer Al Ghosn; and Hubert Rash, who became the company's first Norfolk rate clerk in 1948.

However, not all of the employees were thrilled with Lillian's decision to bring her sons on board. Traffic manager W. O. Malbone, Earl Sr.'s right-hand man, had expected to take over the company's general management.[9] After Lillian brought her sons into management positions instead of appointing him president, he remarked, "If the kindergarten would get out of the way, I could run this company," a comment that Earl Jr. considered a personal insult.[10]

Despite his initial resistance, Malbone, whom the Congdons considered a family friend as well as an employee, eventually came around and agreed that Lillian had made the best decision for the company, remarking a few years later, "Those boys knew what to do the day they walked in the place after Big Earl was gone."[11]

Yet Malbone could not have been alone in his consternation at Lillian's decision in 1950. Not only was it rare for a woman to head a freight line at that time, but it was even more unusual for two teenage boys to take the helm of a growing company. Trucking industry insiders marveled at the situation. In a 1968 profile of Old Dominion, *International Trail* magazine indicated that Lillian's contemporaries insisted that "the pretty matron was 'leading with her chin'" and that the decision to ask her sons to help her run the company "was considered not less astonishing than if the modern-day Chicago Cubs were suddenly to replace Manager Leo Durocher with the batboy."[12]

Financial Woes

Shortly after Earl Sr.'s passing, Lillian received a call from Manchester Board and Paper, a company that the Congdon family had been leasing trucks to for more than 10 years.[13] Manchester's management realized that Earl Sr. and Lillian had been earning $30,000 annually on the six tractors and

Right: Listed is Old Dominion's management team in 1949.

Below: After Earl Sr. passed away, Lillian came out of semiretirement to run the company with her sons.

MANAGEMENT TEAM

E E Congdon.................... General Manager
W O Malbone..................... Traffic Manager
E J Hayes......................... Book Keeper
R H Tiller....................... Office Manager
F P Woodlief.......................... Salesman
J H Callahan....................... Rate Clerk
C E Matthews......... Richmond Terminal Manager
E W Coleman........... Norfolk Terminal Manager
W E Chesnutt.......... Newport Terminal Manager

five trailers that the Congdons had leased to it and said that effective July 1, Manchester would either buy the trucks from the Congdons at book value, or the Congdons could keep the trucks and Manchester would buy their own new trucks.[14]

Considering that the Congdons were only drawing a combined $6,200 annually from Old Dominion, it would have been a huge blow to the family if it lost the $30,000 per-year contract with Manchester.[15] "Our family lived rather well back in the 1940s," Earl later recalled. "Back then, $30,000 a year was a lot of money."[16]

Lillian and her sons knew that the loss of this income stream would prove tough on the family, but she also accepted the fact that it might be inevitable, so she and her sons put their heads together to develop additional financial opportunities within the company.

"We realized that we had to make some improvements at Old Dominion if we were going to be able to continue to live anywhere near the lifestyle we'd become accustomed to enjoying," Earl noted. "I did my best, and she was a pretty good coach, and between her, Jack, and me, and our loyal Old Dominion employees, we made Old Dominion better."[17]

Earl wasn't about to assume that Manchester had valued the leased equipment appropriately, and if Manchester was going to buy it from the Congdons, he wanted to ensure that his family received every penny to which they were entitled. He had the Manchester equipment appraised and realized it was worth more than book value. "We went back to Manchester with appraisals and convinced them that they should pay Mother appraised value for the equipment," he recalled. "I believe she got about $20,000 from the sale of the trucks and trailers."[18]

Making Up for Lost Income

The Congdons and their staffers at Old Dominion found several innovative ways to bring additional money into the company after the loss of the Manchester Board and Paper contract. First, they sold Earl Sr.'s boat, along with the company's Dodge Power Wagon, which Earl had employed as the company's very costly safety vehicle back in 1949. Sales of both items brought in $4,000 in much-needed cash.[19] In addition, Earl discovered surplus equipment parked in the truck yard and suggested that the company sell it to raise funds. Malbone, however, had another

WHAT DID OLD DOMINION HAUL?

TRUCKING COMPANIES CAN CARRY ANY VARIETY of freight. While some specialize in just one type, Old Dominion carried general commodities. Major accounts in the 1950s included tobacco companies, companies that shipped canned goods or paper, and government traffic.[1]

Because Old Dominion's main route in the 1950s ran between Richmond and Norfolk, most of the cargo during that period originated in one city and headed to the other. Norfolk is located on the water and has a central position on the East Coast, so it has always been a major shipping port, where goods arrive on ships and must subsequently be carried to points west. In addition, as the site of a large naval base, government traffic has always traveled to and from Norfolk.

"In those days, the Richmond over-the-road drivers ... would leave Richmond at 5 o'clock in the morning, and they would bring the freight to Norfolk, arriving around, oh, probably 7:30 or 8 o'clock, and then Norfolk employees would unload those trucks and deliver the freight," recalled Earl Congdon Jr., who pinch-hit as a driver and dockworker from time to time.[2]

"The Richmond Road drivers would go down to the steamship piers and pick up loads of canned goods, like pineapple from Hawaii, and burlap out of India, coming to Richmond," where companies would turn the fabric into bags, Earl noted.[3] "Coffee from South America was also a mainstay of our backhaul business."[4]

idea—he decided they should put the equipment to work.[20]

Malbone recalled that back in 1949, Lillian's brother-in-law, a skilled accountant, had told Earl Sr. that he had been losing money on the interline freight. Earl Sr. subsequently told the interline carriers that Old Dominion would require 50 percent of the revenue for Old Dominion's portion of the haul, regardless of the point of origin. "Since all of these interline carriers had a much longer haul than we did, this was the equivalent of telling them that we didn't want their business, so we lost all of our interline freight," Earl said.

Malbone knew that he could get Old Dominion's surplus equipment back in business if he could just resecure those interline freight contracts. He and Earl contacted the interline companies one by one and were able to bring most of the accounts back within Old Dominion and get those surplus trucks back on the road quickly.[21]

Meanwhile, Jack Congdon, who was just 17 years old when his father passed away, finished school and joined Old Dominion, handling operations and safety for the company. "He was the one who really discovered, I think, that we needed some kind of a safety program," Earl later recalled. "We didn't have one. And when he hired our drivers, he interviewed them and pretty much looked after our operations."[22]

Despite Jack and Earl's hard work and intuitive grasp of the trucking industry, in some respects, it was still clear that they were teenagers. During one instance that proved Earl's boyhood innocence, he decided to join a group that would help him further his sales career within Old Dominion, not realizing that his car did not exactly portray him as an executive:

I knew that I had to get involved in sales, and we had something that was called a traffic club. Every city has got them. And in a traffic club, you'd have motor carrier salespeople, trucking owners, railroad people, and then you'd have the shippers that had something to ship, so it was sort of a customer-

carrier type club, and we'd meet probably once a month. Well, the traffic club was having a picnic out in a city park, and I had a Buick convertible, and I had put a gutted muffler on that Buick convertible, and I'm headed for the traffic club, and I'm coming down a long hill—and this was before you had power steering on cars so that you could turn off the engine and still steer the car—and I thought to myself, "You know, here I am a kid about to join the men—businessmen—and I've got this gutted muffler on this car, and it is not going to enhance my image one bit." So I cut the engine off, and I glided into my parking place, and when the meeting was over, I had to wait for everybody to leave before I could go home.[23]

Old Dominion Makes Financial Progress

Several months after Earl Sr. passed away, Earl asked Eddie Hayes, the company's bookkeeper, if he could see Old Dominion's monthly financial statements and was puzzled by Hayes' response.[24] "We don't have any," Hayes told him. "I close the books and give your Dad a sheet of scratch paper with one number on it. If the number is black, it is the monthly profit for that month. If the number is written in red, it means we had a loss."[25]

Earl, who had been attending business school for over a year at that point, knew from his accounting classes that Old Dominion should begin preparing monthly statements and began doing so in August 1950.[26] For that month alone, he discovered that Old Dominion earned $10,000, which was more than the company had earned the entire year before.[27]

Part of that increase was due to the fact that prior to Earl Sr.'s death, Old Dominion had been absorbing all of the maintenance costs incurred in repairing the trucks that had been leased to Manchester. In addition, the changes that the Congdons and the Old Dominion staffers had put into place allowed the company to realize new profits and lower costs, which made a difference.[28]

In addition, Old Dominion had begun to earn additional income from hauling war freight. The Korean War began in June 1950, and because of the company's location, Old Dominion was called upon to carry military items from the Richmond Quartermaster Depot to the Hampton Roads, Virginia, area.[29] "We were getting $120 a load from Richmond to Hampton Roads, and we had about a dozen of those a day for a while," Earl said.[30]

By 1951, Old Dominion was beginning to acquire new business related to the Korean War and from other companies. That year, Old Dominion was awarded a contract by Ford Motor Company to distribute auto parts from the company's Richmond distribution center to dealers throughout Virginia.[31] "We did buy two Ford tractors that year in order to make Ford feel good about giving us such a large contract," Earl recalled.[32]

The additional contracts helped Old Dominion secure its footing under the new, reorganized company management. During the 1950s, Old Dominion averaged 28 trailer loads per day from Richmond to Williamsburg, Newport News, and Norfolk.[33]

As profits began to grow, the Congdons were able to focus slightly less on how Old Dominion would survive after Earl Sr.'s passing and concentrate more fully on how the company could thrive. However, discord among unionized drivers would throw a wrench in the works of Old Dominion's plans.

In 1950, Old Dominion's tractor-trailers traversed all across Virginia.

Teamsters Take Aim at Old Dominion

In 1953, the International Brotherhood of Teamsters realized that its union had no support from Old Dominion employees who worked at the company's Newport News terminal. On February 24, the Teamsters sent a telegram to the National Labor Relations Board renouncing a claim on Old Dominion employees at that location, leaving Old Dominion with union representation in Norfolk only.[34]

At the time, the unionized carriers in Norfolk had been negotiating with the local Norfolk union over its National Health and Welfare Plan. The plan would cost $2 per week.[35] "I had, however, been advised that the Teamsters officials were using pension and welfare money for purposes other than for the employees' benefit and would not agree to joining the Central States Welfare Fund," Earl said.[36]

Old Dominion's labor attorney recommended that the company's managers should take a quick poll to determine which employees would be willing to work if the Teamsters announced a strike, and all 20 of the Norfolk employees stated that they would.[37]

Old Dominion's Martinsville, Virginia, terminal is pictured here in the late 1950s.

On March 12, 1953, the union called a strike on Old Dominion, one of only two truck lines in Norfolk that had refused to sign the Health and Welfare Plan agreement. "During the preceding night, all of our employees were visited by goons at their homes and threatened with bodily harm should they report for work," noted Earl.[38]

The morning of the strike, Earl headed to Norfolk with Eddie Bass, Old Dominion's Richmond dock foreman, while Jack stayed in Richmond and successfully encouraged the company's Richmond drivers to head to Norfolk to help deliver the freight.[39]

When Earl and Bass arrived in Norfolk, they found that none of the employees had reported to work, so the two men drove to an area of Norfolk and recruited workers willing to cross the picket line for employment.[40]

In addition, Old Dominion placed an advertisement seeking employees and received scores of applications. Between the group they recruited, the Richmond Road drivers, as well as Jack and Earl, who were helping out, Old Dominion was able to deliver and pick up 80 percent of the company's freight on the Thursday that the strike began, and by the weekend, the company had caught up with its current delivery schedule. By that Sunday, eight of the 20 striking employees asked to come back to work, and Old Dominion quickly brought them back on board.[41]

Throughout much of the spring of 1953, Old Dominion continued to operate in Norfolk, despite picket lines where union members sometimes yelled threats at the Old Dominion workers.[42] However, despite the union's techniques, it became clear to all involved that Old Dominion was not going to give in.

The picket lines over the next several weeks gradually dwindled down to just one or two pickets, and finally the union gave up the fight, ending Old Dominion's association with the Teamsters union.[43]

Old Dominion Loses Its Only Salesman

In 1954, Old Dominion employed one sales representative. Pete Woodlief was considered a terrific salesman, and other companies quickly took notice of his results. Estes Express, a local freight company, wanted to build its business to compete with Old Dominion's and offered Woodlief $140 per week to join its ranks.[44]

Woodlief, who had been earning $95 a week with Old Dominion, did not want to leave the company but found it hard to turn down such a big pay raise. Earl tried to convince him to stay but could not match Estes' offer because Malbone, Old Dominion's top executive at the time, was making $125 a week, and Old Dominion could not pay Woodlief more than Malbone was earning. Earl offered Woodlief $100 per week and a company car if he would stay with the company.[45]

"This was not enough," said Earl. "He left us, went with Estes, and did a marvelous job of taking Old Dominion freight over to Estes Express over the next several years. In retrospect, we would have done well to have figured out a way to keep Mr. Woodlief."[46]

Earl personally took over Woodlief's role until the company was able to replace him with its new salesman, Hunter MacNamara.[47] By 1954, Old Dominion had regained its footing quite securely following Earl Sr.'s passing, and Lillian and her sons emerged not only as pillars of the freight line community but as highly respected employers who treated their staff like family.

A 1954 profile of Lillian in the *Richmond News Leader* noted that—long before the practice became commonplace—Old Dominion offered profit sharing through retirement funds and a year-end bonus, which "helped make the drivers safety-conscious." In addition, the article indicated that "all of the records of the concern are open to the employees by way of supervisors who discuss operations frankly and openly at monthly all-day meetings."[48]

Noting that Lillian headed into the office every day, the article said she "looks like the star of some dramatic play, with her upswept hairdo, instead of the leader of brawny men. ... And actually, she is the star in a lifetime drama."[49]

TRADE NAMES

WOMAN HEADS FREIGHT LINE

By WILLIAM BIEN
News Leader Business Editor

Most women consider it their special privilege to slice a few years off their calendar age.

Lillian Congdon added a few years. Mrs. Congdon is an unusual woman.

When she went to work—at 13—she never dreamed what the years would turn up. Today she is president of Old Dominion Freight Line, the largest common carrier between Richmond and Norfolk.

At 13, she already had a mind of her own, however. She went to the telephone company and talked herself into a job as an operator. Said she was 16 . . . and who's going to dispute a woman's word?

Before she was 14, Lillian Herbert became a supervisor and instructor.

Then, when she was 17, she decided to marry Earl E. Congdon . . . and a remarkable story of courage and grit began.

They'd made plans for a honeymoon and a little cottage—the things newlyweds always plan.

Then Congdon lost a leg in an accident and spent 10 months in the hospital. They were married anyway, in June, 1928, soon after he left the hospital.

They had nothing. No home, no money, no apparent future . . .

WEDDING PRESENT

But they did have an automobile given to them as a wedding present. They traded that

[Staff Photo]
MRS. CONGDON, SON, EARL, OF FREIGHT LINE

Richmond for a night trip. Over and over, day after day.

"The only time we got much sleep was on week

body trucks. They scratched up enough money to open their own terminal here—on Twentieth

This 1954 profile of Lillian demonstrates the uniqueness of her position, with the title announcing, "Woman Heads Freight Line." *(Image ©* Richmond Times-Dispatch.*)*

A New Acquisition

In 1956, Earl and his brother Jack began looking for ways that they could extend Old Dominion's reach beyond the Richmond-to-Norfolk route and heard that the Bottoms-Fiske Truck Lines was for sale.[50]

Bottoms-Fiske, which was based in High Point, North Carolina, had routes that covered most of North Carolina and Southern Virginia, terminating at Norfolk. The regulation rules stated that a company with an operating certificate that terminates in Norfolk can join its certificate with a different company that operates between Richmond and Norfolk. This meant that acquiring Bottoms-Fiske could legally be a means for Old Dominion to obtain access to the route between Richmond and North Carolina, as long as the drivers traveled through Norfolk.[51]

By that time, Old Dominion had grown its net worth to $350,000, up from $81,000 when Earl Sr. had passed away. However, that was not enough to buy Bottoms-Fiske, which had a net worth of nearly $600,000.[52]

David Fiske, president of Bottoms-Fiske, discussed Old Dominion's financial status with the

Holderness family, which owned the controlling interest in the company. After mulling over the possibilities, Fiske called Earl with a proposal. Bottoms-Fiske wanted $600,000 for the company and asked Old Dominion for a $200,000 down payment. The company would carry the remaining $400,000 balance for eight years at 5 percent interest, after which Old Dominion would own the company free and clear.

Unfortunately, Old Dominion did not have $200,000.[53] Still, that did not dissuade the Congdons from pursuing the acquisition. "Old Dominion had very little debt at that time, and I told them that we would see our bank in Richmond to see if it would lend us the down payment money," Earl said.[54]

A 1969 magazine profile of Earl later likened Old Dominion's interest in buying Bottoms-Fiske to "a goldfish swallowing a trout."[55] Earl himself referred to the acquisition as "sort of like an upside-down merger."[56]

However, the Congdons would not be discouraged by the size of the transaction. After discussing the matter, Earl, Jack, and Lillian agreed that the acquisition would be good for the company, so they procured a loan to fund the purchase.

With Lillian's support, the family took out the loan they needed to offer Bottoms-Fiske the $200,000 down payment. "God bless Mother," Earl said. "She had to put her personal signature on all of our loans. Mother risked everything she had to back Jack and me and let us do what we did."[57]

Lillian also made an offhanded comment that helped Old Dominion gain extra leverage as part of the deal. During the last bargaining session over the acquisition, Lillian expressed concern that if another Depression struck the country, the Congdons would lose Old Dominion.[58] Chick Holderness, the majority owner of Bottoms-Fiske, said, "Little lady, if that's all that's bothering you, here's what I'll do: If you'll keep Bottoms-Fiske

INTERLINE TRUCKING IN THE 1950s

OLD DOMINION EARNED HALF OF ITS REVENUE during the 1950s by partnering with interline carriers to transport freight from one state to another, often with intermediate points in between.[1]

Interline trucking was a crucial factor in the freight industry during a time when trucking companies operated under very restrictive Certificates of Public Convenience and Necessity. Whereas Old Dominion was authorized to carry freight from Norfolk to Richmond, another company that was only able to haul from Richmond to Philadelphia could easily partner with Old Dominion to get freight originating from Norfolk that needed to find a way to Philadelphia, or vice versa. "One of Old Dominion's major interline carriers was Brooks Transportation, which had operations between Virginia and New York," Earl Congdon Jr. noted.

Another was Cochrane Transportation Company, which operated between Richmond; Washington, D.C.; Baltimore; and Philadelphia. "Cochrane Transportation had a very nice movement from Peoples Drug amounting to one or two trailer loads per day originating in Washington D.C., transferred to Old Dominion in Richmond, for delivery to Peoples Drug in Newport News and Norfolk," Earl recalled.[2]

On an average day in the 1950s, Old Dominion averaged 28 trailer loads, but on a very big day, the company could handle as many as 40 loads, half of which came from interline traffic.[3]

separate from Old Dominion until you've paid us off, if something bad happens, as long as you live up to everything you're supposed to do, and we have to repossess it ... why, if you come up short, if we can't sell it for what you owe us, we will not come back on Old Dominion for the deficit."[59]

With that, Old Dominion closed the acquisition of Bottoms-Fiske in 1956, and received Interstate Commerce Commission (ICC) approval of the acquisition in May 1957.[60] Part of the sale agreement was that 61-year-old David Fiske would continue running Bottoms-Fiske for another five years after the acquisition.[61] In addition, Old Dominion would run Bottoms-Fiske as a separate subsidiary of the company and not merge it into Old Dominion until Old Dominion paid off the $400,000 that it owed.[62]

Some of the original employees from the Bottoms-Fiske acquisition included Henry Marshall, vice president of sales and traffic; R. L. Bullard Jr., secretary–treasurer; Fred Peters, assistant secretary treasurer; Jim Pipes, traffic manager; Reid Hanes, claims agent; Paul Pilcher, safety director; Inky Murr, Charlotte terminal manager; C. C. White, Norfolk terminal manager; Clyde Hodges, Eden terminal manager; Lawanna Mooney, secretary; Lucille Kivett, purchasing agent; Cornell Brenson, longtime driver; and W. T. Ellis, who would go on to become division manager.

With the acquisition of Bottoms-Fiske came inevitable management changes, as Old Dominion was restructured to make the two companies work together more smoothly. One major change that took place during that time was the departure of W. O. Malbone.

In 1957, Earl offered early retirement to Malbone, who had suffered several strokes, saying that Old Dominion would continue to pay Malbone a reduced salary indefinitely for health reasons. C. G. "Jerry" Pusey replaced Malbone as traffic manager.

With the Bottoms-Fiske acquisition in the works, Old Dominion staffers began to adjust to operating a major subsidiary located in another state. And the transition would have to take place faster than anyone could have imagined, because a surprise waited just around the corner that would drain the company's resources and threaten Old Dominion's very existence.

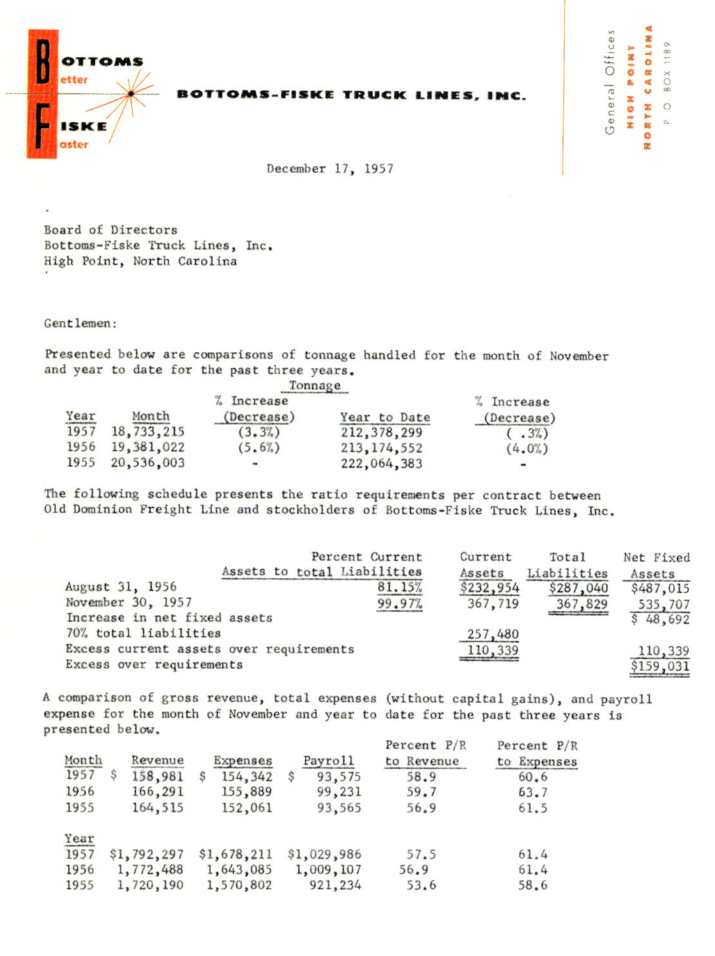

BOTTOMS Better FISKE Faster

BOTTOMS-FISKE TRUCK LINES, INC.

General Offices
HIGH POINT
NORTH CAROLINA
P. O. BOX 1189

December 17, 1957

Board of Directors
Bottoms-Fiske Truck Lines, Inc.
High Point, North Carolina

Gentlemen:

Presented below are comparisons of tonnage handled for the month of November and year to date for the past three years.

	Tonnage			
Year	Month	% Increase (Decrease)	Year to Date	% Increase (Decrease)
1957	18,733,215	(3.3%)	212,378,299	(.3%)
1956	19,381,022	(5.6%)	213,174,552	(4.0%)
1955	20,536,003	-	222,064,383	-

The following schedule presents the ratio requirements per contract between Old Dominion Freight Line and stockholders of Bottoms-Fiske Truck Lines, Inc.

	Percent Current Assets to total Liabilities	Current Assets	Total Liabilities	Net Fixed Assets
August 31, 1956	81.15%	$232,954	$287,040	$487,015
November 30, 1957	99.97%	367,719	367,829	535,707
Increase in net fixed assets				$ 48,692
70% total liabilities		257,480		
Excess current assets over requirements		110,339		110,339
Excess over requirements				$159,031

A comparison of gross revenue, total expenses (without capital gains), and payroll expense for the month of November and year to date for the past three years is presented below.

Month	Revenue	Expenses	Payroll	Percent P/R to Revenue	Percent P/R to Expenses
1957	$ 158,981	$ 154,342	$ 93,575	58.9	60.6
1956	166,291	155,889	99,231	59.7	63.7
1955	164,515	152,061	93,565	56.9	61.5
Year					
1957	$1,792,297	$1,678,211	$1,029,986	57.5	61.4
1956	1,772,488	1,643,085	1,009,107	56.9	61.4
1955	1,720,190	1,570,802	921,234	53.6	58.6

In May 1957, the Interstate Commerce Commission approved Old Dominion's acquisition of Bottoms-Fiske Truck Lines, Inc., which was based in High Point, North Carolina. The company was considerably bigger than Old Dominion, making the acquisition a bit unique, but Lillian's support, and a creative financing agreement, helped make it happen.

The damage to a Bottoms-Fiske office following the union bomb attack was terrible. Strikers threw dynamite through the windows of several Bottoms-Fiske facilities during the strike, which lasted from 1959 through 1961. *(Photo by Jim Wommack.)*

CHAPTER FOUR

SIGNIFICANT TRANSITIONS

1959–1969

High Point got one of its most dynamic young executives, who says, "You either expand or eventually you will go out of the trucking business." And if expansion is the name of the game, Congdon is playing it to the hilt as president of Old Dominion.

—A 1969 profile of Earl Congdon in the *High Point Enterprise*[1]

AFTER THE 1956 PURCHASE OF Bottoms-Fiske, the Congdons continued to run Old Dominion from Richmond, while David Fiske managed Bottoms-Fiske from its High Point, North Carolina, headquarters.

Earl and Jack Congdon checked in on David Fiske from time to time, but Fiske kept the Congdons at arm's length, explaining that the Bottoms-Fiske employees felt concerned about their job security after having been acquired by Old Dominion, which was a considerably smaller operation.[2]

When Jack and Earl did visit the Bottoms-Fiske operation in High Point, Fiske would take them golfing, refusing to show them around the office and introduce them to staffers.[3] However, Jack and Earl knew that operating two truck lines separately would mean redundancies. Therefore, the Congdon brothers instituted some changes from Richmond, to the dismay of Fiske, as Earl later recalled:

My brother and I wanted to merge the Old Dominion and Bottoms-Fiske terminals at Norfolk. That was Mr. Fiske's largest terminal, next to his big one in High Point, and his best buddy in the company was the terminal manager at Bottoms-Fiske. Anyway, we put them together, and we made the Old Dominion manager the sales guy, and the Bottoms-Fiske manager the terminal manager. My brother goes in one day and tells the Bottoms-Fiske manager, "If you don't get your dock costs down to five cents for a hundred pounds, we're going to have to have a serious talk."

The Bottoms-Fiske fellow quit, and a day or two later, I walk into Mr. Fiske's office in North Carolina, and he looks at me. He's livid. And he said, "That brother of yours has caused my buddy in Norfolk to quit. He's no longer welcome down here. ... You can come, but he better not set his foot in my office."

So I go back to my brother Jack, and I said, "Jack, we've got to do something. ... We need Mr. Fiske's goodwill."

We worked it out. We brought the Bottoms-Fiske guy back, and we made him the salesman and

In the 1960s, Old Dominion used posters to remind employees of ways to help keep claims rates low. *(Image repoduced by permission of American Trucking Association, Inc.)*

Mrs. Earl E. Congdon
512 Ridge Top Road
Richmond, Virginia

Dec. 21, 1959

Dear Dot & Henry,

Please give our thanks to all the wonderful folks at Bottoms-Fiske for the lovely time shown to us Saturday last. Putting it mildly, "we had a ball"! The party couldn't have been nicer & the girls' skit was as cute as can be. We all wish it could have lasted longer.

All of us in Richmond hope you all have a wonderful Christmas. Thanks ever so much.

Sincerely,
Kitty

Mr. & Mrs. Henry Marshall
702 Gatewood Ave.
High Point, N.C.

Bottoms-Fiske and Old Dominion operated separately, but the Congdons made occasional trips to High Point to check in. In this handwritten note, Kitty Congdon, Earl's wife, thanks one of the Bottoms-Fiske executives and his wife for their hospitality during a visit.

> *our guy the terminal manager without having to get the thing down to a nickel, and the Bottoms-Fiske guy stayed with us until he retired many years later.*[4]

Although Fiske's contract allowed him to continue managing Bottoms-Fiske for five years, he only stayed with the company for two years following the acquisition.[5] When Jack and Earl received Fiske's April 1959 announcement of his plan to retire to Florida, they were surprised about taking on the challenge of managing Bottoms-Fiske, but "anxious to give it a go," Earl recalled.[6]

On May 1, Fiske retired, and Jack and Earl traveled to High Point to take over the business, with Earl serving as president of Bottoms-Fiske. They met one employee who told the brothers, "We sure hope you boys know what you're doing."[7]

"Little did she know that we didn't," Earl later remarked. "It was going to be necessary to get some on-the-job training quickly."[8]

Teamsters at Bottoms-Fiske

On May 18, 1959, just weeks after Fiske's retirement, Jack and Earl received a letter from the local Teamsters union indicating that it represented a majority of Bottoms-Fiske employees. The brothers, however, knew they needed more than the union's word for the fact that it represented the company's drivers. The Congdons scheduled elections in 1959 for August 27 and 28.[9]

During the interim, the Congdons decided to get to know as many of the Bottoms-Fiske drivers, warehousemen, and mechanics as they could prior to the election. They spent time riding along with truck drivers and working alongside dockworkers, explaining the belief that the employees did not need a union, since the Congdons had their best interests at heart.[10]

Despite their efforts, about 56 percent of Bottoms-Fiske employees voted in favor of the union, forcing Jack and Earl to bargain with the Teamsters over the future of Bottoms-Fiske. The union vote did not involve Old Dominion Freight Line, which was running in Virginia as a separate company.[11]

The Congdons hired a labor attorney, who told the brothers that they had several choices. First, they could sign the union contract, which would increase Bottoms-Fiske's operating costs by $400,000 a year. That was not a viable option, considering the highest yearly profit Bottoms-Fiske ever made was only $125,000. The second choice was that Bottoms-Fiske could let the union shut them down by striking, which probably would have bankrupted the company. The third option was to attempt to operate the company, despite a strike.[12]

The attorney asked the Congdons whether they would be able to run Bottoms-Fiske during a strike. "We think we can," Earl replied. "We did it in Norfolk back in 1953, and that seems to be the only logical thing that we can do."[13]

Due to the Congdons' negative experiences with unions nearly bankrupting Old Dominion in 1946, the family was determined to keep Bottoms-Fiske above water and entered into negotiations, attempting to agree on a contract that would keep Bottoms-Fiske in business.[14]

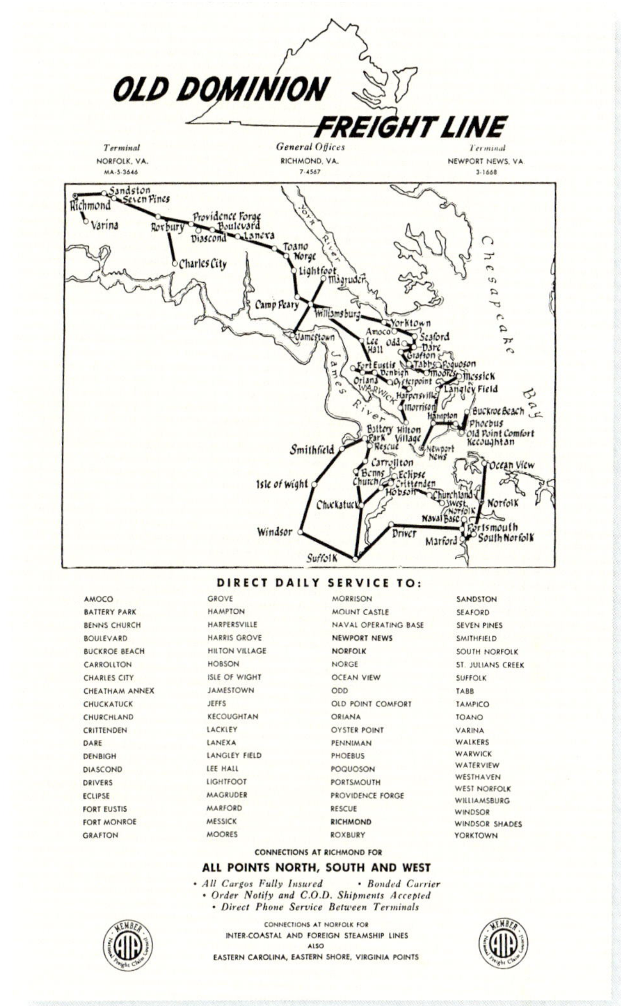

By 1955, Old Dominion offered direct daily service to more than 80 cities throughout Virginia.

Earl feared that unionizing Bottoms-Fiske would prove devastating not just to Old Dominion, but to his own family on a personal level. According to Bob Hoover, who had been with Bottoms-Fiske for a year and a half when the strike took place:

> *Earl told us, when he was at our house one night, "We've lost everything we have in Richmond. We've lost our home, everything we own, to buy Bottoms-Fiske out. If we can't make it and we have to go union, I'm going to*

Unionization in the Trucking Industry

The Congdons had several experiences with unions, both in times of peace and strife. However, unions were widely represented among tractor-trailer drivers, promising them more reasonable working conditions and higher wages. For trucking companies, the prospect of workers unionizing was often a difficult decision.

By 1961, more than 7 million people worked in the trucking industry, with carriers drawing revenues of more than $7 billion.[1] By 1964, the International Brotherhood of Teamsters represented more than 450,000 over-the-road and local cartage drivers across the United States.[2]

The Teamsters maintained local unions in various cities, which individually bargained with companies such as Old Dominion to discuss the rights of their workers. But in 1964, Jimmy Hoffa, then serving as president of the Teamsters, negotiated the union's first national contract, which laid out a uniform set of conditions and timetables for protesting workers.[3]

Under the Master Freight Agreement, the Teamsters gained "power equal and even beyond that of the big trucking companies," making it an important document in the Teamster's history.[4]

For Old Dominion, unionization was not a viable option. "We believe we would have been bankrupt many years ago if our employees had not been convinced they did not need the Teamsters at Old Dominion," Earl Congdon noted. "One [factor] was maintaining that good relationship with our employees."[5]

lose—my family is going to lose—everything we've invested in this."

That was his story, and he said, "I just hope we can survive it."[15]

In 1959, seven bargaining sessions took place between September 29 and November 7. During the meetings, Bottoms-Fiske repeatedly told the Teamsters that the company would be unable to meet the union's demands but had its own proposal to introduce. However, the union considered Bottoms-Fiske's wage offer to be "too vague" and dismissed it. "While we were in the bargaining, of course, we were teaching the men who worked in our office how to run our forklifts out on the dock right in front of the dockworkers," Earl recalled. "We wanted them to see we were serious about operating during a strike."[16]

In addition, Bottoms-Fiske began interviewing prospective employees, while Jack met with Old Dominion's Richmond line-haul drivers to see how many of them would come to North Carolina and drive trucks. Jack also lined up new drivers who indicated that they would be willing to work for Bottoms-Fiske temporarily. "The thing that was really interesting is that there was a Teamster new-car-carrier trucker in Richmond," Earl said. "His union drivers—Teamster drivers—were on layoff because they were having a model changeover ... at the automotive companies, and my brother got the union drivers to drive the Old Dominion trucks between Richmond and Norfolk so that the Old Dominion drivers could come to North Carolina and help us keep Bottoms-Fiske operating."[17]

At the November 7, 1959, bargaining session, the company once again came to an impasse with the union, and Bottoms-Fiske agreed to return to the next meeting—scheduled for December 8—with another offer. However, just two days after the seventh bargaining meeting, the union called the Bottoms-Fiske employees on strike.[18]

On November 9, 1959, Earl went to an evening movie in High Point and decided to stop by the High Point terminal afterward, around 9:00 P.M., to see if anything was happening at the dock. When he arrived, he was "greeted with a sight I shall never forget," he later recalled. "Nearly all of our 41 dockworkers had gone on strike. ... I believe we had only two workers on that dock. God bless them both."[19]

The sight of the striking workers completely stunned Earl. However, what shocked him more than he ever could have expected was the number of reinforcements who bravely showed up to fill their spots not long after:

> *There were probably 50 or 60 drunken picketers. The strike had started, and it was cold that night. ... They had a big bonfire going, and they were whooping and hollering and having the best time. Everybody was happy, and they told us they had shut the damn place down. I walked up on our loading dock, and there were two lone souls standing there that had decided they were going to work, and the rest of the dock crew was on strike. I found out later that we had a one-armed dock foreman who was mean as hell, and apparently nobody liked him, and this had a lot to do with why our High Point dock took such a big hit, because they hated the foreman. Anyway, only two people were there, but I bet, within an hour or two, the dock was full of people, and what had happened was the husbands of the women who worked in the office came to help us on that dock, our mechanics showed up to get those trucks loaded, and the line drivers all came in. They knew that if they didn't work the freight, they wouldn't have any trips to pull that night. And we only had a couple of salesmen, but they were there. ... The problem was, nobody knew what to do.*[20]

Earl believed that in fairness to the drivers who didn't strike, he should personally be the first driver to take a truck past the picket line.[21] "I had a .38 on the seat," Earl later recalled. "I took the first truck through the picket line myself, and I can remember my foot was shaking because I was nervous. ... I figured that I needed to take the first one through there, because how could I ask other people to do it if I wouldn't do it myself?"[22]

Though justifiably nervous, Earl led the way through the line of picketing workers, his truck lurching forward. However, he wasn't completely alone. "The one-armed fellow got in his pickup truck—he was worried about my safety—and he followed me all the way to Winston-Salem just in case somebody wanted to jump me," Earl said. "We went to Winston-Salem with just the tractor and picked up a load of cigarettes over there that was dropped on our yard, and I brought them back, and came back through the picket line."[23] At 4:00 in the morning, Jack arrived at the High Point terminal on a chartered bus with 35 drivers from Richmond. "We were sure glad to see them," Earl said.

The Strike Turns Violent

Once the striking workers realized that Bottoms-Fiske was operating at full capacity without them, violence began.[24] Less than a week after the strike started, Bottoms-Fiske vans were attacked with pistols and rocks, with nonstriking drivers reporting attacks and assaults by striking drivers.[25] "We had 20 drivers shot at," Earl later recalled. "And the strikers would get up on an overpass over the highway with a big chunk of concrete and wait for one of our trucks to come under the bridge, and then they'd drop the concrete and try to time it so that it would go through the windshield."[26]

Not all of the truck drivers who filled in for the strikers were prepared for the intimidation they faced. One of Old Dominion's line-haul drivers, who had come to High Point to help drive for Bottoms-Fiske during the strike, was on his route when a car pulled alongside his truck, containing several men who were pointing pistols at him.

"They scared him so bad that he made a U-turn on the highway," Earl recalled. "[He] came barreling back in through the company gate, nearly running over a couple of pickets, jumped out of his truck, came in my office, and said, 'I'm g-g-g-going back to Richmond.' He left that night. He was one frightened fellow."[27]

The Teamsters did not stop at simply intimidating the drivers. They actually threatened the families of Bottoms-Fiske employees and attacked the terminal itself. According to Hoover:

> *The strikers would go by some of the guys' houses when they knew they were out on their routes and shoot their picture windows out of their houses and just scaring their families.*

Employees survey the damage after strikers threw dynamite through the window of the Bottoms-Fiske terminal, damaging the offices and blowing out windows all across the neighborhood. The perpetrators were never caught. *(Photos by Jim Wommack.)*

> *But the worst thing I remember was, I came in about 4 o'clock in the morning from Newport News, and everybody was all upset. The fire department was there. They put two or three boxes of dynamite at the front of the terminal. Of course, there was nobody in the offices—of the front of the terminal—at that time, and they blew the whole front of the terminal out. I mean, it just took everything off the desk, and tore the desk up, blew the front of the building out. Terrible explosion.*[28]

Not only did Bottoms-Fiske drivers and staff members face intimidation from the union, so did the locals who did business with them. One Bottoms-Fiske striker phoned the local Yellow Top Cab Company, warning the owner that "if he didn't stop sending his drivers to the local trucking terminal with nonstrikers as fares, the cab drivers would be beaten up," a *High Point Enterprise* article noted.[29]

By December 1959, agents for the State Bureau of Investigation had arrived in High Point to keep an eye on the incidents. However, the violence not only continued, it escalated. "We had a watchman down in Charlotte, and they threw a pack of dynamite through a window right over him, and it landed on the floor," Earl said. "I think I would have run like hell, but he picked the dynamite up, carried it outside, and threw it out in the yard. And it blew up and blew windows out of houses in the neighborhood. I mean, it was a pretty big deal."[30] Several additional dynamite blasts took place at the North Carolina and Virginia terminals, but it proved difficult to catch the perpetrators.[31]

Bottoms-Fiske drivers began keeping pistols in their trucks to defend themselves, and companies along their routes took notice. The DuPont plant in Martinsville posted a sign in its guard shack that read, "To the Bottoms-Fiske drivers: Please check your pistols at the guard gate before you come in. We don't want you bringing them into the factory."[32]

At one point, even a man of the cloth commiserated with Earl about the violence:

> *I had a preacher come into my office one day. ... Apparently our truck kicked up a rock, which they do sometimes, and it broke the windshield on this preacher's car, so he tried to stop our truck. Well,*

we had instructed our drivers, "If somebody in a car tries to stop you, don't stop."

So the driver wouldn't stop. But, finally, the preacher must have somehow convinced the driver with a signal or whatever else that he was just a lone person, and so our truck finally pulls over, and the preacher said, when he went up there to the cab, he looked at the end of a pistol. And he wrote me a letter to tell me about it, admitting, "I guess, after the driver told me the story, I can understand."[33]

Organizations around High Point rallied in support of Bottoms-Fiske, with members of associations and the media weighing in. A December 30, 1959, *High Point Enterprise* editorial noted, "The Teamsters' leadership has charted a terrible course. It is incumbent on all thinking men to see that course is not carried to the kind of conclusion that pays off for goons, hoods, and terrorists."[34]

However, Bottoms-Fiske employees did occasionally find ways to fight back. As Bob Hoover recalled:

I'll tell you a little funny instance that happened. The warehouse people were sort of getting tired of the strike, so they loaded a bunch of the warehouse people in the back of a truck, and about midnight, they pulled out like they were going to go deliver something.

The strikers were standing out in the street throwing things. They just thought the driver was by himself. But the truck pulled right out in the middle of the highway in front of the terminal, stopped, and all those warehouse people jumped out of the back, and they ran those strikers all over the countryside there. That was right after the bombing of the front of the terminal, about two weeks later.[35]

As the strike continued into 1960, the violence worsened, with nonstrikers experiencing shots being fired at them, their houses, their trucks, and their cars. They also had sugar poured into their gas tanks, had their tires slashed, and had explosives thrown at the Bottoms-Fiske terminals.[36] On March 25, 1960, Earl asked the High Point police chief to station a police car at Bottoms-Fiske's entrance. Considering the dangerous attacks the company had faced, the chief granted Earl's request.[37]

Bottoms-Fiske continued to participate in bargaining sessions with the union during the strike. By the time the 11th and final session was held on July 27, 1960, the union was no longer haggling over wages and benefits—the strikers were trying to resecure their jobs.

When Bottoms-Fiske had advertised for drivers to replace those who were on strike, the company received more than 500 applications and filled the positions in no time. After a year, many of those strikers wanted their jobs back, but the positions had been filled. "We certainly aren't going to fire men who ducked bullets and dynamite for us, just to hire back those who were shooting the bullets and throwing the dynamite," Earl told a reporter at the time.[38]

By February 1961, the company and the Teamsters still had not come to an agreement, but after 17 months, the striking workers had grown weary. "That big picket line gradually ended up with just two poor, lone pickets walking back and forth after, say, a year," Earl noted. On February 28, the last picketer left the front gate of the Bottoms-Fiske terminal, and the strike ended.[39]

In an interview with the *High Point Enterprise* at the strike's end, Earl said he felt "relief, but in no sense are we gloating."[40] He explained:

A strike is certainly a no-win situation. The union lost its credibility and its treasury. Bottoms-Fiske's finances were so depleted at the end of the strike that no new equipment was ordered for the next two years, and the strikers were forced to find employment elsewhere after having walked the picket line for months on strike for benefits which were not nearly as much as those being earned while employed. Bottoms-Fiske had to rebuild its customer base and its treasury. We shall never forget those loyal employees who stood by the company and took great risks to keep their company and their jobs secure.[41]

Whereas Bottoms-Fiske had a net worth of $614,497 at the end of 1959, 1960 closed out with a net worth of $537,467—a net loss of $77,030.[42] Because the strike did not occur at the Old Dominion headquarters in Richmond, Old Dominion still posted a net profit of $38,622 in 1960.[43]

A Merger in Mind

In 1961, with the strike behind them, the Congdons were able to get back to running two separate freight companies—Bottoms-Fiske in High Point, North Carolina, and Old Dominion in Richmond, Virginia. However, by the next year, it was decided that the best option would be a merger that combined Old Dominion Freight Line and Bottoms-Fiske Truck Lines, resulting in a company known simply as Old Dominion Freight Line.[44]

After the merger was finalized on July 1, 1962, the Bottoms-Fiske name and insignia were dropped from the company's equipment.[45] Earl became the president of the newly formed company, with Lillian serving as chairman of the board and Jack as executive vice president.[46] Earl and Lillian settled into new residences in High Point, North Carolina, while Jack remained in Richmond.[47] By that point, Earl was married with three children, and Lillian had married Emmett Clyde Crowder.

Crowder had been a friend of Earl Sr. back when both were terminal managers with Virginia Motor Express in the 1930s.[48] "In the very late 1940s, Mr. Crowder came to Richmond, and he was with the Wilson Freight Forwarding company out of Cincinnati, and they wanted a cartage agent to do their pickup and delivery work in Richmond," Earl later recalled. "So my dad agreed to do that and they renewed their acquaintance. When Dad died in March 1950, Clyde Crowder was working in our facilities because we were doing his pickup and delivery work, and maybe a few months after my dad's death, when my brother and I were trying to entertain our mother to do the things that good sons would do, Clyde Crowder asked if it would be alright if he came around."[49]

Earl and Jack were delighted to have Crowder take their mother out, and Lillian began a courtship with him. The two married shortly after Lillian moved to High Point, and Crowder joined Lillian there as they set up a new home in North Carolina.[50]

Lillian worked in the office alongside the Old Dominion staffers, where she recorded the company's freight revenues every day by hand.[51] Joann McMillan, who currently works in Old Dominion's claims department and has been with the company since 1967, recalled the excitement around the company when Old Dominion experienced its first $1 million month. Lillian bought hamburgers for the whole office. "I remember she'd take breaks with us in the break room. She just acted like one of the crew. I mean, she worked as hard as anybody else did," McMillan noted.[52]

With total revenue of more than $4 million by the end of 1962, Earl and Jack decided to add to the fleet.[53] The company operated gas-powered tractors and began the conversion to White diesel tractors over a several-year period.[54] By the end of 1962, Old Dominion's fleet included 101 tractors, 217 trailers, 87 straight trucks, and 24 service cars.[55] To house the ever-growing fleet, Old Dominion built a 30-door terminal in Charlotte, North Carolina, and a 24-door terminal in Durham, North Carolina.[56] By 1963, the company operated out of 18 terminals in Virginia and North Carolina.[57]

Despite being chairman of the board at Old Dominion following the merger with Bottoms-Fiske, Lillian Congdon Crowder went into the office every day, recording freight revenue by hand.

The Birth of Old Dominion Truck Leasing

With Lillian and Earl settled into the High Point office, Jack was left with little to do back in Richmond, but his family was happily settled there, and he had no interest in leaving Virginia. While trying to determine what his role could be within Old Dominion, despite the geographic difficulties, Jack got a call from Earl that piqued his interest.

An Old Dominion truck in Mebane, North Carolina, in 1964. *(Photo courtesy of Eastern Alamance High School.)*

In 1964, Earl told Jack that Thomas Built Buses, a High Point–based company, had asked him whether Old Dominion would be willing to lease a truck, but Earl said he didn't know anything about the leasing business. Thomas Built told Earl, "Well, we'll let you experiment with us. You charge us a rate that we've been quoted and then you run it and see how it goes, and if you can do it, fine. And if you can't, tell us how much more you've got to have and why."

Earl considered Thomas Built's proposal and called his brother. He said, "Jack, you could start with that. You have a truck, you have a customer. Why don't you try that and make it grow, go all over Richmond and get you some leases?"[58]

Jack liked the idea, but told his brother that he was also interested in starting a tire company. The brothers decided that Jack could continue to run the Richmond to Norfolk operation for Old Dominion as well as start the leasing and tire companies. The combination provided an excellent full-time job for Jack.[59] So in 1964, Jack created Old Dominion Truck Leasing, for which he was the CEO.

"The first lease wasn't but one truck, and Old Dominion Freight Line was so small at the time that we needed diversification if it were possible," Jack explained. "However, the biggest problem we had was money, since Old Dominion Freight Line couldn't lend the leasing company any money, and the leasing company's credit was quite limited because it hadn't been in business."[60]

Jack set up a meeting with truck manufacturer International Harvester Company, which agreed to finance the leasing company. In exchange, International Harvester asked Old Dominion to assign the leases directly to their company as collateral. Jack agreed. "One of the first leases was Dixie Container Corporation, which had 14 tractors," Jack said, getting the company off to a very good start.

Shortly thereafter, Jack heard that a friend of his father's, who had been leasing trucks to a grocery warehousing company called Richfood, wanted to get out of the leasing business. With financing from International Harvester, Jack bought the fleet. "That grew in a very short period of time to pretty close to 100 [trucks], which really gave us a big boost," he later said.[61]

This advertisement for the Fuller Transmission Division of Eaton Manufacturing shows how dependable the transmissions were in Old Dominion's tractors, which hauled "everything from cigarettes to furniture." *(Image © 1963 Eaton Manufacturing Company.)*

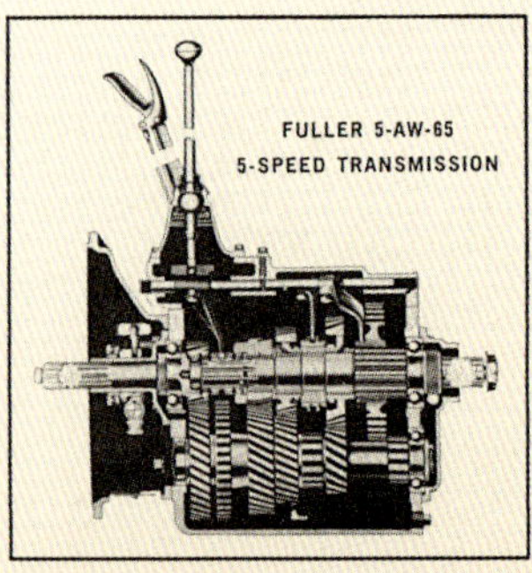

Pinning Down the Route

With the former Bottoms-Fiske routes under the company's belt, Old Dominion's operating authority during the 1960s spanned from Charlotte, North Carolina; north to Martinsville, Virginia; east to Norfolk, Virginia; and back from Norfolk to Charlotte, "serving most points in that triangle," Earl recalled. "Then, of course, there was the dogleg from Norfolk up to Richmond, which was the original Old Dominion authority."[62]

By 1964, Old Dominion's revenue topped $4.3 million, with a pretax profit of $187,770.[63] The following year, Old Dominion hired a Chicago-based management consulting firm called Sadler & Associates to create reports on Old Dominion's management. Sadler & Associates analyzed such traits as temperament, non-irritability, self-respect, cordiality, poise, and sympathy.[64]

The analysis of Earl Congdon revealed that he has "very proper attitudes of motivations for the business world … much patience for details and numbers … and scores in the upper 9 percent of the population in speed of thinking." However, it noted that the 34-year-old company president was "bothered by a fair amount of worry."[65]

Earl faced many new challenges on the job. In 1966, Old Dominion posted revenue of $5 million, up from $4.8 million in 1965. However, higher costs in transportation, terminals, traffic, sales, and operating licenses took their toll, decreasing the company's pretax income to $82,013, as opposed to the 1965 level of $116,549.[66]

Old Dominion acknowledged the challenges of 1966 in an April 3, 1967, letter to new members of the company's profit sharing plan, which stated: "As you already know, 1966 was a hard year to produce a big profit—even though we all worked as hard as ever. … In spite of depressed business last year, Old Dominion Freight Line—and its profit sharing plan—came out looking pretty good, compared with others."[67]

Perhaps in response to the tough year that the company endured, in 1966, Old Dominion hired

A view of Old Dominion's Newport News, Virginia, office in 1962.

CPA firm Leach, Calkins & Scott to perform a survey of the accounting-related activities in the High Point office "for the purpose of evaluating the operating efficiency of the office staff."[68]

The survey found that "work groups are too great in number and too small in size" and that employees should have written instructions for their positions.[69]

It appeared that Earl, as the company president, not only took the outside consultants' opinions in stride, but also to heart. The company financials improved significantly, with 1968 revenue at $6.1 million and a pretax income of $263,898.[70]

Need for Expansion

Despite the company's ability to haul freight within a geographic region that spanned farther than ever before, Old Dominion faced a significant challenge in the 1960s with a drop-off in the interline freight business.

"At one time, interline traffic was over half of our revenue, and these interline carriers were gradually opening up in Newport News, Virginia, and Norfolk ... and all over North Carolina," Earl said. "There was a time at Bottoms-Fiske when Carolina freight carriers would drop by our High Point terminal and drop off freight going all over North Carolina and Virginia."

Later, however, those freight carriers opened their own terminals, diminishing Old Dominion's workload and serving as an impetus for the Congdons to decide to expand their operating territory.[71]

In 1968, Old Dominion showed interest in purchasing the Bruce Johnson Trucking Company, which would have opened up the option of Old Dominion traveling between North Carolina and Virginia without having to travel through Norfolk. However, the sale fell through.[72]

The following year, Earl learned that the Barnes Truck Line, based in Wilson, North Carolina, was for sale. The company operated throughout Virginia and the Carolinas, and held a separate certificate spanning across Philadelphia, Pennsylvania; Baltimore, Maryland; and eastern Virginia.[73]

Three Barnes brothers—Roy, Eddie, and Henry—owned the truck line, and Jack and Earl traveled on the Old Dominion company aircraft to Wilson to meet with the majority stockholder, Roy Barnes.

Upon arriving, Roy did not greet them. When the Congdons called his office to inquire why, they were told that he had just died. Stunned, Jack and Earl returned home.[74]

Later in 1969, Eddie Barnes, who by then owned 83 percent of the truck line, also passed away, and the remaining brother, Henry, who owned 17 percent of the business, contacted Earl about selling.[75] Henry wanted to buy the company himself, but the bank wouldn't lend him the money unless he had a buyer for the company. The Barnes bookkeeper called Earl and said, "Why don't you come over, and we'll talk?"[76]

Old Dominion agreed to buy Barnes from Henry, but there was an important caveat to the sale: Roy's children had a right of refusal to buy the company after they turned 21, which was still seven years away. "It appeared that they would never exercise this right, but you can never tell," Earl recalled. However, Old Dominion took the chance and proceeded with its purchase of Barnes.[77]

Kitty and Earl Congdon, standing at center, and Jack and his wife Natalie, sitting at the far right, with executives of Old Dominion Truck Leasing at a March 1968 national lease meeting in Arizona.

Meanwhile, by the time Old Dominion had gotten the call from Henry Barnes, Earl was already negotiating to purchase Nilson Motor Express. Based in Charleston, South Carolina, the acquisition of Nilson would have given Old Dominion a certificate to travel between Savannah, Georgia; Charleston; and Wilmington, North Carolina; and to all points in Georgia and the Carolinas, with a separate certificate to travel between Charleston, Norfolk, Richmond, Baltimore, and Philadelphia.[78]

As if Old Dominion weren't juggling enough potential acquisitions, another company entered the picture, and it proved too attractive for Earl to pass up. Old Dominion learned that the White Transport Corporation, which had been Old Dominion's cartage agent in Greenville, South Carolina, was for sale and signed a contract to buy it.[79]

If it could acquire all three companies, Old Dominion would be able to operate between eastern Pennsylvania, Baltimore, Virginia, and throughout the Carolinas—an exciting route that would open up additional business opportunities.[80] By the end of 1969, Old Dominion purchased White Transport Corp. and applied to the Interstate Commerce Commission (ICC) to acquire both Barnes and Nilson. Old Dominion would be granted the temporary

WHAT IS LTL TRUCKING?

OLD DOMINION IS KNOWN INTERNATIONALLY for its strength in less-than-truckload (LTL) shipping. LTL companies specialize in collecting freight from different shippers and placing it together on the same truck, then line-haul drivers usually deliver it to hub facilities to sort and then redirect, or they can personally deliver all of the items on the truck, depending on the destination and the freight involved.[1]

Because LTL drivers usually drive the same routes from one day to the next, they typically get to know their customers along the route, which is an advantage for shippers. Not only do the customers benefit from creating a rapport with their drivers, but they also save money by using LTL. That's because the shipper is only paying for a portion of the truck, rather than having to pay for an entire trailer, as a full truckload freight company would require.[2]

operating authority to operate both companies in 1970.[81] Little did Earl know that Old Dominion would end up battling the ICC for full control of Barnes for several more years. Instead, by the end of the 1960s, the company felt good about the new territory it would be able to cover.[82]

A 1969 profile of Earl in the *High Point Enterprise* noted that he "just recently announced the acquisition of three more truck lines, which will roughly double the volume of business from about $6 million last year to more than $11 million. … Perhaps more importantly, the acquisitions will extend the territory of Old Dominion from Philadelphia and York in Pennsylvania south along the Eastern Seaboard into Savannah and Atlanta in Georgia."[83]

When Old Dominion announced that it was negotiating to buy the three additional truck lines, an August 10, 1969, company press release indicated that between the four carriers, about 800 people were employed, with more than 1,000 pieces of equipment used. The release also noted that "no changes in management or employees are contemplated at present."[84]

Earl and Jack considered the acquisitions part of the company's strategic vision for growth. "Almost all of the LTL truckers were unionized, and we didn't feel that we could acquire a unionized truck line," Earl said. "Barnes happened to have had a certificate that called for general commodities. … We used their general commodities certificate to expand Old Dominion over the territory and let Barnes stay in business hauling full truckloads and lumber and steel. They were not an LTL carrier. So we both used the same authority, and that was how we ended up being in the truckload business."[85]

Old Dominion closed out 1969 with revenue of $6.8 million and a pretax income of $294,729, allowing the company to enter the new decade with confidence, a full fleet, a growing operating authority, and money in the bank.[86]

Following Old Dominion's acquisition of Deaton Truck Line in 1979, the company promoted its expanded service area, which included 46 service centers in 15 states.

CHAPTER FIVE

UNPARALLELED GROWTH

1970–1979

My dad, he's been out having meetings with truck drivers since as long as I can remember. I was out with him when I was 10 years old, going to the Christmas drivers meetings and learning how to shake hands with truck drivers. ... This feeling of family and this feeling of openness and honesty and just laying the cards on the line is a tradition that we've continued.

—David Congdon[1]

As OLD DOMINION ENTERED THE 1970s, the company was unable to finalize the purchase of Nilson Motor Express and the Barnes Truck Line. Because of the red tape involved in the regulated trucking environment, Old Dominion had to wait until the government approved the acquisitions before the company formally owned the other truck lines. Until that happened, the previous owners of Barnes and Nilson continued running day-to-day operations.

On June 30, 1970, Old Dominion finally acquired permanent authority for Nilson and purchased all of the company's stock, with Nilson completely merging into Old Dominion effective July 1, 1970. The net purchase amount of the Nilson acquisition without liabilities assumed was $940,480, and that investment helped Old Dominion expand into another previously unexplored area.[2]

The Nilson acquisition gave Old Dominion the authority to handle furniture, and the company expanded that opportunity into a new, large-scale furniture-hauling business.[3] The furniture division would serve all of Florida, New Jersey, Connecticut, Massachusetts, and Rhode Island by 1978, and took advantage of Old Dominion's location in High Point, considered the "furniture capital of the world."[4]

While Old Dominion continued to patiently wait during what would become a seven-year interval before the Interstate Commerce Commission (ICC) granted the company final authority to operate Barnes, Henry Barnes continued as president of the company, with his son Louis serving as general manager.[5]

"It was kind of interesting," Earl Congdon recalled. "The price was set at the beginning of the seven years, and the seller had a choice: Did [the seller] want to gamble and have the profits or losses, whatever they might be, until we got final approval from the Interstate Commerce Commission? And we didn't know it was going to be seven years. Nobody did at the time."[6]

Government approval for the Barnes acquisition proved such a slow process because it was opposed by approximately 12 carriers due to the extensive operating authority it would have granted Old Dominion, and the fact that Old Dominion was considered a more aggressive LTL carrier than Barnes had been.[7] During the seven-year waiting period, Old Dominion developed "considerable traffic" between Baltimore and Virginia, as well as points between the Carolinas and Georgia.[8] In fact, for two years, Barnes earned higher profits than Old Dominion, making it "a really good purchase for us," Earl recalled.[9]

Earl Congdon enjoys Old Dominion's 1972 holiday party.

Old Dominion closed out 1970 with a generous profit, with terminals in Atlanta and Savannah, Georgia; Charleston and Columbia, South Carolina; Wilmington, North Carolina; and Baltimore, Maryland.[10] "Our revenue jumped from $6.8 million to $7.4 million in 1970, a heck of a big increase," Earl later noted. "Our profit before taxes increased nicely, and our operating ratio dropped a little from 93.8 down to 92.7, which was nice."[11]

A New Employee

In 1971, Earl was elected president of the North Carolina Motor Carriers Association.[12] He dedicated his administration to "improving the state trucking industry's public image, securing adequate rate relief, and obtaining other decisions from regulatory agencies that will make possible increased productivity."[13]

Even while hard at work as both the president of Old Dominion and the North Carolina Motor Carriers Association, Earl also enjoyed his growing family, which included his wife Kathryn (Kitty), daughters Karen and Audrey, and son David.

In the summer of 1971, 14-year-old David began working for Old Dominion on the docks to earn enough money to travel to Japan with the Boy Scouts.[14] "My original application shows that I was 5 feet, 6 inches, and a 112 pounds, so a hand truck weighed probably as much as I did," David later recalled. "I really enjoyed working out there on the dock and working side by side with some of the same great people who work for us now on the dock."[15]

David earned $1.65 per hour for his 40 hours per week, and by the end of the summer, he had earned enough money to go to Japan.[16] "I would say that was when my work ethic was born," David said. "I never even had a paper route before that."[17]

When he returned from his trip to Japan, David wanted to continue working at Old Dominion and learn more about the inner workings of the business while earning some pocket change. By the time he was 16 years old, David was working as a mechanic in the company's shop and "began going to service centers and working on the dock and riding with pickup and delivery drivers because I had a driver's license and a car," David recalled with pride. "I thought, you know, I'm going on an adventure at age 16, to go to Durham. I drove up to Baltimore; I went to Greenville, South Carolina; I went to Atlanta; I went to Charleston."[18]

David would continue taking on new roles at Old Dominion, working under not only his father's eye but under the tutelage of the company's longtime staffers, who aimed to teach him all aspects of the business.

Additions to the Old Dominion Family

In 1971, Old Dominion enjoyed another revenue increase, with profits jumping up to $1,428,000 and its operating ratio down to 87.3 percent.[19] "Any carrier that can operate below

Old Dominion opened a new 117-door service center in Greensboro, North Carolina, in the summer of 1975.

MAKING IT WORK

THROUGHOUT THE 1970s, OLD DOMINION MADE acquisitions and worked on its fleet, but in some respects, Earl Congdon Sr.'s Yankee ingenuity was still in place long after his passing. Since Old Dominion was committed to long-term growth and to investing in many expansion opportunities that existed at the time, the company had to make do when it came to certain upgrades. Although today Old Dominion is known for its state-of-the-art technology and top-notch equipment, that was not always the case in the 1970s.

For instance, Brian Stoddard, Old Dominion's current vice president of safety and personnel, began working at Old Dominion in 1969 and started driving a truck for the company in the early 1970s. He recalls driving a split-axle International Harvester gasoline tractor, "but I had to bring coat hangers to work with me because if I didn't, when I would stop at a light, the doors would fly open," he recalled. "I mean, it was old equipment, and it was outdated, but, you know, we were making it work."[1]

Likewise, Ernie Benge, who started at Old Dominion in 1975 and now serves as the company's claims director, recalls that "at one point when I came here, we used to have as much water damage from the floor of the trailer as we did from the roof. If you walked in the trailer and you saw a piece of cardboard on the floor, you'd better not step on it because you might go through the floor."[2]

90 percent is really, really, exceptional," Earl said. "The lower the operating ratio, the better."[20]

The following year, Old Dominion saw the company's net worth increase to a record $3.47 million, with an operating ratio of 89.7 percent in 1972. "In 1973, we had a fair increase in revenue, but our before-tax profit actually dropped a little bit because we let our operating ratio get up some. We were beginning to spend money trying to open operations in new areas," Earl recalled.[21]

Star Transport had been Barnes' interline partner in Baltimore and held an operating authority that ran from Baltimore and Washington to Philadelphia, New Jersey, part of New York state, most of Massachusetts and Connecticut, and all of Rhode Island. This operating authority could have greatly expanded Old Dominion's range. "This was indeed a very handsome operating certificate," Earl said.[22]

But there was a small catch: Star, which had sales of $2.5 million, operated just five of its own trucks but partnered extensively with other carriers who operated under Star's authority.[23] A question arose regarding whether Star's operating certificate could withstand the government's "dormancy test."

"There were farmers all over the country who were granted a piece of paper back in 1935, when regulation came in of the motor carriers, who had never operated a truck," Earl explained.[24]

In some cases, these small ventures, which may have had a truck or two on the road but had never planned to operate in the freight industry, stuffed their operating certificates in drawers and forgot about them. After a certain period, the government would declare an unused certificate to be dormant, and the business was unable to sell such certificates to another trucking company.[25] Old Dominion expressed concerns that Star's certificate might be in danger of this type of restriction, since the company did not operate many of its own trucks on the road.

After researching the issue, Old Dominion agreed to acquire Star Transport in 1974, and prior to the company's hearing before the ICC to apply for approval, Earl and Jack Congdon learned that about 25 other trucking companies were protesting Old Dominion's acquisition of Star.[26]

"Jack and I got in our company airplane and traveled from one protestant to the other in an attempt to get them to withdraw their opposition,"

Earl said. "Fortunately, we were able to get all of the protestants to withdraw and received ICC authority to acquire Star Transport in 1974."[27]

Bill Chestnutt, originally a Newport News terminal manager who later became operations manager, served as president of the newly acquired Star Transport.

Rough Times

Despite the successful acquisitions that Old Dominion completed, the company, like all businesses, was never guaranteed that any particular newly acquired operation would be financially prosperous.

The year 1974 began well, but as the year progressed, Earl expressed concern about the company's revenue, noting in a November 1974 letter to Old Dominion Vice President Henry Marshall, "I am afraid we are in for some pretty rough times. Business in general will most probably be pretty poor for the next nine months, and we must draw our belts tight in order to come through in the

Above: One of Old Dominion's brand-new straight trucks is ready for work at a terminal in 1974.

Below: In both good times (left) and bad (right), Earl sent updates to Old Dominion's staff members to let them know how the company was doing.

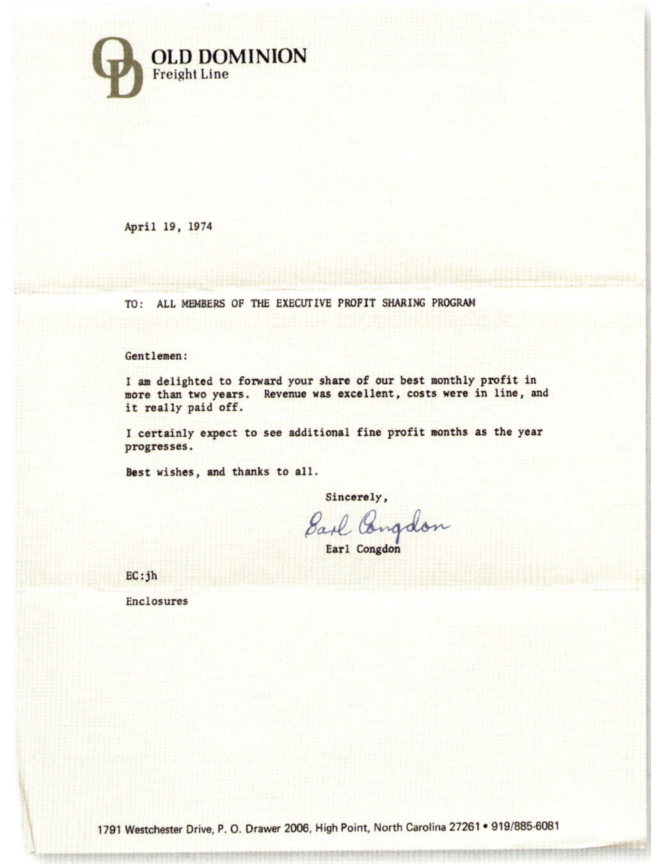

OLD DOMINION
Freight Line

April 19, 1974

TO: ALL MEMBERS OF THE EXECUTIVE PROFIT SHARING PROGRAM

Gentlemen:

I am delighted to forward your share of our best monthly profit in more than two years. Revenue was excellent, costs were in line, and it really paid off.

I certainly expect to see additional fine profit months as the year progresses.

Best wishes, and thanks to all.

Sincerely,

Earl Congdon

Earl Congdon

EC:jh

Enclosures

1791 Westchester Drive, P. O. Drawer 2006, High Point, North Carolina 27261 • 919/885-6081

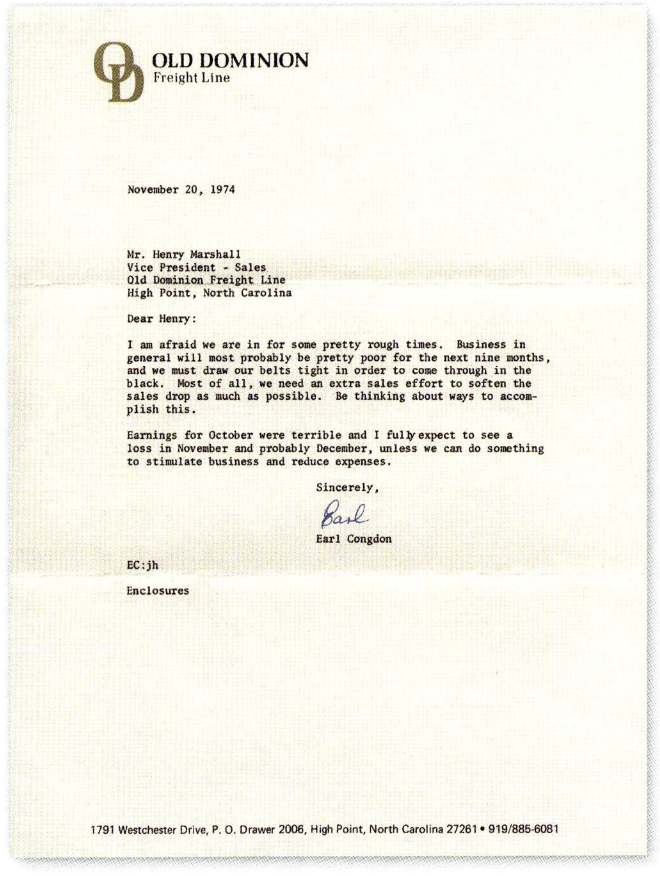

OLD DOMINION
Freight Line

November 20, 1974

Mr. Henry Marshall
Vice President - Sales
Old Dominion Freight Line
High Point, North Carolina

Dear Henry:

I am afraid we are in for some pretty rough times. Business in general will most probably be pretty poor for the next nine months, and we must draw our belts tight in order to come through in the black. Most of all, we need an extra sales effort to soften the sales drop as much as possible. Be thinking about ways to accomplish this.

Earnings for October were terrible and I fully expect to see a loss in November and probably December, unless we can do something to stimulate business and reduce expenses.

Sincerely,

Earl

Earl Congdon

EC:jh

Enclosures

1791 Westchester Drive, P. O. Drawer 2006, High Point, North Carolina 27261 • 919/885-6081

By 1975, Old Dominion tractor-trailers featured the same distinctive green-and-white appearance that they do today. The circular Old Dominion symbol is emblazoned on the side of each trailer.

black. ... Earnings for October were terrible, and I fully expect to see a loss in November and probably December unless we can do something to stimulate business and reduce expenses."[28] A separate 1974 letter from Earl to Marshall indicated that the company's No. 1 problem was "not enough LTL traffic."[29]

By the end of 1974, revenues were still positive, and the company closed out the year with a net worth of $15.1 million, which was a $3.4 million jump to top 1973's net worth of $11.7 million.[30] However, as Earl predicted, the company did head into rougher territory in 1975.[31]

The number of claims that Old Dominion was paying in 1975 did not help the company's bottom line either. Claims for 1975 totaled $280,000, recalled Ernie Benge, retired director of claims with Old Dominion, who has been with the company since 1975. The company was battling a 1.47 percent claim ratio against revenue in 1975, which was very high. By comparison, the 2010 claim ratio would be 0.47.[32]

Although 1975 was overall a difficult year, Earl felt that business was improving by the second half of the year, noting in a letter to the company's profit sharing plan that he was "delighted" with June results and that revenue was increasing and more business was becoming available.[33] That upswing continued, and by 1976, the company's net worth was boosted to $17.4 million.[34]

Part of that improvement was due to Old Dominion's focus on building more interline business. By the mid-1970s, that segment of the company had all but disappeared, and the company wanted to acquire more hauls in New Jersey, New York, and New England. However, Old Dominion did not want to risk unionization, fearing that it could bankrupt the company—and most cartage agents in the North were unionized.[35]

"In fact, our truck drivers didn't want to go [to the North]," Earl later recalled. "That was a time when the Teamsters had guards on the bridges into Manhattan, you know, and would say 'You show me your union card, or we're not letting you in.' "[36]

To expand its direct traffic base while avoiding the risk of dealing with unions, Old Dominion beefed up its operation in Baltimore and acquired non-union cartage agents in Philadelphia and Edison, New Jersey, followed by a subsequent agreement with Textile Delivery Service of New York, which made New York City deliveries on Old Dominion's behalf.[37]

In the late 1960s and early 1970s, Old Dominion was a pioneer in the ocean container drayage business. The company was also one of the first trucking companies to adopt the aerodynamic air shield on top of their cabs.

After making arrangements with additional cartage agents, some successful and some less so, Old Dominion eventually "overcame [its] fear of unionization in New England, and [we] opened our own operations in Rhode Island, Connecticut, and Massachusetts," Earl recalled.[38]

Old Dominion also benefited in the mid-1970s from making new business agreements with additional customers. For instance, Old Dominion entered into an agreement with the Borden Company to haul milk from Borden's plant in High Point to the A&P stores in Virginia.[39] Old Dominion acquired a dozen used refrigerated trailers, handling the milk delivery for Borden and A&P for five years, never missing a delivery.[40] "We had a lot of fun delivering milk and made a lot of money during the five-year period," Earl said.[41]

"Tears in My Eyes"

By 1976, Old Dominion had been waiting for seven years to determine whether the ICC would finalize its purchase of Barnes—but that long wait would soon come to an end. The Barnes acquisition was finalized on May 3, 1976, with a total purchase price of $2.1 million.[42]

But working with the ICC was never simple. Even after Old Dominion had patiently worked with the ICC for seven years while awaiting approval, the government had another trick up its sleeve. After approving the acquisition, the ICC alerted Old Dominion that it planned to remove the company's Richmond to Washington route. "They left us with an operation from the Carolinas and Georgia to Richmond, Virginia, and then another certificate from Washington, D.C., north all the way to New England," Earl said.[43]

Not only did the ICC plan to decimate Old Dominion's hard-won route, but the government agency also planned to make the change almost immediately. "We got a telegram from the commissioner of the ICC saying that we had to cease operations in two weeks," Earl recalled. "Imagine losing a fourth of your business and all that equipment. It would have bankrupted us."[44]

Earl could not bear to see 25 percent of his business simply disappear. After all, the intent of buying Barnes was to expand the business, not add in one direction while removing routes in another direction. He decided to take action.

"I went to the ICC with tears in my eyes, on my hands and knees, to see the commissioner, and she sent me to the Interstate Commerce Commission's chief counsel," Earl recalled.[45] After telling his story to the counsel, the attorney suggested that Earl go down the hall and explain his situation to an examiner in a different office.

The examiner told Earl that since Barnes had mostly handled forest products and steel in full truckload lots, one of Old Dominion's competitors at the original hearing had predicted that Old Dominion would take the Barnes certificate and use it to become an LTL carrier in the area, creating new competition like they had never seen before.[46]

Earl remained convinced that the ICC had been wrong in gutting the company's certificate, and he pleaded his case to the examiner:

> *So I'm telling this guy across the desk, and he listens to my tale of woe, and he says, "Wait a minute. ... Hey, Pete, you and Ralph come in here."*
>
> *These two other guys come in, and they sit down, and I go over the whole tale again. What I didn't know was that these guys were some kind of a hearing board, and it was illegal for me to be meeting with them because we didn't have our lawyer,*

Government approval of Old Dominion's acquisition of Barnes Truck Line was slow because several competitors opposed the purchase, fearing that Old Dominion would create LTL competition in the Northeast.

KEEPING PACE WITH VEHICLE MAINTENANCE

By 1977, Old Dominion operated approximately 1,500 pieces of equipment, "including one of the largest fleets of flatbed equipment in the East."[1] Not only did the company employ 1,000 people to run the business, dispatch the units, and drive the trucks, but Old Dominion also had to make sure the vehicles stayed on the road, a major evolution from 1946, when the very first tire specialist, Stuart Robinson, was hired. After all, a broken-down truck did not help the company earn money.

Enter Old Dominion's "major maintenance facility," which sat on 85 acres and spanned 45,000 square feet, all under one roof. Run by H. H. "Mac" McNorrill, Old Dominion boasted that the facility maintained better quality work because of the facility's layout.[2]

The maintenance shop served 150 units a day, handling overhauls and repairs for Old Dominion. Custom-designed by a shop foreman, the facility was built in the shape of a large letter "T" and had two floors. The first floor housed the parts room and the rebuild shop, while the second floor contained offices, a training room, a lunchroom, and a parts storage area.[3]

In one wing of the "T," the company housed a power shop with 14 bays, as well as a bay for wheel alignment and another for forklift repairs. The second side of the "T" held four drive-through check and service bays and a tire shop, and the third wing contained a 10-bay trailer repair shop.[4]

Rounding out the facility, Old Dominion housed a drive-through wash rack, a chassis dyno, and a paint shop directly behind the building, leading McNorrill to comment at the time that the building was "just right."[5]

John Pye stands to the left and Larry Perdue stands second to last on the right, alongside Old Dominion's tire department, which had the benefit of working in a new, custom-built facility in the 1970s, servicing 150 units per day.

and all the protestants' lawyers from seven years ago should have been there in a meeting like this. ...

I finished my story, and the first guy said, "Tell you what you do: Go see your lawyer right now, and tell him that you want him to apply for an emergency certificate of public convenience and necessity for you to operate between Richmond and Washington, and we're going to grant it."

I went to the lawyer, and he was kind of an arrogant guy. He said, "You can't do that. The only way you can get one of these things approved is if there is no service available, and there's plenty of service between Richmond and Washington."

And I said, "You do it anyway."

I didn't tell him that they had assured us they were going to approve it. I didn't know whether I was supposed to. But it was granted.[47]

Despite the time and expense involved in finalizing the Barnes acquisition, the deal ended up being a bargain for Old Dominion. "We let the surviving Barnes brother and his son run the company, and they made enough profit during the seven years that we ended up getting it for nothing," Earl later noted.[48]

Family Dynamic Shifts at Old Dominion

In 1976, Lillian Congdon Crowder, who had been a driving force behind Old Dominion's early successes, decided it was time to enjoy her twilight years. At 67 years of age, Lillian resigned from her position on the company's board and from employment with Old Dominion and transferred her stock in Old Dominion to the company. Not long after she moved on from Old Dominion, her grandson stepped in and took his place at the company.[49]

In May 1978, David graduated from the University of North Carolina at Wilmington with a bachelor of science in business and a concentration in management. "I proceeded to do my graduate work at the North Carolina Truck Driver Training School," he said. "I graduated second in my class."[50]

David then began working at Old Dominion full-time in the fall of 1978 as a truck driver, followed by time in the industrial engineering department, performing many responsibilities, including "doing time and motion studies and looking for ways to improve

Left: Thanks to several acquisitions, Old Dominion tractor-trailers were able to operate almost all the way up and down the East Coast by the mid-1970s.

Below: Lillian Congdon Crowder (right), with husband Emmett Clyde Crowder, attends an Old Dominion party in the 1970s. Howard Teal, vice president of sales, stands at left.

efficiency on the dock and in the pickup and delivery operations, as well as implementing the first daily profit and loss system in our service centers," he said.[51] David also became a trained pilot. He had learned to fly at the knee of his father and had flown with Earl many times as a child, so it came naturally to David to fly himself from terminal to terminal during the course of his career with Old Dominion.[52]

As David worked in different departments within Old Dominion, he helped develop the company's "family" atmosphere and continued his father's and grandfather's goals of ensuring that the company's managers were accessible to every employee across the board.

To that end, near the end of the 1970s, David started a newsletter "as part of our communication efforts to try to maintain a union-free company," he explained. "So that's when the true Old Dominion family culture really became publicized," which included not only the newsletter to keep the staff informed of corporate news, but also company picnics, awards, and other events.[53]

"The whole concept of family is very deeply rooted in our culture," David said, explaining why the company newsletter was named *Old Dominion Family*. "We have been viewing ourselves as a family, so when you come down to the root of this family culture, part of it is Earl and Jack and family to family, and it was a family business. And then, I think, through the 1960s and 1970s, we still always had a nice family feel."[54]

David Congdon joined Old Dominion full-time in 1978 following his graduation from the University of North Carolina at Wilmington and his completion of the North Carolina Truck Driver Training School.

New Acquisition Helps Old Dominion's Bottom Line

In 1977, Bill Carpenter, Old Dominion's vice president and general manager, left the company to serve as president of a different freight company, Deaton Truck Line, which was based in Birmingham, Alabama. After working at Deaton for a period, Carpenter grew unhappy and decided to return to his old position. He contacted Earl and asked if there might be an opportunity to return to Old Dominion. After Earl agreed to take him back, Carpenter mentioned that Deaton was potentially available as an acquisition target if Earl were interested in buying its holding company, Expediter Systems.[55]

Deaton had operating rights throughout the 48 states, making it "pretty darn valuable," Old Dominion later noted in company documents.[56] Deaton operated as a truckload carrier, with vans comprising about one-third of the business and flatbeds taking up the other two-thirds.[57] Buying Deaton would allow Old Dominion to expand its LTL routes into Alabama, Mississippi, and Louisiana,[58] so in June 1979, Old Dominion acquired Expediter Systems for $8.7 million.[59]

Along with Deaton Truck Line, the Expediter acquisition included Expediter-owned businesses such as Skeeter Bass Boats, a concrete products company, Vulcan Trailer Manufacturing, and a truck body plant.[60] After Old Dominion's purchase of Expediter was complete, it divested itself of all the businesses except Deaton and Vulcan.[61]

The timing could not have been more fortuitous. Although buying Expediter was expensive and

Jerry Wilson, one of Old Dominion's dedicated mechanics, works on a tractor in the 1970s.

involved a lot of attention since Old Dominion had to market the unrelated divisions, the Deaton acquisition proved a blessing to Old Dominion's bottom line during a period when the trucking industry was taking a financial hit.

By the end of 1979, trucking companies' profits were down 2.5 percent, with some down as much as 7 percent.[62] With a recession looming across the United States, many companies were choosing to haul their own freight, leaving trucking companies short on business.[63] Old Dominion was no exception, with a pretax income of $2.8 million in 1979, down from $4 million in 1978.[64] But as Old Dominion's profits shrank, the company's Deaton business more than made up for the shrinkage.

As the 1970s came to a close, it was becoming clear that the government was considering deregulating the trucking industry, which could have a huge positive impact on Old Dominion. Moving into the 1980s as a larger, stronger company than ever before, Old Dominion relished the opportunity to seize an even larger market share, should deregulation materialize.

Old Dominion instituted its Express Service to California in 1983 and advertised it to customers with pictures showing palm trees along the road.

CHAPTER SIX

GOVERNMENT DEREGULATION CHANGES EVERYTHING

1980–1987

Deregulation came in 1980, and obviously, it was very, very lucky that we made it through. I remember the first day that Overnite came out with its 10 percent "across-the-board" discount—scared everybody to death.

—Buddy McBride
Old Dominion vice president of transportation[1]

EARL CONGDON SR. AND HIS WIFE Lillian founded Old Dominion during a time when freight companies were free to travel wherever they pleased. However, that freedom did not last long. After the tightening of government regulations in 1935, Old Dominion was restricted to traveling between Richmond and Norfolk, Virginia. Old Dominion spent the better part of the next 45 years making acquisitions, spending more than $6 million to help expand the company's reach beyond that original route.[2]

However, the operating authorities that Old Dominion had so painstakingly collected might end up becoming worthless if the proposed government deregulation of the transportation industry came to fruition, as many predicted would happen in the 1980s.

Transforming the Industry

Earl Congdon knew a good acquisition when he saw one, and had a sense of how a particular company would fit in with Old Dominion's structure. When he heard that Johnson Motor Lines, a North Carolina–based LTL shipping company, had shuttered its doors in 1980, he wondered whether portions of Johnson's business would be a good fit with Old Dominion.

Johnson offered a "special commodities division" that piqued Earl's interest. The company handled "only truckload traffic utilizing the services of owner-operators and 'trip leases,'" Earl later recalled.[3] Old Dominion acquired Johnson's special commodities division and its owner-operators, renaming the division "Rapid Transport."[4] Jack Davis, division manager and vice president of operations, would go on to serve as manager of Rapid Transport.

Old Dominion invested in 50 flatbeds, 200 vans, and 35 refrigerated trailers for the Rapid Transport group. The company's owner-operators proved to be more accident-prone than Old Dominion was accustomed to, so it became a challenge for Old Dominion to ensure the company's profitability.[5]

However, Old Dominion worked to assimilate Rapid Transport into the Old Dominion family because Earl realized that major changes were ahead.

Whereas the 1970s were marked by considerable growth for Old Dominion, the 1980s proved

The Rapid Transport subsidiary bled money throughout the 1980s, forcing Old Dominion to liquidate its assets in 1985. Earl Congdon later described the Rapid Transport acquisition as the "worst mistake of my career."

a vastly different landscape. President Carter had indicated that he was committed to removing price controls and improving competition in the marketplace, so trucking deregulation was one area where he focused.[6]

Analysts began to consider the potential impact of the Motor Carrier Act (MCA). If passed, such a bill would eliminate the need for operating licenses, in which Old Dominion had invested heavily, and would prohibit carriers from collectively setting rates through rate bureaus.[7]

Earl investigated the likely effect that deregulation would have on Old Dominion's future, and in 1979, he attended a weeklong conference at Harvard University on the topic to find out more.[8] "We came out of that meeting with 25 truckers, and we determined that, in the event that we were deregulated, which we were the following year ... probably the three largest carriers, Consolidated Freightways, Yellow, and Roadway, would survive," Earl recalled later. "The rest of the Teamster carriers were going bankrupt, and we had the chief financial officer of the Teamsters union in our group, and we told him that 'you have some real troubles ahead.' ... When I came out of that one-week session up there, I was convinced that most of the Teamster carriers were going bankrupt, and it's turned out that way. They were."[9]

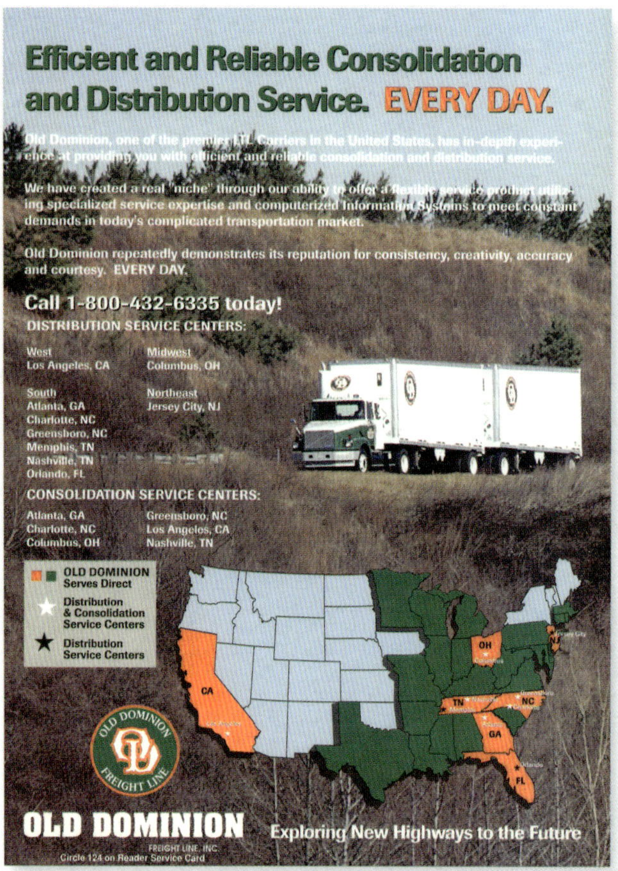

Part of Old Dominion's marketing strategy in the 1980s was to advertise its LTL service in national magazines, such as this ad which ran in *Distribution* magazine.

Based on what Earl learned at the session, he was not opposed to deregulation, noting, "When Congress regulated us in the first place, it was supposed to be to protect the public against predatory pricing and all those things. Instead, it looked to me like they were protecting the haves, meaning the carriers that had the good operating routes. And little fellows like ourselves struggled to acquire more operating authority because we only started out with a route from Richmond to Norfolk."[10]

Earl spoke to the Rowan Traffic and Transportation Club in Salisbury, North Carolina, on April 10, 1980, to discuss the topic of deregulation. During his speech, Earl expressed concern that many LTL truckers would attempt to extend their service into new areas, which, he predicted, would create "entirely too many carriers offering service in some traffic lanes."[11] However, he also predicted that "carriers with mediocre management, Teamster contracts, and limited markets will fail" and also suggested that "nonunion carriers like Old Dominion will have a cost advantage and will use it to dominate markets in nonunion areas."[12]

Earl's studies of the potential impact of deregulation did not turn out to be for naught. President Carter signed the MCA into law on July 1, 1980, as part of his pledge to "remove anticompetitive government regulations wherever possible," the media noted at the time.[13] Deregulation had become law, and trucking businesses would either flourish or fail in its wake.

Freight Companies Face Losses

As the reality of deregulation set in among freight carriers, it became clear that the industry as a whole would suffer for an uncertain time period from the effects of deregulation.

"As a result of deregulation, the nation's trucking industry faces extraordinarily huge losses this year—perhaps totaling as much as $785 million," noted an October 23, 1980, article in the *Winchester Star*. "The reason: Truckers are now writing off Interstate Commerce Commission operating licenses for which many of them paid millions of dollars. With the new regulatory climate making it much easier for new firms to enter the business, these operating certificates, which specify the routes truckers serve and the commodities they haul, have little or no value. The write-offs come at a time when the economy is soft and the trucking industry is suffering along with other businesses."[14]

Studies showed that LTL carriers in particular "faced considerable turmoil in adjusting to the highly competitive postregulated environment. The new competitive circumstances were particularly harsh for managers of firms with the most protection in a regulated environment."[15]

Freight companies, including Old Dominion, faced significant challenges regarding the empty trucks they had on the road. "At one time, we had more truckload freight than we had LTL because we owned three or four truckload carriers at one time, and we didn't do very well with them," Earl later said. "Many of the truckload carriers had authority that would only let them go in one direction, and they were having to come home empty. So what happens? You have to double the rate so that you've got enough to pay you to come home empty. Well then, after deregulation and everybody now had authority to haul in both directions, what happens? The price starts coming down. You don't charge for double the miles anymore."[16]

As a result, freight companies lost a significant portion of their income because they were forced to run empty trucks back to the terminals. "Barnes had a problem being able to deal with that, and so did the other truckload carriers that we were dealing with," Earl said. "They didn't cope well after deregulation, and Werner did. They did a hell of a job, as we all know, as did several other truckload carriers, including J.B. Hunt and Schneider National. But our guys that were running our truckloads just didn't do well. Barnes started losing money after deregulation, and Deaton, which was a big acquisition for us, had the same problem. They started losing money."[17]

Despite the problems that deregulation created for Old Dominion, including the threat of unlimited competition on the roads, Earl also envisioned a future where the company could move into previously uncharted territory. "When it finally became apparent that the Interstate Commerce Commission was going to grant a nationwide, unrestricted certificate to any motor carrier requesting one, Old Dominion was able to develop its expansion strategy."[18]

Overexpansion Hurts Old Dominion

Old Dominion decided to take advantage of deregulation by expanding into every possible market as Teamster lines across the country faced bankruptcy.[19] The company rapidly expanded into Florida, Tennessee, the Midwest, Dallas, and California, at a huge financial cost to the company.[20]

Unfortunately, the strategy did not work as well as Earl had hoped. "What, in fact, happened was that the big three got that business," he recalled. "We didn't have a strong enough name. ... We weren't recognized in all these new areas that we had opened."[21]

Larger trucking companies with more coverage had an advantage over Old Dominion post-deregulation and began offering deep discounts. For example, Overnite Transportation of Richmond offered a 10 percent rate cut on LTL traffic, allowing the company to increase volume and revenue, while smaller businesses, including Old Dominion, struggled to keep up.[22]

Prior to deregulation, salespeople such as David Penley, who began as a salesman in 1975 and would go on to become vice president of general sales, "were pretty much just real salespeople," recalled Mike Wood, Old Dominion's current vice president of the Midwest region. "They built relationships, and it was entertainment and everything else to get the business, because the discounting wasn't there and everyone charged basically the same rate."[23]

Changes had to take place across the board, creating a ripple effect from the sales department on out through the rest of the business. "We, as trucklines, had to become productive because, prior to 1980, it was really this: If you had a good personality and you got along well with customers, you got business because the price was the same," noted

Operating in the Wake of the Energy Crisis

In the 1970s, the United States faced an energy crisis because of several factors. OPEC placed the US under an embargo due to geopolitics, depriving the country of oil in 1973. Although the embargo was lifted in 1974, the country underwent another oil shortage in 1979, when Ayatollah Khomeini of Iran slowed exports to the United States.

The US government instituted several programs in an attempt to improve fuel efficiency during those intervals, but companies such as Old Dominion, which used substantial amounts of fuel in the course of its normal operations, suffered due to the shortages. As the company moved into the 1980s, fuel became more abundant, but Old Dominion continued many of the fuel-saving strategies that it had implemented.

In 1981, David Congdon wrote that "trucking companies are using every fuel-saving device they can get their hands on—clutch fans, air shields, fuel squeezer engines, radial tires, etc."[1] Old Dominion equipped all new trucks with fuel

John Yowell, Old Dominion's executive vice president and chief operating officer, who joined the company in 1983 and tragically, and unexpectedly, passed away in 2010.[24]

In response to the competition, Old Dominion reduced its LTL class rates by 10 percent as of September 1980.[25] In addition, Old Dominion established terminals throughout Tennessee, in Memphis, Nashville, Johnson City, and Chattanooga in 1980, which represented a "financial drain on the company, which continued until they became profitable," Earl later recalled.[26] The combination of these factors made profits almost nonexistent in 1980.

Earl predicted that 1980 "may well turn out to be one of the most critical years ever for Old Dominion," due to inflation, higher interest rates, and slowed business.[27]

Despite revenues dropping drastically between April and June 1980, Earl reminded Old Dominion employees that the company was in better shape than most other carriers, offering the example that Spector had laid off 22 percent of their employees and that Old Dominion was only beginning to consider layoffs as of June of that year.[28]

By the end of 1980, Old Dominion had $8.8 million in total assets, a drop from the $9 million that the company had when the year began.[29] Overall, the company lost $386,337 in ordinary income before taxes in 1980.[30] Whereas in the past, the company could have procured loans to make up the losses, the lending environment was not as free in the early 1980s. One of the biggest causes of Old Dominion's loss in net worth that year was the fact that it had to write off its $6 million operating authority following deregulation.[31]

Borrowing money was very difficult in 1980 because not only were interest rates higher due to the economy, but freight companies were no longer able to use their operating authority as collateral to borrow from banks, since operating authority became worthless following deregulation.[32]

In response to the difficulties the company was facing, Old Dominion hired a consulting firm to perform a "Traffic Quality Analysis" study to evaluate the cost of shipments in late 1981.[33] In addition to analyzing costs, the company also continued its acquisition strategy, and on August 1, 1981, Old Dominion acquired All-Pro Transport Lines, Inc., which operated out of Miami.[34] The carrier was a small intrastate freight line, with LTL terminals throughout Florida in Miami, Fort Myers, Tampa, and Jacksonville.[35]

Things did not improve significantly in 1981, which proved to be a "most difficult year," Earl wrote squeezer engines in 1981, adding air shields to almost all trucks, and educating drivers on how to achieve optimum fuel efficiency.[2]

Old Dominion asked drivers to eliminate all unnecessary idling, defining "necessary idling" as a three-minute idle prior to shutdown of a hot engine on a truck with a turbocharger. In addition. Old Dominion asked drivers to keep bias-ply tire pressure to 90 pounds and radials to 100 pounds to maximize fuel efficiency.[3]

David Congdon also aimed to keep mileage low by instructing drivers to operate their trucks at low rpms. "The new fuel squeezer engines are designed to operate and have peak torque and horsepower in the lower rpm ranges of 1,300 rpm to 1,500 rpm," he said. Therefore, he asked drivers to shift at the lowest rpm possible when up shifting on a flat road or downhill and to let rpms drop as low as 1,300 when climbing a grade, which could eliminate the need for shifting while going uphill.[4] Truck engines in 2011 should be lugged to 1,000 rpms to 1,100 rpms on hills.

Drivers were also asked to keep an accurately recorded "mpg record" in their vehicles so they could write down their miles per gallon, making it easier to detect when a change occurred so the cause could be pinpointed. Plus, they were asked to avoid filling their gas tanks all the way to the top so leakage would not occur, and to maintain the 55 mph speed limit to maximize fuel efficiency and avoid tickets.[5]

"At Old Dominion alone, a mere one-quarter mile per gallon increase will save us approximately $260,000 in 1981," David wrote to employees in February of that year. "Your company is doing its part by equipping the trucks with fuel-saving devices, and it is you, the driver, who must make them work."

to employees in a company newsletter.[36] Earnings in 1981 dropped by 22 percent, due mainly to poor economic conditions and freight rate reductions. However, Earl continued to encourage employees, noting confidence in the team when he said, "We don't intend to merely be a survivor; we are going to grow and prosper."[37]

Earl planned to grow with the strong Old Dominion team supporting him, including his son David, who worked as director of employee relations from 1980 to 1981 and subsequently ran fleet maintenance and equipment from 1981 to 1986.[38]

Slight Improvements Help Make Gains in 1981

Old Dominion celebrated the fact that it was granted a small freight rate increase in 1982, hoping that it would make up for the discounts it had offered and add to profitability. However, in a message to employees in the spring of 1982, Earl noted that the trucking industry was in a "crisis situation" and acknowledged that Old Dominion was working to make the business profitable.[39]

To that end, the process of consulting continued into 1982 to optimize efficiencies and improve savings.[40] Old Dominion also stepped up its sales force and its marketing strategies,[41] acknowledging in an internal company memo, "There is no question that we must consider the marketing function as our primary tool for growth and direction in the future, as have other carriers."[42]

The revenue-growing strategies in early 1982 were helpful, allowing the company to earn profits of $1 million during the months of March, April, May, and June, but it was not enough to overcome the $1.6 million loss that the company had experienced between November 1981 and February 1982. Earl remained confident that by the end 1982, Old Dominion would be at a break-even point or would earn a small profit.[43] However, he was not as certain that the company would have any surplus to share with employees, as it had done every previous holiday season.[44] "This means that there will be little or no profit to share, so each of you should plan your finances accordingly," Earl warned.[45]

Despite the financial setbacks, Old Dominion was able to keep almost all of its employees as of the summer of 1982 and continued to increase revenue by expanding its territory and adding sales representatives.[46] Although acknowledging that sales were not strong, Earl chose to look at the bright side, telling employees, "Our business is better than that of any carrier I have talked with."[47]

Above: Old Dominion executives gather for a group photo in 1983. From left to right: Everett Barber, Charles Pearson, Fred Meredith, Rod Hall, Tom McCauley, Gene Campbell, Stan Koerner, Jack Wolverton, Jerry Pusey, David Penley, Jerry Nussbaum, Bob Owens, Campbell Ramsey, and Earl Congdon.

OLD DOMINION FAMILY

Vol. 1 No. 10 — Summer Issue, 1982

MESSAGE From The President

Earl Congdon
President

Folks, things are better now for Old Dominion. We earned profits in March, April, May and June totaling $1,000,000. While July may not be profitable, we expect fairly good profits for the balance of the year if there is no further rate cutting.

The bad news is that our company lost $1,600,000 in November, December, January and February. Since our "Profit Sharing Year" runs November 1 thru October 31, we are still showing a $600,000 loss for the year. We should earn enough between now and the end of October to break even or show a very small profit. This means that there will be little or no profit to share, so each of you should plan your finances accordingly.

We are fortunate at Old Dominion that virtually all of our people are working. We are even hiring additional people at some locations. Our business is better than that of any carrier I have talked with.

You all know that the economy is horrible. Most of our customers' business is simply terrible. Since my Spring 'message,' our industry has lost TIME-DC Spector-Red Ball, Hemingway and several other good carriers.

Our revenue is holding up because we have expanded our territory and because we are not cutting back in Sales. We are adding sales representatives as fast as we can find good people. We have an excellent sales force and it's getting better. We can see it gaining strength almost by the hour.

A sales force, of course, is no better than the product it sells. That's where we come in because we are the product. Our salesmen are selling "The Old Dominion Team." They are proud of our team and the product is selling because we have the best team in the league.

Our California service is now profitable and so is our new Service Center in Roanoke. We are now in a position to proceed with further expansion of our service area.

In order to expand our coverage in Georgia, a new Service Center will open in Columbus, Georgia in early August. This will be followed later in August by another Service Center in Johnson City, Tennessee to service northeastern Tennessee, including the cities of Kingsport, Bristol, Greenville and Elizabethton. Also during August and September, we will be opening Service Centers in Chicago, Illinois, Indianapolis, Indiana and Louisville, Kentucky.

It will take about six months and a lot of hard work by all of us to make these new areas profitable. We're counting on each of you to "pitch in," as you always have, to make the new areas profitable as soon as possible.

LTL Marketing Strategy

By David Congdon

A lot of thought has gone into our PLAN. Our local sales force, Regional Sales Managers, National Accounts Executives, and top managment personnel have determined from talking with our customers what they are looking for in a carrier.

The term "marketing strategy" is relatively new to the trucking industry. Before the Motor Carrier Act of 1980, carriers had certain routes over which they ran and everyone had the same rates. All that could be sold was service. Today the carriers (Old Dominion and major competitors) can go anywhere in the U.S.A. and we have pricing flexibility. Today's "freedom" is why we must have a "marketing strategy."

Marketing strategy has been the topic of numerous top management and regional sales meetings for the last year and a half. A marketing strategy is basically this. First, decide what kind of carrier you want to be; small regional, large regional, short haul, long haul, etc. Secondly, after defining your market and researching differences in rate levels between certain geographic areas, determine the best locations for new service centers in terms of producing immediate profits and contributing to the growth of existing service centers. Thirdly, poll the customers within your market area to determine their needs as to service and price. Then it is necessary to develop ways to match our company's capabilities with those needs.

Further, I want to expand the four most important ingredients of our strategy: 1. Flexibility 2. The Plan 3. Pricing 4. Teamwork.

Management believes that our marketing and expansion strategy has to be flexible. We have not set an absolute one-year, two-year, three-year, etc. plan that we will follow to the letter. Market conditions are continually changing. New businesses open up, new carriers emerge, carriers and customers go out of business,special situations and opportunties arise. We must be flexible to react and sometimes change our time schedule to take advantage of existing opportunities. Top management is attuned to this flexible approach.

A lot of thought has gone into our Plan. Our local sales force, Regional Sales Managers, National Accounts Executives, and top management personnel have determined from talking with our customers what they are looking for in a carrier. We have tailored our plan to these needs. We call our plan 'The Heartland-Spoke Strategy." We want to be a large regional carrier in our "Heartland" states in the Southeast. Our plan is to develop nearly total coverage in all of these states. Existing service centers in Florence, South Carolina and Roanoke, Virginia and future service centers in Columbus, Georgia and Johnson City, Tennessee are examples of improved statewide coverage.

In today's market the National Accounts are looking for a carrier who can blanket a state. We began "spoking out" about ten years ago with the service centers in Baltimore, Philadephia, Jersey City, New York and New England selling service to and from our Heartland southern states. Our expansion this fall to Louisville, Kentucky, Indianapolis, Indiana and Chicago, Illinois is another example of other spokes on which we will sell service to and from our Heartland. Another area we are pursuing which relates to our Heartland spoke strategy is that of consolidation and distribution accounts. A consolidation is where we pool LTL shipments, that either we pick up or that are brought to our dock, into a truckload to destination, usually a distribution center. The distribution center may be our service center. The shipments are then broken out and shipped again as LTL. Blanket coverage in our Heartland allows us to consolidate and distribute for many National Accounts.

The third important ingredient of our strategy is Pricing. We have the ability to match handling expenses with any LTL shipment and compare cost to revenue to determine profitability of the shipment. As you all know, price is a major factor which determines the shipper's choice of carriers. We have computerized cost-based pricing capability.

The fourth and probably most important ingredient is **Teamwork.** It has taken a great deal of teamwork through good communication to develop this strategy. Our teamwork between the Operations Department and the Sales and Traffic Departments is at an all-time high. Each department understands the other's needs. A great deal of teamwork goes on between National Accounts Executives and the local sales force. It takes National Accounts efforts to get into a big account, but the National Account can easily be lost because of lack of attention or service at the local level. The most important aspect of teamwork is between management and the work force. Our non-union status allows for one-on-one contact between management and labor without the interference of a third party in settling our individual problems. Being non-union is a great asset to our flexibility.

In closing, there are a couple of very important things I must mention. Over the last few years, we have noticed a deterioration in some of our traditional market lanes, i.e. Charlotte to Norfolk, Norfolk to Richmond, Richmond to Greensboro, Durham to Norfolk, etc. This is mainly due to increased competition in these lanes. It is very important that this stop and that we begin to regain traffic in these lanes. What I'm saying is that while we are pushing these new spoke areas, we must not neglect our Heartland. Another thought is that while we expand, we must continue to give superior service as we have in the past. Deterioration in service would hurt us terribly.

This article should give you some idea of where we are headed and how we plan to get there.

Equipment Update

With our upcoming expansion plans, we have found the need for fifteen (15) additional tractors and thirty-six (36) additional trailers in 1982. Our team tractors are getting quite a few miles on them. Due to the critical nature of team operations, the team equipment will be updated with 1983 White Road Commanders as pictured. The old team tractors will continue to be used in single operations. We are also taking on lease thirty-six (36) Spector trailers within the next thirty days.

Left: By 1982, Old Dominion had realized that a solid LTL marketing strategy was essential to capturing market share and announced the philosophy to staff members in this article by David Congdon in the *Old Dominion Family* newsletter.

Old Dominion's revenue-building strategy included unloading any subsidiaries that might be holding the company back. After reviewing the profits within all of the divisions of the company, Old Dominion decided to sell the Vulcan Trailer Manufacturing Company in May 1983 after the subsidiary faced actual losses of more than $200,000, and estimated future losses of $400,000 "arising from the company's guaranty of certain obligations of Vulcan," Earl said.[48]

All of the improvements continued to pay off as the calendar turned to 1983.[49] By that point, Old Dominion had become one of the nation's two largest privately held trucking companies, and in September 1983, Old Dominion opened terminals in Dallas, Texas, as well as in Commerce and Albany, Georgia.[50]

As 1983 came to a close, Old Dominion was pleased to finish the year with a 27 percent increase in growth, with Earl noting that the revenue increase was one of the best in the industry.[51] Many Old Dominion staffers sighed with relief—the negative effects following deregulation were behind them.

A Father-Son Expedition

As Old Dominion entered its 50th year in business in 1984, the company had many reasons to be proud. Because its rapid expansion coincided with deregulation, Old Dominion drove ahead into the decade with a goal to branch out across the country and be a successful nationwide trucking company.

In 1983, Old Dominion had launched a twin trailer sleeper operation traveling to California and back every five days.[52] Not long thereafter, Congress introduced the Tandem Truck Safety Act of 1984, which allowed twin-trailer runs nationwide.[53]

To celebrate the possibilities of cross-country twin-trailer routes for Old Dominion, Earl and David climbed into a twin-trailer rig loaded with 39,000 pounds of freight in November 1983 and embarked on a transcontinental run from Greensboro, North Carolina, to Los Angeles.[54]

"Trucks hauling cargo are a common sight on the country's highways and byways, but the two men who rotated driving chores on this rig were an unusual pair of long-haul drivers," wrote a reporter in *Business North Carolina* magazine.[55] However, Earl, who was the company's president, and David, then the vice president for equipment and maintenance, did not find it strange to share driving responsibilities as they made the trek to California.[56] After all, both men were veteran drivers, and with Earl Sr. having started the company more than 50 years prior, it was a great way to celebrate their family's ties to the industry that made the business successful.

In 1984, to celebrate the 50th anniversary of Old Dominion, the company presented Earl Congdon with a fully restored 1946 Ford straight truck.

The father and son took turns driving, with one resting in the cab's sleeper compartment while the other took the wheel. As the truck passed "Hotel Row" in Sweetwater, Texas, Earl admitted, "I'd be lying if I told you those hotels didn't look good."[57]

After delivering the freight, which totaled a record $11,300 in revenue, to Old Dominion's Los Angeles Service Center, Earl remarked, "It was an unforgettable experience for both of us."[58]

Company at a Crossroads

By 1984, Old Dominion had installed Bill Carpenter as the company's executive vice president and general manager.[59] Old Dominion had hired Carpenter in the early 1970s, "and he pretty much ran the day-to-day operations of the company like a chief operating officer would," Earl said.[60]

Thanks to his confidence in Carpenter and his interest in spending more time with his family, Earl began to stay at his home in Florida more often than ever before as Carpenter got a handle on operations at Old Dominion.[61]

But as Earl pulled back from his daily responsibilities, Old Dominion's sales slowly began to fall. In particular, 1984 was a difficult year for Old Dominion, with Rapid Transport bleeding money, causing Earl to tell employees in a fall 1984 newsletter message, "Rapid is the big loser and is the biggest cause of our poor earnings performance."[62]

While Rapid lost money, the company's Deaton acquisition, under President Buddy Moore, brought in revenues and profits, which allowed the company to stay afloat.[63] However, banks were growing impatient with Old Dominion after the company "lost money in 1984 and in the early part of 1985, and the banks suggested that maybe we ought to bring a consultant in," Earl recalled.[64]

Old Dominion had already undergone a review from a consulting firm in 1984, which reported, "It appears you need to have someone go through each department and clear out the excess people. There are a lot of people sitting around talking."[65]

In the spring of 1985, the consulting firm started interviewing employees, resulting in Old Dominion eliminating about 37 employees, all from the general office. "For whatever reason, they didn't get out into the field to try to see what might be available in the way of savings out there," Earl recalled.[66] The cuts brought the company back to profitability, but at a cost. Bill Carpenter and several other top managers were let go during that time.[67]

Despite sales of $173 million in 1984, Old Dominion still lost money that year, leading to further staff reductions. By June 1985, Old Dominion had eliminated 146 positions throughout the company.[68] Fifty of those positions were eliminated at the company's High Point headquarters, while the other 96 positions were cut from the company's service centers.[69]

"It's one of those things that businesses have to do," Earl told a *High Point Enterprise* reporter in 1985. "We bit the bullet and did it, and we'll be a better company for it."[70]

Not long afterward, Old Dominion's once-flourishing Barnes business became unprofitable, and Old Dominion merged it with the Rapid Transport business, "causing considerable confusion and resulting in even further losses," Earl said.[71]

Unable to keep Rapid afloat, Old Dominion liquidated Rapid Transport in November 1985, following losses of $6 million during the years that Old Dominion owned it.[72] "Old Dominion's adventure with Rapid Transport was the worst mistake of my career," Earl later reflected. "I believe to this day that full truckload is easier to operate then LTL, but it is certainly very different and can't be operated on a part-time basis with LTL executives."[73]

A New President for Old Dominion

Following the Rapid Transport liquidation and the high number of layoffs that Old Dominion endured, the company's consulting firm told Earl, "If you want to pull this thing out, we think you can do it, but you're going to have to sell your house in Florida and go back to work."[74]

Earl's singular goal was to keep Old Dominion profitable and propel the company back to being a powerhouse in the freight industry. But a wave of self-doubt made him reconsider whether he should be at the helm.[75] "I thought, 'Well, we're trying to grow Old Dominion into something really big, and do I have the skills to take us to the next level or two?' " Earl recalled. "And I thought it might be smart to bring in a president and chief operating officer, so my brother and I started searching for that fellow."[76]

It was unusual—but not unheard of—for an Old Dominion tractor to feature a color other than green. This furniture division truck features a red cab.

The Congdons set their sights on John Ebeling, a trucking industry veteran who had served as the regional vice president for Consolidated Freightways, after which he served as CEO for ANR, which owned several Midwestern unionized trucking companies.[77] Ebeling had been unable to make ANR profitable, but that did not sway Earl and Jack in their decision to hire him. "My brother and I chose to believe that the Lord Himself could not have made ANR profitable under the circumstances," he said. "We ended up hiring John Ebeling as Old Dominion's president and appointing him as a member of the board on September 1, 1985."[78]

With Ebeling in the president's position, Earl stepped back, giving Ebeling free rein over the daily operations of the business. "John pretty much made it clear that he would really like for me to stay out of the way, and I sort of felt that maybe I should, too," Earl said. "I was still the CEO and the chairman. John was president and chief operating officer. But he had his own ideas on what he thought ought to be done, and so I enjoyed my stay in my house in Florida and spent some time with John Ebeling, too."[79]

Ebeling soon instituted weekly executive staff meetings, and he was known around the company as being proficient at making successful sales calls.[80] Some of Ebeling's contributions to Old Dominion throughout the years included establishing official regions organized by area managers, supporting the company's sales incentive plan, and promoting the exclusive use of twin trailers for line-haul use. Ebeling would remain involved with the company long after he retired, serving on the board of directors until he fell ill and passed away in 2009.

Ebeling and Earl began building a strong management team that included hiring Wes Frye in 1985 as controller, who would go on to become senior vice president of finance, chief financial officer, and play an important role in banking, finance, and investor relations, and serve as a liaison to analysts;

Old Dominion hired John Ebeling to serve as the company's president on September 1, 1985. *(Photo by Bachrach.)*

Joel McCarty, who came on board in 1987 as vice president, general counsel, and secretary and would later be promoted to senior vice president, while playing a key role in in real estate development and 11 acquisitions; and Ed Richardson, who joined in 1986 as director of maintenance and was later promoted to vice president of equipment and maintenance, focusing on building a fleet to accommodate future growth.

One of Ebeling's greatest successes was keeping the Old Dominion team intact. "A lot of times, when someone—especially on a president's level or even on an executive vice president's level—comes into a company, they bring a lot of the people that they've worked with previously," noted Old Dominion's former executive vice president and chief operating officer John Yowell, who sadly passed away in 2010. "John did not do that. He kind of did it on his own, and I thought that was pretty neat because he didn't tear up the team."[81]

Old Dominion in Crisis

Unfortunately, installing a new president did not give Old Dominion the quick turnaround Earl had hoped for. In 1986, the company faced a 99.6 percent operating ratio, the worst Old Dominion had ever experienced.[82] That year, Old Dominion's bank told Earl and Jack, "You will either have to sell Deaton or infuse $5 million of capital into Old Dominion Freight Line."

The only place Old Dominion could get the capital was from the privately held truck leasing company Jack and Earl owned.[83] "We decided that it was better business to infuse $5 million of capital into Old Dominion than it was to sell Deaton," Earl explained. "In retrospect, we maybe should have sold Deaton. We had two offers of $20 million for Deaton in 1986, and we ended up five years later selling it for $11 million because it had started losing money, so in retrospect, we probably should have sold Deaton for $20 million in 1986. At the time, we owed North Carolina National Bank $26 million, so we could have paid that loan from $26 million down to $6 million and we wouldn't have been carrying such a high debt load."[84]

The company's largest losses occurred in 1987, making Old Dominion's financials worse under Ebeling's stewardship rather than better. "This, of course, was naturally bothering us all," Earl recalled. "Ebeling didn't think that we could save Old Dominion, and he suggested that we try to sell it."[85]

Reluctantly, Old Dominion went through the process of meeting with several trucking companies about the possibility of selling Old Dominion, but the company couldn't find a buyer.[86] Earl felt like Ebeling had run out of options for bringing the company back to profitability. "In my opinion, he gave up," Earl said. "In fact, he was even looking for a job."

However, despite the problems Old Dominion was having, the team worked together, determined to succeed, and John Ebeling proved instrumental in helping Earl guide the company to profitability."[87]

Old Dominion got an opportunity to merge with Thurston Motor Lines in the first quarter of 1987, and they began to negotiate. By October 1987, at which point Old Dominion knew it was about to lose almost $4 million for the year, Old Dominion got a letter from International Utilities, which owned Thurston, saying that it was selling Thurston to

KEEPING TIRE EXPENSES IN CHECK

IN THE 1980s, OLD DOMINION'S MAINTENANCE COSTS were topped by the cost of fuel, and coming in second as most expensive for maintenance purposes was tires. "The cost of a new drive tire is now in excess of $200," Old Dominion's Tire Shop Foreman John Pye announced in Old Dominion's internal company newsletter in August 1980.[1]

In 1980, Old Dominion employed eight repairmen who were responsible for maintaining the company's 16,000 tires. Between that department's efforts, the good efforts of the drivers, and the work of the maintenance and operations departments, the company was able to significantly reduce tire expenditures.[2]

Eliminating flat tires was one way that Old Dominion saved money. Drivers were trained to avoid allowing their tires to run flat, which, over a three-year period, reduced the number of flat tires by 315 and saved the company $63,000 in replacement costs. During the same period, "tires destroyed by road hazards have been reduced by 250 tires, for a savings of $50,000," Pye wrote in the 1980 newsletter. "And finally, tires cut and destroyed by tow motor forks have decreased from 12 tires per year to two per year."[3]

Old Dominion also sought to repair tires when possible, rather than unnecessarily replacing them outright. The company would attempt to recap tires at least three times—costing the company $80, a significant savings over the $200 cost of a new tire.[4]

"Don't neglect your tires," Pye implored drivers in his 1980 article. "Your life is riding on them!"[5]

Old Dominion employed eight repairmen whose sole responsibilities were ensuring that the company's tires were safe.

Brown Transport, and the company's deal with Old Dominion was dead.[88]

"This was two weeks before the trigger was being pulled to announce the merger," David Congdon recalled.[89] And that wasn't the worst part.

"Then we got a letter from our bank about the same time," Earl said. "And I don't know whether they knew about the Thurston deal being dead or not, but they suggested that we get another bank, and we owed them $26 million."[90]

Old Dominion was only capable of borrowing $1.8 million at the time. "So we were on thin ice, all right," Earl recalled. "I told John Ebeling that if he couldn't find some economies, that we had to erase this loss and that I was going to propose a 10 percent pay cut, which is what some of our competitors had been doing during this recession."

Although Ebeling did not agree with the idea, he had no other suggestions. Earl decided to move forward with the plan.[91]

Saving the Company

In November 1987, two Old Dominion executives, Buddy McBride and Bill Barley, got wind of the news that Earl might be thinking of cutting employees' pay and were concerned over the impact that might have on the business. They invited Earl to lunch and asked him about his plans.[92] He warned that he planned to institute a 10 percent pay cut.[93]

"And they said, 'My God! Please don't do that. It will destroy the company,'" Earl recalled later. The two men suggested that Old Dominion could find $4 million in cost reductions, but Ebeling had led Earl to believe that was not possible. However, McBride and Barley promised to call their terminal freight managers and find the money.[94]

"So we came back from lunch and went in our office," McBride said. "All four of us sat there, and we came up with a game plan of how much had to be cut. ... And Bill Barley and I laid out a plan to Earl, and it had to do with a lot of changes."[95]

Based on the suggestions of Barley, McBride, and Earl, several decisions were made that subsequently saved the company. First, Old Dominion instituted a freight rate increase which brought in about $2.6 million.[96] Earl also realized that Old Dominion was suffering serious losses serving New York City, so the company raised prices by 25 percent to New York. Old Dominion then proceeded to raise prices by 25 percent in Washington, D.C., to make up for previous losses, raise rates to New England by 14 percent, and raise rates to Florida by 10 percent to 12 percent to make up for the fact that empty trailers were running back from Florida.[97] Although some of Old Dominion's management worried that rate increases might scare away customers, those fears proved unfounded. In fact, some Old Dominion executives realized that they might have been underpricing the company's services to begin with.[98]

Earl then created a study of Old Dominion's use of owner-operators in Florida and determined that Old Dominion could save $400,000 by replacing those vehicles with company trucks, as well as closing a terminal in Columbus, Georgia, to save another $300,000.[99]

No one in the company was allowed to hire or give a pay raise without approval from McBride or Barley during that period. "It kept us in business,"

Buddy McBride, Old Dominion's current vice president of transportation, proved instrumental in helping save the company during the crisis of 1987. *(Photo courtesy of Snow Photo and Digital Imaging, Inc. [formally Snow Studio].)*

McBride recalled. "Obviously, to get where we are today, to start making money, a lot of things happened, but that gave us the foundation to give us the time that it would take to start doing things we're doing today."[100]

When Earl and his management team finished instituting the cost reductions, "we came up with a number that we were going to change that $3.7 million loss to a profit of, oh, a million or two," Earl recalled later. "We were really cooking."[101]

Between McBride, Barley, and Earl, Old Dominion was thankfully back from the brink, and the company learned many important lessons. Old Dominion's financials broke even by January 1988, and the company steadily made money thereafter.[102]

"I think you have to give a whole lot of credit to Earl, with his pencil, his legal pad, his calculator, and his studying of freight bills," David recalled. "It was our internal cost reduction deal and a major step forward with rates, those two things did it. We were sticking our necks out by jacking these prices up."[103]

Total Quality Management

During the 1980s, an initiative gained momentum throughout the service industry, known as Total Quality Management (TQM).[104] TQM's central tenet is that long-term success can be achieved through customer satisfaction, and charges all of an organization's members to participate in improving processes, services, products, and company culture.[105] Because everyone within a TQM-structured business is responsible for the company's quality, each member of an organization works to ensure that the company is operating at its highest levels.

David Congdon became a student of TQM and wanted to institute it within Old Dominion but knew that Ebeling's style didn't quite match the TQM philosophy. "We were just managing in an older, autocratic style of management: Everybody do what we tell you to do. Just punch the clock, come in and do your job, and leave. Follow instructions," David said. "And that was basically the way the company was being run, and I was trying to raise the issue of how to be more participative."[106]

David used the TQM management style in the maintenance department, over which he had control in the 1980s, and hired Ed Richardson in 1986, future vice president of equipment and maintenance, who took maintenance to another level. As David noted, "The best thing to ever do as a leader is to hire people who are smarter than you are."[107]

It was a philosophy that would serve the company well as it ventured into new territory, with the thought of going public on management's mind.

Information contained herein is subject to completion or amendment. A registration statement relating to these securities has been filed with the Securities and Exchange Commission. These securities may not be sold nor may offers to buy be accepted prior to the time the registration statement becomes effective. This prospectus shall not constitute an offer to sell or the solicitation of an offer to buy nor shall there be any sale of these securities in any State in which such offer, solicitation or sale would be unlawful prior to registration or qualification under the securities laws of any such State.

Subject to Completion
September 20, 1991

2,000,000 SHARES

OLD DOMINION

COMMON STOCK

Of the 2,000,000 shares offered hereby, 1,250,000 shares are being sold by Old Dominion Freight Line, Inc. (the "Company"), and 750,000 shares are being sold by the Selling Shareholders. The Company will not receive any part of the proceeds of the shares being sold by the Selling Shareholders. See "Use of Proceeds" and "Principal and Selling Shareholders".

Prior to this offering, there has been no established market for the Company's Common Stock. It is currently estimated that the initial public offering price will be between $11.00 and $13.00 per share. See "Underwriting" for the factors to be considered in determining the initial public offering price.

See "Investment Considerations" for information that should be considered by prospective investors.

THESE SECURITIES HAVE NOT BEEN APPROVED OR DISAPPROVED BY THE SECURITIES AND EXCHANGE COMMISSION OR ANY STATE SECURITIES COMMISSIONER NOR HAS THE SECURITIES AND EXCHANGE COMMISSION OR ANY STATE SECURITIES COMMISSIONER PASSED UPON THE ACCURACY OR ADEQUACY OF THIS PROSPECTUS. ANY REPRESENTATION TO THE CONTRARY IS A CRIMINAL OFFENSE.

	Price to Public	Underwriting Discounts and Commissions	Proceeds to Company (1)	Proceeds to Selling Shareholders (1)
Per Share	$	$	$	$
Total (2)	$	$	$	$

(1) Before deducting expenses estimated at $ payable by the Company and $ payable by the Selling Shareholders.
(2) The Company has granted the Underwriters a 30-day option to purchase up to 300,000 additional shares to cover over-allotments. To the extent that the option is exercised, the Underwriters will offer the additional shares to the public at the Price to Public shown above. If the option is exercised in full, the Price to Public, Underwriting Discounts and Commissions and Proceeds to Company will be $, $ and $, respectively. See "Underwriting".

The shares of Common Stock are offered by the several Underwriters, subject to prior sale, when, as and if delivered to and accepted by them, and subject to the right of the Underwriters to reject any order in whole or in part. It is expected that delivery of the shares will be made at the offices of Alex. Brown & Sons Incorporated, Baltimore, Maryland, on or about , 1991.

ALEX. BROWN & SONS
INCORPORATED

WHEAT FIRST BUTCHER & SINGER
CAPITAL MARKETS

The date of this Prospectus is , 1991.

In 1991, Old Dominion listed 2 million shares of its stock for sale to the public for the first time in the company's 57-year history.

CHAPTER SEVEN

GOING PUBLIC

1988–1993

When I got here, we started growing, and we were able to give the customers more and more of what they were asking for. The customer was always first. Out of all the things we had to do, the customer came first, and to this day, it's still that way. I've never had to say no to a customer.

—John Yowell,
former Old Dominion executive vice president
and chief operating officer, who sadly passed away
December 30, 2010[1]

AFTER OLD DOMINION EMERGED from its financial crisis still intact, the company's management felt that the best way to bring in revenue without further cuts or layoffs would be to improve efficiency within the company across all divisions, including a commitment to lowering the claims rate.

"Do any of you believe that a 'busted up' shipment which arrives on time is good service?" Earl Congdon asked in a letter to employees in spring 1988. "We must be careful to load our freight so that it won't become damaged."[2]

In addition, Earl told staffers, shipments that ended up at the wrong destination had become a growing problem that cost the company money and took time to resolve.

Old Dominion's new strategies to improve the claims rate and cut costs worked well, and in 1988, profits reached $2.8 million.[3] John Ebeling credited the turnaround to better pricing during the second half of 1987, tighter cost controls for the year, revenue growth due to sales and marketing efforts, and improved service.[4] With business on the upswing in 1988, Old Dominion committed more than $9 million to replace outdated equipment.[5]

"In 1988, our losses ceased, and the operating ratio dropped to 96 percent," Earl later said. "We made almost $3 million before taxes in 1988. We had a definite turnaround."[6]

Also helping profits in the late 1980s was David Congdon's commitment to making the company's furniture division profitable. David had moved to Old Dominion's furniture division in 1987 and proved successful after placing more emphasis on quality than the previous furniture manager.[7]

The furniture division had been sending empty trailers back to Old Dominion after making deliveries, and Old Dominion had been using owner-operators at the time to make the deliveries.[8] The owner-operators would leave North Carolina on a Sunday night, drive to Philadelphia, and begin making deliveries to customers by Monday. They would deliver the entire load by Tuesday morning, drive home empty, and begin the cycle again on Wednesday.[9]

Each of the division's 150 trucks made two trips out in a week. When David took over, the division was earning $12 million in sales but still losing millions every year.[10] David knew he could turn those losses into profits. He took the division from losing

Old Dominion's trucks were a familiar sight both in the city and on the highways by 1993. *(Photo © 1994 Jim Stratford.)*

Above: A set of pup trailers parked outside of Old Dominion's headquarters in 1989.

Below: Old Dominion President John Ebeling and Chairman Earl Congdon standing by an Old Dominion truck in 1993. *(Photo © 1993 Jim Stratford.)*

$2 million, "to making maybe—maybe—a couple hundred thousand a year but still doing roughly $12 million in sales," he recalled. "It was a pretty slim margin."[11]

Operating in a Bad Economy

By 1989, Old Dominion had 2,800 employees, a fleet of 1,300 tractors, and 3,000 trailers—all twins—and the company had an 88 percent on-time record, compared to the industry average of 85 percent.[12] At that point, the company's furniture division accounted for 8 percent of its revenues.[13] Old Dominion was also finding recognition outside of the South and across the industry. In 1989, *Transport Topics* magazine ranked Old Dominion as No. 49 of the top 100 carriers on its annual list, noting Old Dominion's revenues at the time as $127 million.[14]

As Earl told employees, Old Dominion posted a 21 percent increase in revenues, "one of the best revenue increases in the industry" during the first half of 1989. However, Earl foresaw that the national economy was weakening.[15] A 1989 *Time* magazine article indicated that 10 of the top US economists were predicting an upcoming recession, noting that "all segments of the US economy—consumers, corporations, the federal government—are laboring under heavy debt loads."[16]

With 1990 came the beginning of the Gulf War and a resulting increase in oil prices, which boosted inflation. Add to that the savings and loan crisis, which involved the failure of more than 700 savings and loan associations, and the financial landscape was ripe for an inevitable recession in 1990.[17] The trucking industry did not fare any better than the rest of the national economy, and by that spring, just eight of the companies that had been considered the top 50 freight carriers in 1980 remained.[18] "Things have gotten so bad in our industry that the Interstate Commerce Commission (ICC) is scheduling Sunshine Hearings to determine how to keep the motor carrier industry from destroying itself," Ebeling wrote to employees in spring 1990.[19]

Old Dominion management felt grateful the company survived. However, Old Dominion still maintained its goal to reduce its large debt load.[20] "To survive, we must grow with profitable freight and a very efficient operation," Ebeling said. "I am confident that our team is up to the challenge as each of us goes that extra mile to survive this marathon."[21]

One way that Old Dominion found to optimize cost controls was to begin installing inspectors in its largest terminals who would verify shippers' weight using the proper freight classification and oversee a freight reweighing process. Old Dominion had found that in some cases, customers would either intentionally or unintentionally misjudge the weight of their freight, and Old Dominion had not been double-checking the numbers until the early 1990s.[22]

If a customer documented that his freight weighed 1,500 pounds when it actually weighed 2,000, that customer was receiving a 25 percent to

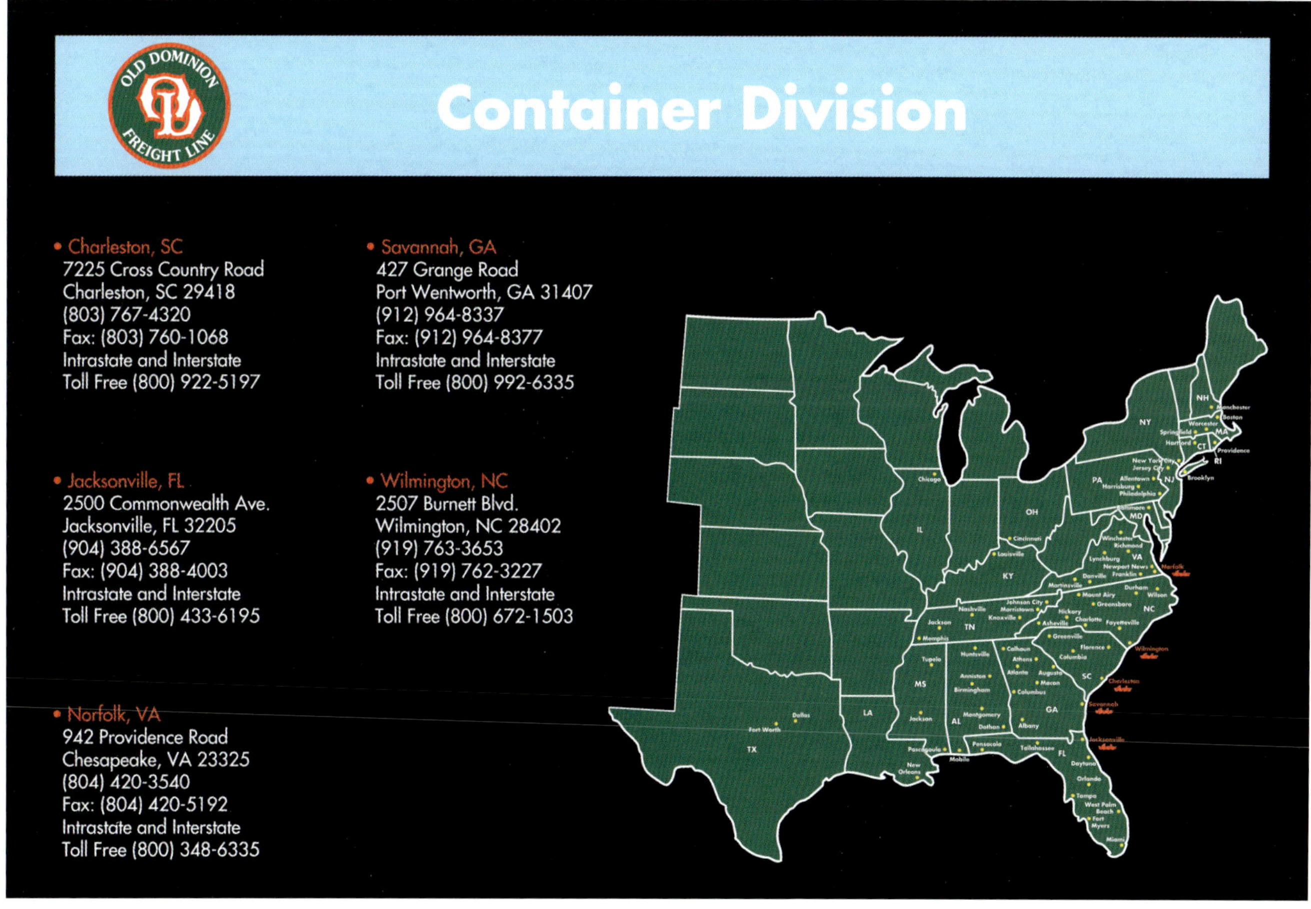

In 1991, Old Dominion's container division operated a brisk business, particularly along the East Coast.

ERROR-FREE WORK

Old Dominion's pledge to make its workplace "error-free" involved extensive staff training exercises in both the classroom and the warehouse.

According to Earl Congdon Jr., "quality service" is Old Dominion's only product.[1] In an effort to improve the company's quality of service, Old Dominion created the Error-Free Work (EFW) program in 1988. The company projected that the new initiative would earn Old Dominion $2.5 million within the first year of implementation.[2]

Ernie Benge, then Old Dominion's claims manager and currently director of claims, challenged the company's employees to dive into the initiative by asking them one simple question: "If payment for every mistake that is made by you was being paid by you, would

30 percent discount by understating the weight. Earl learned that most other carriers were using inspectors in their terminals, and once Old Dominion followed suit in the early 1990s, the company started saving significant amounts of money.

Earl said, "If we had been doing this back in the 1980s when we were losing money, we would have been looking at three or four operating ratio points."[23]

Thanks to a variety of strategies, including the installation of freight inspectors, 1990 revenues came in at $134 million, with a 91.8 percent operating ratio.[24] This was despite the fact that the US was in a recession throughout most of 1990 and 1991.[25] The lessons that Old Dominion had learned about controlling costs and operating a lean business during the company's own financial crisis in 1987 were extremely valuable as Old Dominion operated throughout the recession. "While other carriers are experiencing layoffs, we're hiring," Earl told employees in 1991.[26]

Since the company was experiencing such success at a time when other trucking companies were floundering, Old Dominion's officers thought it might be the best time to implement new capital-building strategies.

Wall Street Beckons

By 1991, Old Dominion executives felt that the company was undercapitalized and realized that one effective way to raise funds was to go public.[27] As a company that had operated privately for more than 50 years, "we had a certain amount of net worth on paper and no money to spend," Earl later recalled.[28]

your present level of efficiency and accuracy be acceptable?"[3]

To prevent errors, Benge advised Old Dominion's employees to focus on three areas:

- *Avoid carelessness—Staff members who simply don't pay attention could fail to record what they're receiving or delivering or how much weight they're loading on a trailer.*
- *Train employees well—An employee who doesn't know how to perform the job can easily make mistakes.*
- *Expect high-quality work from others in each employee's department—There is nothing worse than a bad attitude.*

As Benge reminded staffers, the $2.5 million that Old Dominion paid in claims in 1987 "did come out of your pockets—and mine, and everyone else who is an employee of Old Dominion."[4]

Under the guidance of Benge and the rest of the claims department, as well as the participation and commitment of Old Dominion's entire workforce, the company did reach its goal of lowering its error rate, and by 2010, Old Dominion's claims rate was the lowest in the industry.[5]

Old Dominion made a strong commitment to "Error-Free Work," which involved hard work from employees at all levels of the company and included steps such as installing inspectors at its largest terminals to check the freight.

Old Dominion was in a strong position to go public, with operating revenue for the first six months of 1991 at $74 million, a 14.9 percent increase over the $64 million during the same period of 1990.[29] Those numbers, coupled with the Congdons' interest in raising equity, made it an easy decision to go public. According to Earl, the company was "sitting with maybe a $16 million net worth and debt that was still probably running at maybe three times our equity, and it wasn't healthy. We felt strongly that we needed more capital in Old Dominion, and so we decided to do a public offering."[30]

In preparing to go public, Old Dominion had to show a history of profitability for the previous four years, and the company discovered that its furniture division would be viewed as a liability by investors. Analysts suggested that if Old Dominion could show the furniture division losses as losses from a discontinued operation, Old Dominion would be worth $20 million more. However, it would mean that the company would be forced to shut down the furniture division entirely or try to sell it.[31]

The fact that the company's furniture segment had been making any money to begin with was a testament to David's hard work. "We didn't give David any capital at the furniture division, so every cent that he needed to operate the division had to be borrowed—that was the first thing we did to him," Earl later recalled.[32]

Despite the fact that he was operating the division with limited resources, David was committed to making the furniture segment a success. He was disappointed when faced with the prospect of losing the division. David considered cashing in some of his Old Dominion stock and spinning off the furniture division as his own company, but after much consideration, he realized he would be spending $1.5 million on the venture, and he did not foresee a proper return on investment.[33] "It was a very emotional day for me when I went over and met with my people, brought them into the break room, and said, 'Guys, we're shutting this thing down,'" David recalled.

He found jobs on the freight side of the business for the displaced staff so that they maintained employment. David took a new position as vice president of line-haul with Old Dominion, where he ran central dispatch.[34]

Selling the Shares

On October 24, 1991, Old Dominion released its initial public offering of 2 million shares of stock at $12.50 per share.[35] When the stock went up for sale, the company found that "there turned out to be four times more demand for the stock than stock available," the *Greensboro News & Record* reported at the time.[36]

David recalled that Wes Frye, now senior vice president of finance and chief financial officer, was instrumental in getting Old Dominion's financial house in order so that the company would be in position for a public stock offering. Wes worked with the company's banks, underwriters, and outside accountants in developing the documentation and marketing strategy in preparation for the initial public offering. David said, "Wes has continued to play a key role in Old Dominion's banking and financial matters as well as investor relations and liaison with analysts who write on the trucking industry. In fact, in 2011, Wes was recognized by *Institutional Investor* as being the best chief financial officer in the LTL Trucking Segment."

Following the IPO, the Congdon family continued to own 73.4 percent of the stock,[37] but Old Dominion had long-term plans to work the ratio down gradually to where the family would own 55 percent of the company, and the public would own 45 percent.[38] Overall, the public offering brought in about $25 million, of which about $9.3 million went to the Congdon family, and the rest went to pay down debt.[39]

After the stock sale took place, Ebeling told Old Dominion staffers: "I believe our public offering is probably one of the most significant events in our company's history. The fact that our investment bankers and the individuals who invested in our stock believed enough in Old Dominion to buy our stock is a true compliment to all of our employees."[40]

The stock sale set Old Dominion up for future success as well. "When we went public, it put us in a position of financial stability that became stronger and stronger as time went on. It enabled us to grow and expand our ability to purchase equipment and real estate necessary to accomplish our objectives. As information, when Old Dominion went public, we had 47 service centers and 2,400 employees. Now there are 216 service centers with 13,500 employees," recalled Joel McCarty, Old Dominion's current senior vice president, general counsel, and secretary.[41]

The stock sale also gave the company additional unexpected advantages, Earl later noted:

> *It's made us a better company because the analysts and the investors keep our feet to the fire. I think it has made us far more disciplined than we might have been if we owned it all and we felt that we could operate like we wanted to. I think that we forewent a heck of a lot of profit in the early days because we were growing and growing and growing, and it kept us off balance. We didn't manage as well. ... But when you're publicly held and the stockholders are wanting growth, but they don't want you to say, "Well, we're going to spend it now so that we'll be bigger later." Somehow you've got to learn how to be profitable now as well as have a long-term plan, so I think it's been good for us.*[42]

Old Dominion closed out 1991 with record earnings, posting revenues of $155.8 million, a 16 percent increase over 1990.[43]

Finding Out What Fits

During the period when Old Dominion went public, the company analyzed several divisions to determine how they would fit into the overall structure at Old Dominion. As with the furniture division, Old Dominion had to make some tough decisions when it came time to review profits within its Deaton

John Ebeling and Earl Congdon during a strategy meeting in 1993. *(Photo © 1993 Jim Stratford.)*

subsidiary.[44] After reviewing Deaton's financials and what it could offer the corporation as a whole, Old Dominion decided to sell Deaton "because it did not fit into our overall strategy of being a fast-growing LTL carrier with solid performance," Ebeling noted in 1992.[45]

All of Old Dominion's adjustments were improving the company's profile nationwide. In 1992, *Forbes* magazine ranked Old Dominion 92nd among the "200 Best Small Companies in America."[46] The company had an average return on equity of 17.9 percent and a five-year compound earnings per share growth rate of 80 percent, making it very attractive to investors and a standout among LTL carriers.[47]

By that point, Old Dominion was using a distribution network arrangement with other carriers that allowed the company to ship to or from all 50 states and Canada. Interregional deliveries made up 60 percent of the company's business, meaning most trucks traveled 500 miles or more from one of the company's 47 terminals.[48] As Earl told a reporter in July 1992, "Our game right now is

OLD DOMINION'S TRUCK DRIVER TRAINING SCHOOL

IN 1988, EARL CONGDON CALLED FUTURE VICE President of Safety and Personnel Brian Stoddard into his office and asked him if he could teach others how to drive a truck.[1] Stoddard replied, "Well, somebody taught me, so, yeah, I'm sure we could do that."[2]

From that simple conversation, the class of ODTDT-8/88 was formed. The name stood for Old Dominion Truck Driver Training–August 1988, in recognition of the very first class. The program, which remains in place today, provides employees with training on driving a truck professionally, all free of charge.[3]

The program launched with just eight students, five of whom graduated and became qualified drivers for the company.[4] By 2010, the program had trained nearly 3,000 drivers, providing students with training manuals, a video library, and teaching aids.[5] Old Dominion has opened up the weeklong classroom portion of the program to students almost anywhere, as long as they have access to a classroom. Students learn about regulations, company policies, safe driving, keeping logs, Department of Transportation requirements, and the handling of hazardous materials. Students also prove their commitment by donating the first 25 hours of supervised training to gain experience familiarizing themselves with the equipment.[6] A minimum of 240 total course hours are required to receive a final road test by a safety manager, nearly double the hours required by many other professional driving schools.

Since the class is free of charge, Old Dominion asks students to stay with the company for 12 months after they receive their certificates. If they leave before that, they must reimburse Old Dominion for the cost of the class, which by 2010 reached $3,500.[7] The course has trained scores of responsible and committed drivers for Old Dominion since 1988 and is considered one of the most innovative programs in the industry.

As Stoddard explained, "At Old Dominion, we grow our own qualified truck drivers."

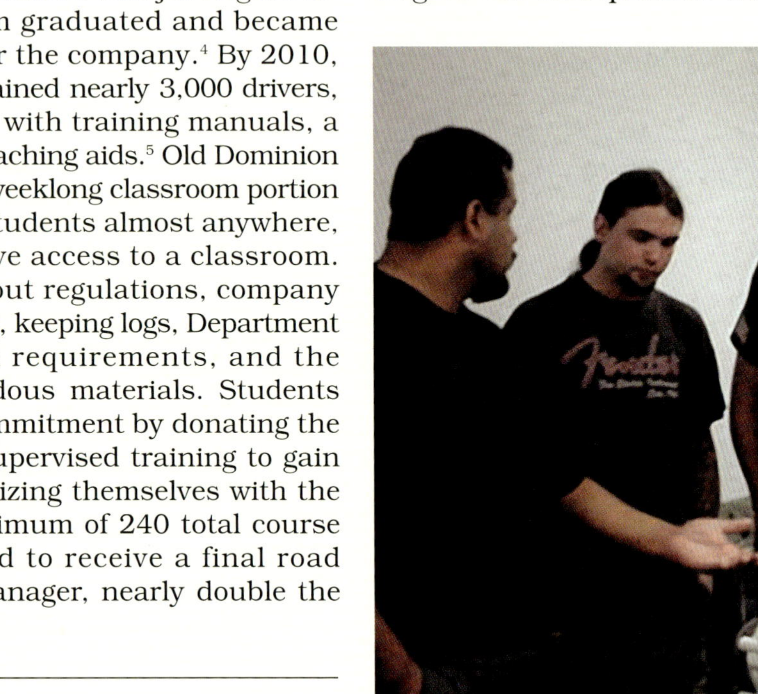

Old Dominion established its Old Dominion Truck Driver Training program in 1988. Drivers study at no cost to them, and in return, they make a commitment to work for Old Dominion for one year following graduation.

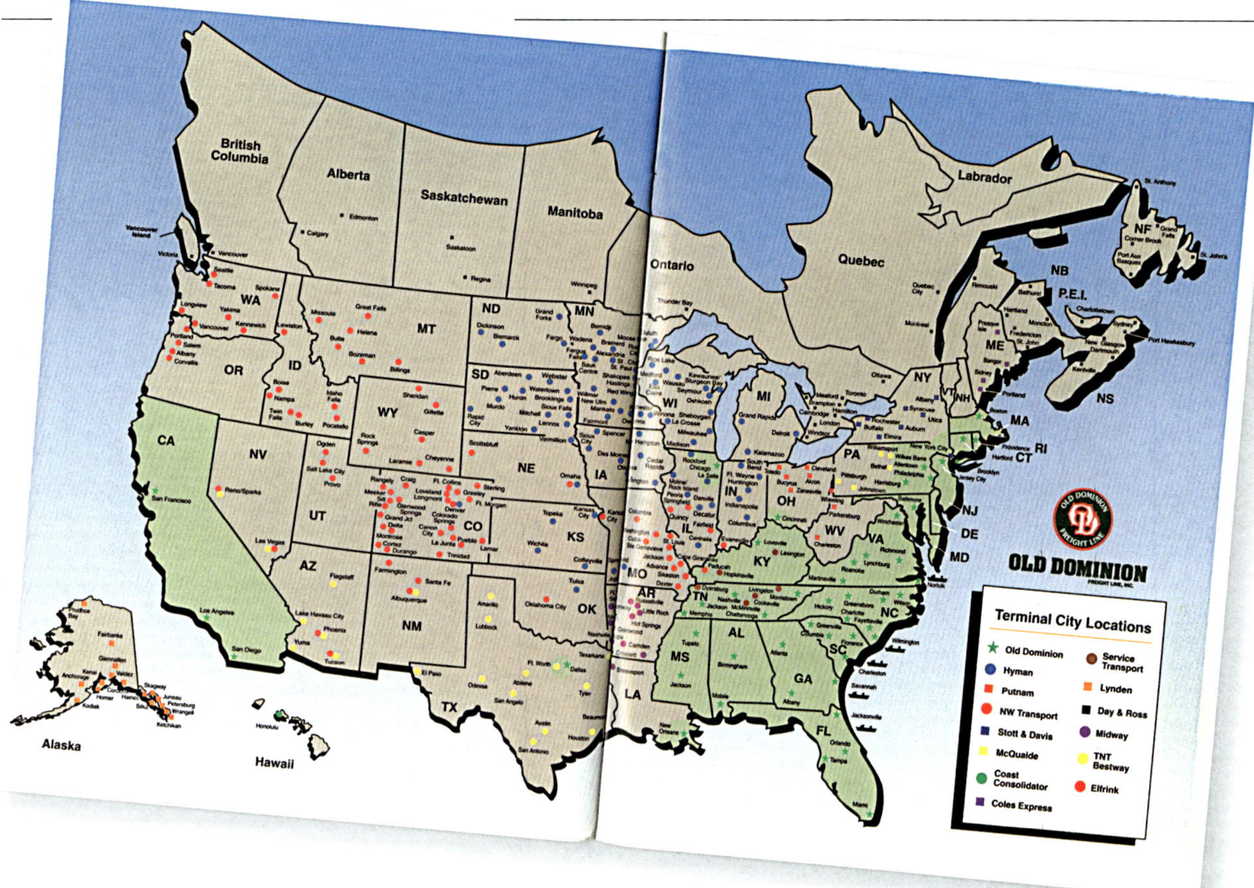

This map shows the broad reach of Old Dominion's terminals in 1991, throughout the United States and into Canada, through interline partnerships.

to increase density by putting more shipments and dollars of revenue into our existing fleet. This helps our profit ratio because we have already incurred a lot of overhead in our initial investment."[49]

The investment to which Earl was referring involved the $16.4 million purchase of 316 tractors and trucks from Freightliner, Volvo GM, and Navistar, as well as 380 trailers, bringing Old Dominion's fleet to nearly 1,000 tractors and 3,000 trailers in 1992.[50]

The investments turned out to offer the company excellent returns. Total revenues in 1992 reached $183 million, and the company's top 15 customers made up only 19.1 percent of total revenue, with no single customer making up more than 3.89 percent of revenue volume.[51] As Earl told a reporter with *Southern Motor Cargo* magazine, "We believe we can grow revenues 15 percent to 20 percent each year for the next three to five years within our existing area of operations, and we want to stay within that area as long as we can because most of our overhead has already been incurred."[52]

Taking TQM Company-Wide

The Total Quality Management (TQM) philosophy, which David had successfully instituted in the maintenance department and the furniture division years before, made its way into the way Old Dominion did its business in 1992.[53] The development took David by surprise and allowed him to seize a new opportunity at Old Dominion:

> *In the fall of 1992, we had a management retreat in Myrtle Beach, which combined a golf outing with a business meeting. It was at this meeting in the fall of 1992 that John Ebeling made a proclamation. He said, "I think it's time for us to change our management style and to adopt quality management."*
>
> *That came out of the blue. I'd been talking about this since probably 1986 or 1987 and practicing it in my respective areas of responsibility, trying to tell Earl and John that we needed to implement it sometime. I wasn't getting anywhere with them, but he*

FOUNDATION OF SUCCESS

Old Dominion's secret to success—the Quality Management Process

CUSTOMER FOCUS

The pillar of *Customer Focus* represents key functions Old Dominion emphasizes to satisfy customer needs. Marketing and sales are the ways in which Old Dominion listens to the specific needs of their customers and determine what they must do to satisfy those needs. Best-in-class service, claim-free handling, accurate billing, and cost-effective pricing represent the four primary and universal needs of Old Dominion customers.

TOTAL INVOLVEMENT

The pillar of *Total Involvement* might be termed Old Dominion's "people" pillar. It is through people—the company's most valuable asset—that we focus on the needs of our customers. Internal and external communications keep everyone informed of what's going on and what each person needs to do to satisfy Old Dominion customers. Old Dominion's Safety Program is one of the best in the industry. Old Dominion's in-house Driver Training School allows the company to develop safety-conscious drivers and to promote from within. It is through communications and the family atmosphere that Old Dominion remains union free. Old Dominion is dedicated to promoting from within through opportunities on all levels in our company.

MEASUREMENT

The pillar of *Measurement* tells everyone at Old Dominion if our improvements are working and if we are accomplishing our objectives. All employees are held accountable for satisfying internal and external customer needs.

SYSTEMATIC SUPPORT

The *Systematic Support* pillar represents the elements that are provided primarily by and through effective management to the organization. Financial stability is the cement that binds all the success elements that built the Foundation of Success. Through equipment maintenance and replacement, Old Dominion operates one of the newest, greenest, and most dependable fleets in the industry. Old Dominion is continuously updating its facilities to sustain growth and provide a premier service. We recognize the need to continue the development of employees through an ongoing educational process. The focus on Information Systems Technology provides customers with necessary information, electronically, to properly manage their link in the total logistics process, in addition to assisting in the efficient movement of their goods.

CONTINUOUS IMPROVEMENT

The Quality Management Process is summarized with the *Continuous Improvement* pillar. Old Dominion understands that we must never be satisfied with status quo. We must continuously strive to improve customer service, employee relations, and labor efficiency. Old Dominion believes that the people who do the work, in conjunction with those who manage it, are best qualified to improve their work process. Through team-based problem solving and the planning process, Old Dominion accomplishes continuous improvement.

Since Old Dominion Freight Line's inception in 1934, the company founders have desired to deliver quality service to their customers. Earl and Lillian Congdon had a "do whatever it takes" mindset, and they were determined to make their customers' priorities their own priority. That tradition carried forward in the hearts and minds of Old Dominion employees throughout the years, and in 1992, the company decided to formalize that storied tradition into a process that would formally promote quality service at the highest level.

Led by David Congdon, the company's executive team embarked on a search to find a quality model that would represent the company's values, vision, and mission to serve. Their search led them to ODI of Boston, Massachusetts, and the study of ODI's Total Quality Advantage (TQA) process. Soon after, Old Dominion adopted the TQA methodology as its own and, with the help of senior management, the company began to build what is known today as the Old Dominion Foundation of Success. Once the initial model was built, the entire company was introduced to the Old Dominion Foundation of Success.

Since that time, the Foundation of Success has become a living, breathing process that has grown and evolved as the company has changed. The Old Dominion Foundation of Success is neither an afterthought nor a separate or standalone function at Old Dominion. Company employees have integrated it into the way they operate their business. Its Vision, Mission, Values, and Success Elements are incorporated not only in the Foundation of Success model, but they are also part of who Old Dominion's employees are as promise keepers.

Old Dominion's Vision and Mission represent the company's aspirations and steps for achieving them. The Success Elements, each of which are "owned" and led by an officer of the company, are portrayed within the five pillars of Old Dominion's Quality Management Process: Customer Focus, Total Involvement, Measurement, Systematic Support, and Continuous Improvement, all of which are supported by the company's Values—those ideals which are behind every decision made at Old Dominion.

proclaimed it at this meeting in front of management, and when we got back to the office on Monday, I asked John if I could have a word with him and Earl. We went into Earl's office, and I volunteered. I said, "I am delighted that you feel the way you do about quality management, and I want the job. I want to lead this."

And so, lo and behold, they said yes, and effective January 1993, I became vice president of quality for the company.[54]

At the time, Earl stressed that TQM was a "process that involves everyone, every day, and is not a program."[55] Several national publications reported on Old Dominion's commitment to TQM, with *Business Life* noting that Old Dominion planned for all employees to complete the course by July 1994.[56] Although Old Dominion may have been slow to adopt the TQM dynamic, Ebeling and Earl became fully committed to the philosophy once it was adopted. "We've created a participatory environment," Ebeling told a *Southern Motor Cargo* reporter in 1993. "Take a mechanic in our shop, for example. His customer is the driver who brings a truck in, and his job is to satisfy that driver. Historically, a company would not think that way, but we've got to get our mechanics to recognize that drivers are their customers and to satisfy them."[57]

In his new role heading up quality management, David visited other companies and observed their positives and negatives, and through that, he involved senior management in the development of Old Dominion's Foundation of Success Model, which encompasses the company's vision "to be the premier transportation solutions provider in domestic and global markets served, and our mission statement, and then five pillars of quality: customer focus, total involvement, measurement, systematic support, and continuous improvement—all built on a foundation of underlying values of respect and courtesy and honesty," David said.[58]

By 1992, Old Dominion's fleet consisted of nearly 1,000 tractors and 3,000 trailers. Pictured below is the Greensboro, North Carolina, service center.

Old Dominion executives gather in 1993. From left to right: Terry Hutchins, Buddy McBride, Wes Frye, Tim Turner, George Crawford, John Ebeling, Don Souza, Earl Congdon, David Congdon, Ed Richardson, Ernest Brantley, John Yowell, Joel McCarty, and Charles Lanier. *(Photo © 1993 Jim Stratford.)*

Record Revenue

Between the public offering, Old Dominion's commitment to TQM, and the company's investment in its fleet, Old Dominion was on a roll by 1993. At the end of that year, revenue had risen to an extraordinary $205 million, with trucks logging an average haul length of 671 miles.[59] The company's 12 percent revenue increase over 1992 levels was attributed mainly to a 14 percent increase in LTL tonnage.[60]

In addition, 1993 had been a year during which Old Dominion was able to experiment with ways to save costs and improve efficiencies in its truck components. Ed Richardson, Old Dominion's vice president of equipment and maintenance, told a reporter in 1993 that the company was testing antilock brake systems (ABS) to determine whether they would offer the company a return on investment and was researching whether onboard automatic chassis lubrication systems could allow the company to cut inspections in half. He also indicated that Old Dominion switched entirely to hub-piloted wheels in 1993.[61]

"We see hub-piloted wheels as being a real labor and cost-saving device in the future, and we've gone to them 100 percent now," Richardson told the reporter for *Southern Motor Cargo*. "With hub-piloted wheels, you have only 10 studs and 10 nuts. In other systems, you have 10 studs, 10 inner nuts, and 10 outer nuts. So, what you've done is essentially cut the work in half or better, in taking a wheel off or mounting it."

In Memorium

1948

1993

Lillian Congdon Crowder

We are greatly saddened by the passing of Lillian Congdon Crowder on December 26, 1993, at the age of 84. Lillian and her husband, Earl, my parents, founded our company in the summer of 1934 with a single truck. Their original operation was between Richmond and Norfolk, VA. Dad drove the truck while mother answered the telephone and did the paperwork from her home. They had no terminal that first year, and no money either.

In 1936, they moved into a two-door terminal in Richmond which they shared with Overnite Transportation Co. – one door for each company. They bought our first water cooler that year. It cost $35 and they had to finance it. A new truck could be bought for less than $1,000.

Old Dominion grew nicely during the late 30s and throughout the 40s. Lillian partially retired during the 40s because she had my brother, Jack, and me to raise, and apparently we required some supervision.

Tragedy struck in 1950 when Dad (Earl, Sr.) died accidentally at age 43. Mother was 40, I was 19, and Jack was 17. What would become of Old Dominion?

Mother never blinked and there was never a moment of indecision. When offers to buy the company came in, she said NO! – Old Dominion is not for sale; my boys and I are going to run it. We had 100 loyal employees, 23 tractors, 37 trailers, 25 straight trucks, and 3 little terminals. Sales for an entire year were $450,000.

Lillian Congdon returned to work full time, took charge and was the glue that held our company together for 4 or 5 years while Jack and I gained a little maturity.

She served as our Chairman and President until 1962 and as Chairman until she retired in 1975.

Even after she retired and moved to Florida, she remained very interested in what was happening at Old Dominion. She was proud of each and every one of us and of the progress of Old Dominion.

Somehow, I believe that she will continue to know how things are at O.D.

As you can see from the picture, our flag at the corporate office flew at half-mast for the week following her death as a tribute to the lady who created Old Dominion and preserved it for the 3,000 families who now make up our family.

We're going to miss her and our prayers go with her

Her Loving Son,
Earl Congdon

Opposite: In 1993, 84-year-old Lillian Congdon Crowder passed away, leaving her sons to carry on the legacy of the company that she and her husband founded in 1934.

Loss of a Matriarch

Everyone involved with Old Dominion Freight Line acknowledged that Old Dominion would never have survived without the hard work and dedication of the company's cofounder Lillian Congdon Crowder. Lillian contributed the company's start-up money in 1934, handled all of the orders and paperwork from her dining room table while raising her two young sons, and even drove the company's sole truck when her husband was sick. After Earl Sr. died, Lillian "was the glue that held our company together for four or five years while Jack and I gained a little maturity," Earl later wrote.[62]

She was a powerful force within the company, determined to make Old Dominion a success and refusing lucrative offers to sell. When times were tough, Lillian was even tougher, always willing to help, even coming out of retirement when Old Dominion was in need.

It was with extreme sadness that the Congdon family announced Lillian had passed away on December 26, 1993, at the age of 84.[63] Old Dominion flew the corporate office's flag at half-mast for a week after her passing "as a tribute to the lady who created Old Dominion and preserved it for the 3,000 families who now make up our family," Earl wrote to employees.[64]

As Old Dominion moved into a new era without its founding matriarch, the company focused its concentration on growth and service. The new century would also hold management changes that would bring the company, and the Congdon family, full circle.

In 1997, David Congdon became president of Old Dominion. *(Photo © 1993 Jim Stratford.)*

CHAPTER EIGHT

DAVID CONGDON LAYS THE FOUNDATION

1993–1999

David is a visionary. He wanted things to be bigger and better. ... Somewhere in all the strategy, and the changes in the market, David was determined to put service at the forefront. And that's what we did.

—Greg Gantt, executive vice president of operations and chief operating officer[1]

DESPITE THE FACT THAT OLD DOMINion was a firmly union-free carrier, union operations did affect the company from time to time, particularly when Teamsters strikes created new opportunities for Old Dominion.

On April 6, 1994, the Teamsters union called for a strike against 22 LTL trucking companies, sparking a walkout by approximately 70,000 union members. "A handful of large, nonunion trucking companies are among those winning the business that would have gone to the striking carriers," according to an article in the *Memphis Commercial Appeal*.[2]

Among those benefiting from the strike was Old Dominion—being nonunion would once again prove to help Old Dominion forge ahead, and by the end of the first quarter of 1994, Old Dominion would show revenue rising to $55 million.[3] When the dust settled following the strike, Old Dominion and others in the freight industry witnessed a major change that had begun to permeate the trucking sector. "The last Teamsters strike probably set the stage for the fate of unionized companies in the trucking industry, and further confirmed to many trucking analysts and shippers that unionized trucklines are following the same ultimate extinction as the dinosaur," Old Dominion President John Ebeling told employees in summer 1994.[4]

Earl Congdon later reported that the Teamsters went on strike for nearly a month and ended up getting a 25-cent-per hour raise for their efforts, whereas Old Dominion employees received much larger increases as a nonunion company.[5] Old Dominion employees were appreciative of their working conditions, but some still seemed apprehensive about the management style of the company. An employee survey performed in 1994 revealed that 96 percent of employees believed that Old Dominion was a good company to work for. However, employees reported lower satisfaction scores when asked about how management was doing.[6]

Old Dominion's increasing emphasis on Total Quality Management (TQM) would serve to change the management atmosphere for the better.[7] According to the company's internal newsletter, "The Quality Advantage Workshop is our first step toward developing a consistent and positive management culture throughout our organization."[8]

In 1994, David Congdon conducted a Total Quality Advantage Workshop that left participants completely energized. "Most importantly, they left

In 1994, Old Dominion celebrated its 60th year in business, a remarkable feat that the company commemorated with lapel pins.

with a clear game plan and the tools necessary to lead positive change through Quality Action Teams, for our customers, our employees, and Old Dominion," the Old Dominion newsletter reported.[9]

The company's commitment to improving quality led to stellar sales in 1994. The year came to a close with revenues of $243.5 million, an 18.6 percent increase over 1993 levels, and net income of $10 million, a 21 percent increase—marking record financial performance for the company.[10] Because income rose in 1994, Old Dominion was able to grant a generous wage increase to its employees in 1995.[11]

In addition to benefiting from a new focus on quality, Old Dominion also realized pricing adjustments may have been long overdue. The company had increased LTL prices by 4.6 percent during 1994, which brought in additional cash. Although the price increases led to approximately $12 million in lost business, overall, the increases still helped Old Dominion's bottom line, and led the company to develop more accurate charges going forward.[12]

As part of the pricing changes, Old Dominion also created a new type of rate structure, streamlining rate classifications from 18 classes to just four rate levels. The 18-class system had originally been put in place by the National Classification Committee 50 years prior, so paring the class offerings down dramatically proved to be a difficult sell to customers at first.[13]

In response, Old Dominion offered its customers the alternative of using either the old classifications, or the new system, which reduced the options to four density-based class scales and featured two levels of rates that depended on the maximum value of the goods being shipped. Initially, only international freight forwarders, whose weight was measured in metric units, took the company up on it.[14]

The Economy Weakens

Effective January 1, 1995, Congress required states to deregulate intrastate commerce, allowing Old Dominion the opportunity to enter the huge new markets that awaited thanks to the ruling.[15]

As a result of the good news from Congress, Old Dominion expanded into the Midwest and the West later in 1995 as part of a plan to offer "an intra-regional operation in the Western area of the country."[16] The expansion began with Old Dominion buying certain assets of Navajo LTL, Inc., based in Commerce City, Colorado.[17] The purchase gave Old Dominion six new service centers, additional tractor-trailers, office and computer equipment, and 150 of Navajo's employees.[18]

But quick expansion would not solve the problems that were bubbling under the surface due to a slowing national economy, and 1995 proved a difficult year for Old Dominion. Not only was the US economy weakening, according to Ebeling, the trucking industry was "probably financially in the worst condition it had been in since we were deregulated in the early 1980s."[19]

In addition to the fact that the US was drifting toward a recession, the intrastate deregulation ruling ended up causing many trucklines to expand their territories, "creating greater discounting which continues to put pressure on our profits," Ebeling told employees.[20]

In 1995, financial analysts predicted that the average full truckload carrier would show a

In 1994, *Distribution* magazine honored Old Dominion with its multiregional and interregional LTL Quality Carrier Award.

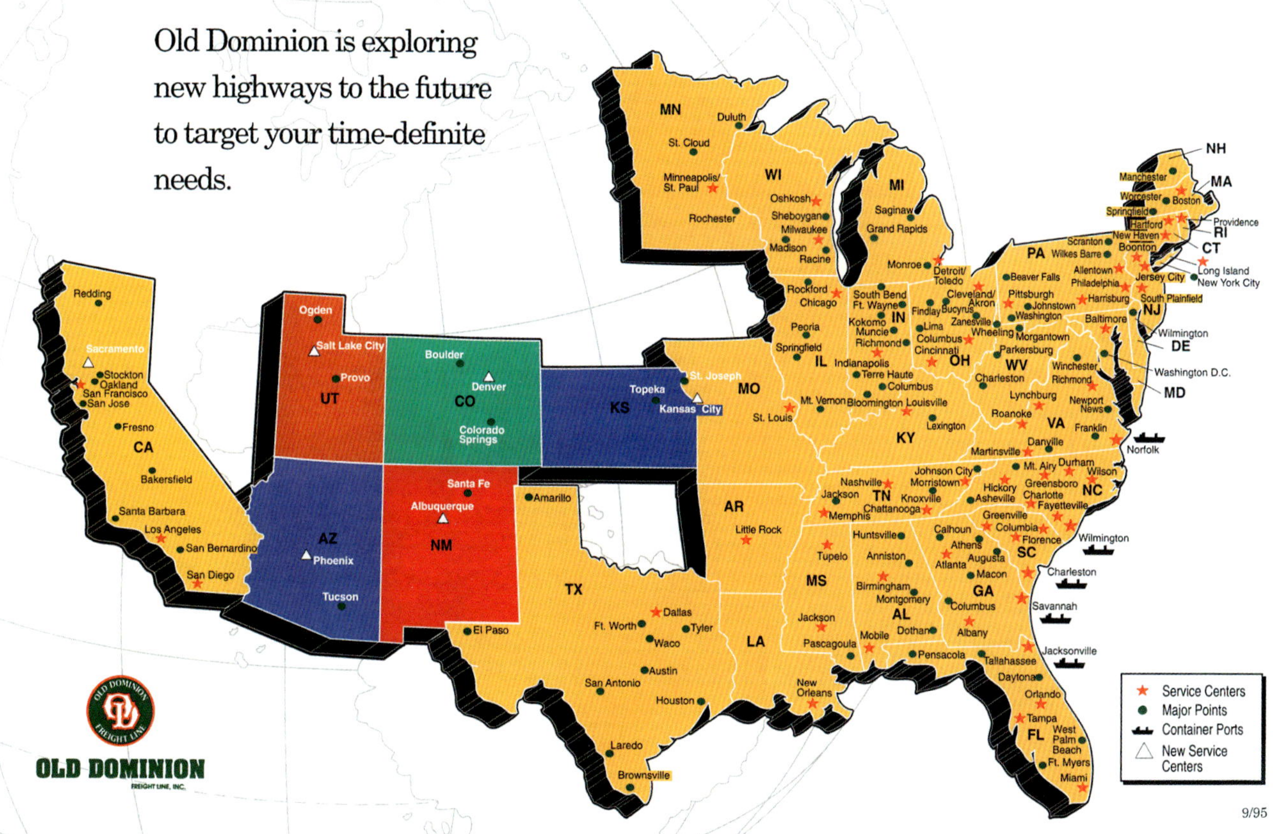

Following the 1995 acquisition of Navajo LTL, Inc., Old Dominion began to promote its capabilities across the West.

28 percent earnings decline, while the average LTL carrier was expected to post a startling 40 percent decline.[21]

A *Denver Post* news reporter speculated in 1995 that the cause of the freight industry's problems was due to freight companies "still suffering from the intense pricing pressures, chronic excess capacity, and weak shipper demand," and that Old Dominion in particular faced increased operating expenses in 1995 following its geographic expansion.[22]

Earl echoed that sentiment in 1995, telling the *Journal of Commerce* that "higher overhead associated with the company's ongoing geographic expansion has penalized profitability."[23]

Old Dominion closed out 1995 with revenues of $248 million, a $5 million increase over 1994, even with the slow economy affecting the US.[24] The average haul in 1995 was 731 miles.[25]

Old Dominion managed to remain profitable in 1995, a year that Earl described as "a real struggle."[26] After opening 15 new service centers, mostly in the West, Old Dominion added 500 new employees in 1995 during a slow economy. According to the company newsletter, "We certainly can't be satisfied with our performance, but we can be proud that we work for a carrier that expanded at the rate we did and was still able to show positive results."[27]

The year 1996 also proved exceedingly challenging for the trucking industry, with analysts predicting that a large number of nonunion carriers were at risk of bankruptcy, due to overcapacity and shrinking rates.[28] In addition, rising diesel prices in 1996 hit the industry hard, prompting Old Dominion and other freight companies to impose a surcharge to make up for the increase in fuel and other petroleum related cost increases.[29]

However, thanks in part to the wide expansion that Old Dominion completed in 1995, the company finished 1996 with a profit, taking in $293 million in revenue and $6.1 million in net income.[30]

Bringing the Congdon Family Full Circle

In May 1997, John Ebeling retired as president of Old Dominion and moved into the role of vice chairman of the board. He told staff members that he had been planning the decision for years. "My decision to step out of the day-to-day management was delayed from my being 55 years old, then to 57 years old, and now finally to 60 years old," Ebeling wrote to employees in June 1997. "Probably the most important criteria in allowing this succession to happen was my confidence in the future of Old Dominion Freight Line, Inc."[31]

The future looked bright for Old Dominion as a Congdon family member once again took the wheel. David Congdon, who had started at the company as a 14-year-old dockworker in 1971, was promoted to president and chief operating officer.[32] At the relatively young age of 40, David wanted to take Old Dominion in a fresh direction, with a renewed focus

Old Dominion's service centers, which spanned across the country in the 1990s, remained active even late at night, as shown below at the Greensboro, North Carolina, service center.

on making service the driving force behind the company's brand identity.[33]

Part of David's management style included delegating to people who were experts in their roles within Old Dominion. "I know a lot about many things, but the people who surround me know a hell of a lot more about the details of what they do, and I don't have to know the details," David said. "I expect them to know the details. My key leadership role is to build consensus around where we're headed, and then make sure we've got the right people, the right players in all the key positions."[34]

Those who kept a close eye on the transportation industry paid careful attention to David during those early days. John Larkin, managing director of the Transportation Research Group for analyst firm Stifel Nicolaus, had known David for years because Larkin helped handle Old Dominion's IPO in 1991. However, at that point, he was unaware that David had such strong management skills, since Larkin had previously only talked to David about his work as a skilled pilot.[35]

In 1997, Larkin visited Old Dominion headquarters in North Carolina and was impressed to hear David's views on the company:

> *Here I thought he was just a pilot and really had no interest in trucking, and I hear him waxing eloquently about his vision for a system strategy, which would be the backbone of this structure that would allow Old Dominion to grow, and then I heard him talk about strategic planning policies that would more or less help provide direction to the company's growth strategy so that they were adding terminals in the right place with the right number of doors and adding the right number of salespeople and telemarketers at each location.*
>
> *And, really, what has driven the excellent performance were those two building blocks that David Congdon talked about on that day back in 1997. He said, "We're going to spend the money, you know, regardless of what Wall Street thinks of it, by putting together the best system in the industry."*
>
> *I said to myself, "Man, that's the way to do it, isn't it?"*[36]

Just one month after coming into his new role, David called for the company's first major strategic planning meeting. "I had been preaching quality, and we had come a long way, but this is where, for me personally, I was able to really take hold and really begin to apply it and be in charge and weave the quality process into the way that we do business," David recalled, noting that he took the quality process from a company philosophy into the fabric of the brand.[37]

When David Congdon was named president of Old Dominion, it brought the company full circle, as David's grandparents, Lillian and Earl Congdon Sr., founded the company in 1934.

The company's strategic planning meetings have continued into the 21st century and provide valuable insight into the company's long-term projections. According to Chip Overbey, senior

MAINTAINING DRIVER RELATIONSHIPS

FOR A TRUCK DRIVER, A CAREER HANDLING AN LTL rig is different than driving a full truckload, since LTL drivers drive shorter distances and don't have to be away from home as often.[1] Add to that the fact that Old Dominion pays well, and the company enjoys very low turnover among its drivers.[2]

One case is the career of Cornell Brenson, who has been driving for Old Dominion since 1949. As of 2010, 80-year-old Brenson was still driving 600 miles a day, five days a week, and had safely driven over 6 million miles behind the wheel with Old Dominion during his 61-year career.[3]

Brenson started as a driver with Bottoms-Fiske when he was 19 years old and worked on the dock briefly before settling behind the wheel of a Corbitt truck. At the time, Old Dominion did not have sleeper trucks, so when Brenson got tired, he would pull over to the side of the road, roll down the window, and stretch out across the front seat to rest.[4]

Brenson became known throughout the company for his positive attitude and his willingness to help others. "Like I tell people, you always smile," he said. "If people pull out in front of you, you smile. If people cut you off, you smile. Cussing and raising sand, it doesn't help you."[5]

If he sees a driver in distress, Brenson has been known to stop and check on them. "I couldn't live with myself if I passed by someone, believing they'd be okay, only to see a story in the next day's paper about something happening to them," Brenson told a *High Point Enterprise* reporter in 1999.[6]

By 2010, Brenson was driving a Freightliner from Charlotte, North Carolina, to Perry, Georgia, and back every day, logging about 10 hours on the road daily.[7] He credits his longevity with Old Dominion to the company's well-known family atmosphere.

"Old Dominion, they're good people," he explained. "I remember years, going way back, when the union came in here—they had different bathrooms for people to use," Brenson recalled. "A bathroom for whites and a bathroom for blacks. At Old Dominion, everybody would use the same bathroom."[8]

In addition, Old Dominion would invite all of the drivers to a holiday party and a family picnic in High Point every year, "and all the families, regardless of what color you were, everybody sat down and ate together," Brenson said.[9]

According to Brenson, "I could have made more money working for other trucking companies who were unionized, but Old Dominion has always taken care of me and my family and allowed me to run the routes I liked."[10]

Old Dominion's Cornell Brenson was honored as the North Carolina State Truck Driver of the Year in 2000. By then, he had been driving for Old Dominion for 51 years. *(Republished by permission of Transport Topics Publishing Group.)*

Volume 5, No. 2 Published by Old Dominion Freight Line, Inc. Summer 1999

PEOPLE FIRST at Old Dominion

"When people are placed first, they will provide the highest possible service, and profits will follow."

"The foremost detail to be addressed by ANY service organization is not the product or process, it's the people. Absolutely. Positively.

Fred Smith, Chairman & CEO
Federal Express

I just finished reading a fantastic book entitled "Blueprints for Service Quality" The Federal Express Approach. This book is a synopsis of their success. Believe it or not, there are no magic formulas or fancy tricks. Everything boils down to four basic things that set them apart. *First* is a consistent, clearly stated service quality goal of 100% customer satisfaction. *Second* are mathematical measurements of service failures that act as a stimulus for continuous improvement. *Third*, employees feel empowered through open communications, training opportunities, quality improvement tools and excellent leadership. Finally, and most fundamentally, a "**People First**" philosophy and environment that acknowledges *employee satisfaction as the primary corporate objective* from which customer satisfaction and profits develop.

Fred Smith summarizes the corporate philosophy by saying, "When people are placed first, they will provide the highest service, and profits will follow". Today virtually every quality initiative, management guideline, compensation or recognition program within Federal Express touches one, two or all three of these **People-Service-Profit** goals.

Now for the big question, "So what?" "What's this got to do with us?" I believe it has very much to do with us. Look at the similarities of our business. We both move customer's goods from point A to point B within a specified amount of time. They happen to handle letters and small packages, we handle larger shipments. Both of our customers expect us to handle their merchandise without loss or damage. We both utilize a lot of equipment and require service centers or depots for the movement of goods. We both have, need and utilize computers for tracking shipments. Lastly and most importantly, both our organizations require ***people working as a team, 24 hours a day, 7 days a week*** to produce consistent ***Customer Satisfaction*** and ***Profitability***. Fred Smith says, "The foremost detail to be addressed by **ANY** service organization is not the product or process, it's the **People. Absolutely. Positively**."

I have seen, as many of you have, Old Dominion evolve for the last thirty years. Similar to Federal Express, we have the same "People" philosophy through our dedication to Old Dominion's "Family" environment and "Open Door Policy". However, I have sometimes noticed us getting caught up in focusing on "day to day" activities without regard for the "People" side of the equation. The ultimate goal is ***SATISFIED PEOPLE***. In the **Quality Advantage (TQA) Process**, we learn about the Customer-Supplier Chain. We understand how the work of one person is passed along to his or her Internal Customer. The end product is delivered to the External Customer.

David Congdon

In closing, I want to make a bold statement. ***I am personally committed to the philosophy that Internal Customer Satisfaction drives External Customer Satisfaction, which in turn drives Growth and Profitability. PEOPLE ARE FIRST at Old Dominion.***

David Congdon
President
Reporting from High Point

As president of Old Dominion, David Congdon took quality seriously, and one of his goals was investing in people who could capably take the company to the next level.

vice president of marketing, pricing, and strategic development:

> *At our annual strategic planning meetings, we try to look at where we are, where we're going, and we try to keep a five-year plan in focus, and it was time for us to revisit our five-year plan, and as we look at that, you know, we try to say, "Okay, what can we be, what should we look like, and what can we accomplish over the next five years?"*[38]

At the very first strategic planning meeting, David focused on three important questions that he wanted to ask management: Who are we today in the marketplace? How did we get here? Where are we going? Furthermore, he asked each department head where they saw their departments five or 10 years down the line so he could more accurately predict what Old Dominion would need to be successful going forward. "I was also asking a question about head count," David later recalled.

The company was having space issues in its corporate office, and David wanted to ascertain whether departments saw themselves adding staff in the near future so he could appropriately predict the space required for future growth.

David also had a vision that would take Old Dominion into virtually uncharted territory—a plan to make Old Dominion a top competitor in both the short-haul and long-haul trucking sectors:

We wanted to become known in the future as a viable and competitive player in regional markets. We wanted to expand nationally and create additional regional markets, but we wanted to maintain the strength of our interregional presence, our freight lanes, because that's what got us to the dance. ... We could not throw the baby out with the bathwater, and we're not at all planning to discontinue interregional and start focusing on regional. We wanted to do both. And that's what was so unique about the company, because it's always been said that you can be a short-haul carrier or you can be a long-haul carrier, but it's hard to do both.

It used to be said it's impossible to do both because the operating methods and the sense of urgency and the culture is different in a short-haul company versus a long-haul company. I would agree that's true, but we decided that we disagreed that you can't do both. ... Another tenet of our strategic plan was that we wanted to do this expansion in such a way as to not destroy our operating ratio, and we wanted to be careful in our expansion and not expand too rapidly where we'd start losing a lot of money in the new geography and cause our profits to suffer.[39]

Renewed Focus on Technology

One area where David refused to compromise was investment in technology. Prior to David's presidency, staffers faced senior management resistance to spending money on technology, primarily from Ebeling. "He was just a lot more cautious than I think even my dad might have been," David said. "He didn't fully understand or appreciate technology, but thank goodness Earl let John Yowell and I loosen the purse strings a little bit because we convinced him and the board that we needed to do this. We showed what we thought operational cost savings would be. That's when we really started investing in freight-handling technology."[40]

Yowell played a major role in guiding Old Dominion through that transformation. According to Rick Keeler, retired senior vice president of pricing and strategic development:

John Yowell came to the company a number of years before I did, and his principal activity was in data processing and IT, so he was responsible for all of the programmers, the hardware, and the programs of the company, as well as trying to direct the future that we had as technology changed. In 1995, he had been given a role as an area vice president, and he had responsibility for the Carolinas and maybe a little fringe territory beyond that.

That was his first real experience of working day to day with the terminal managers, with the people in the field on a one-to-one basis and understanding the business and supporting their processes. He was very much involved in what an area vice president should do. He had a little bit of a learning curve to start with, but he did an excellent job. John was very dedicated to the people, very dedicated to being a support person, very dedicated to working with the customer and to offering solutions.[41]

Although upgrading the company's technology represented an investment, Old Dominion was prepared for the benefits that the investment would eventually bring. "I think we all sort of looked at it as, 'If we really want this company to be what we say we want it to be from a vision standpoint, this is what it's going to take, and it may require an investment right now, but in five, 10 years, we're going to get that back several fold,'" said Chip Overbey, Old Dominion's senior vice president of marketing, pricing, and strategic development in 2010. "And we have."[42]

The first priority from a technology perspective was to invest in the company's dockyard management system and convert from a paper-based tracking system to a computer-based one. David and Yowell worked with the company's technology department to make that a reality, implementing a state-of-the-art, real-time tracking system that kept freight in check. Known as "DYMS" (Dock Yard

Management System), the system involved using bar codes to track company freight and equipment.[43] As freight entered, the dock employees swiped the bar code, "and the system automatically identified the shipment, and instructed the dockworkers where to load it, and automatically updated our track and trace system," Terry Hutchins explained.[44]

In 1996, Ken Erdner started as manager of Old Dominion's computer department. A year later, he was promoted to director and subsequently to vice president of information systems and technology. Under Ken's leadership, the IT department has developed many of the electronic systems which have distinguished Old Dominion from its competitors in-house. As a consequence, the company has been recognized as a leader in this field and has won awards such as the CIO 100 Award.

Next, Old Dominion focused its attention on creating an inbound planning system. According to David, when freight is due to come into an Old Dominion service center, "We have to determine how to plan the routes, and instead of getting a bunch of paper and freight bills and throwing them out on a big table and putting them into piles and then lining up the paper freight bills, we created a computerized methodology for routing our freight."[45]

Another element of David's strategic plan was establishing a revenue quality improvement process. "With Rick Keeler's leadership, and the top-level team that we put on it, we started addressing the cost model and what we needed to do to improve the accuracy of it," David said. "We started focusing on the accounts where we were losing money and the types of freight where we were making money through a continuous process that still exists today."[46]

Another problem that had been a struggle for Old Dominion was that each of the company's terminals had its own routines and processes, so if an employee went from one terminal to another, he might have to learn new methods of recording freight. One of David's first quests, which began back when he first became vice president of quality, was to establish the field services team, which he directed from 1994 to 1997. Terry Hutchins, as vice president of field services, assumed responsibility and continues to do so today. The team standardized the day-to-day processes so each service center

Under David Congdon's leadership, Old Dominion began to invest more money in technology, including the "DYMS" system, which tracked freight as it came in and moved through and out of a facility.

had an Old Dominion way of doing things.[47] The standardized processes helped make all of the divisions more efficient as the company moved forward.

Expanding Old Dominion's Reach

In 1997, a *Distribution* magazine reader survey ranked Old Dominion as the second-best multiregional and interregional LTL carrier.[48] David sought to become a national carrier "with multiple regional operations, all connected interregionally, with best-in-class transit times across any particular length of haul."

Acquisitions would prove an essential part of that strategy.[49] "My dad had used acquisitions in years past to open up a geography because if you can buy a company that already has a base of business and you can integrate it into your company fairly rapidly, it's a cheaper way to expand than to start from scratch," David said.[50]

In a quest to achieve that goal, in 1997, Old Dominion acquired most of the assets of America Central Express, expanding business in the Midwest. In addition, Old Dominion opened new terminals in Kentucky, Indiana, and Texas, bringing the company's staff up to 6,000 employees.[51]

Integrating Acquisitions

Old Dominion is fairly cautious when it considers a company for acquisition, and the organization looks at every aspect of the business before making a purchase.[1] Old Dominion management conducts investigations, "considering the potential acquisition's strength, its history, whether it has vulnerabilities, and other factors," said Bill Cranfill, Old Dominion's vice president and assistant general counsel.[2]

According to Leo Suggs, a trucking industry veteran who has served as an Old Dominion board member since 2009:

> *In the late 1990s, Old Dominion started an acquisition program, and acquisitions, in this business, have never been easy. In fact, there have been many more failures than there have been successes, but they figured out how to buy small companies they could tuck in, and so they were growing rapidly. Their profitability was unequaled. They had a great reputation from the standpoint of their service. Things like their claims ratio was the best in the industry. ... They were a very forward-thinking company, but they were also a company that was conservative. ... They didn't try a lot of crazy things and didn't make many mistakes.*[3]

Once it was determined that a company would be a good acquisition, Old Dominion worked hard to integrate the new business into Old Dominion's structure so that both companies could benefit from the deal. David Congdon noted that Old Dominion's LTL acquisitions have been very important in filling out the company's footprint "as we were pursuing our strategy to become multiregional, interregional, and a national player."[4]

When it came to ensuring that acquisitions fit well into Old Dominion's existing structure, David would confirm that Old Dominion's various departments were prepared for the integration. "Everybody on our team knows what their role is in one of these deals," David explained.[5]

Revenue in 1997 set new records for Old Dominion, topping $328 million, with a net income of more than $10 million, both significant improvements compared to the previous year.[52]

Building a Brand

Until 1998, the notion of building a brand at Old Dominion did not exist. Like most traditional transportation companies, Old Dominion was focused on operational concerns that delivered quality service to its customers, but the idea of brand-building and communicating the heart of the brand was not in play. As a result of a strategic planning session in the fall of 1998, the company made the decision that if Old Dominion was to truly be the carrier espoused in its vision to be the premier transportation company, then it would have to become more market focused and brand-centric.

The senior management team decided that in order to build the premier brand in the transportation industry, the company would have to focus on four key elements:

- *Build the very best service product in the industry, providing competitive best-in-class transit times, claims-free handling, and superior customer service.*
- *Focus on technology to enhance the customer experience and drive down cost to produce a sustainable financial model.*
- *Communicate the brand proposition in as many strategically targeted channels as possible.*
- *Build confidence and loyalty to the brand internally. If the Old Dominion family believes in the brand, then the customer will ultimately be convinced.*

Page 6 — January 18, 1999 TRANSPORT TOPICS

FINANCE

Old Dominion Acquires Skyline's LTL Assets

By Daniel P. Bearth
Staff Writer

Old Dominion Freight Line, High Point, N.C., boosted its freight hauling operations in the Southeast with the purchase of assets from Skyline Transportation's less-than-truckload operations on Jan. 18.

Skyline, based in Knoxville, Tenn., will continue to offer truckload and other transportation services, said J. Wes Frye, senior vice president of finance for Old Dominion.

Skyline President W.H. Reed Jr. declined to elaborate.

Old Dominion will merge Skyline's LTL terminal operations into its network. It also will purchase additional tractors and trailers, whose numbers depend on the amount of business Old Dominion retains, he said.

Mr. Frye said he hopes that Old Dominion can keep 50% to 70% of Skyline's LTL freight business, which constituted a large part of the company's total revenue. He said Skyline generated revenue of about $25 million in 1997.

The deal is the third in the past 12 months for Old Dominion, which acquired the assets of Fredrickson Motor Express of Charlotte, N.C., in January 1998 and purchased Goggin Truck Line of Shelbyville, Tenn., in August (TT, 8-10-98, p. 61).

Earl E. Congdon, chairman of Old Dominion, said the latest transaction is consistent with the company's strategy of increasing its market share in its business areas.

"The combination of the two operations will provide for increased density within the current Old Dominion structure and provide customers with more direct service points to both metropolitan and rural areas throughout the southeastern U.S.," Mr. Congdon said in a statement.

"The move will also provide increased next-day service from selected points in the Midwest into strategic areas of Tennessee, North Carolina, South Carolina and Georgia," he said.

For instance, Old Dominion's acquisitions of Fredrickson Motor Express and Goggin Truck Line in 1998 and Skyline Transportation in 1999 provided positive examples of how to integrate a company. "We go out there and execute the deal, make the announcement," David said about the procedure following the Skyline acquisition. "Friday is the last day of operations. We combine all the terminals over the weekend. During that week before Friday, we've put all the computers in place to convert them totally to Old Dominion systems on Monday morning, and it's pretty damn smooth. You know, nothing is perfectly smooth, and you have a couple of weeks of additional acclimation and training and maybe up to a couple of months, especially with the new service centers and brand new people, but the team knew what to do, and we basically executed that one flawlessly."[6]

Three major acquisitions that Old Dominion completed in the late 1990s helped the company expand its geographic reach quickly and efficiently.

These four initiatives became cornerstones of the Old Dominion brand and they remain the foundation of the brand today. As Chip Overbey explained, "We believe in the brand, we believe in building the brand, and we believe we can accomplish something. I think knowing you can do it in your heart is important. You can't convince anybody else unless you're the most convinced."

Growth Through Acquisitions

In 1998, Old Dominion bought selected assets of Charlotte, North Carolina–based LTL company Fredrickson Motor Express and subsequently bought Goggin Truck Line, an LTL carrier based in Tennessee.[53] Rumors abounded about Fredrickson, including news of bounced paychecks to employees. The company seemed on the verge of bankruptcy, and a Chicago-based broker called Old Dominion to ask whether it might be interested in buying the small trucking firm, which had a reputation in the Southeast for next-day service.[54]

Earl and David, along with Joel McCarty and Wes Frye, traveled to Charlotte to hear more, and David was surprised to learn how quickly Old Dominion was expected to move on the purchase:

> *One of my dad's first questions—he always gets right to the point—was, "Well, how much time do you need for us to make a decision on something like this?"*
>
> *And they said, "A matter of hours."*
>
> *They were going to shut it down the very next day. We confirmed the day before going to Charlotte for the meeting that the company was Fredrickson Motor Express. We were familiar with their service product and recognized it was actually better than ours, with more next-day lanes than we provided within their territory.*

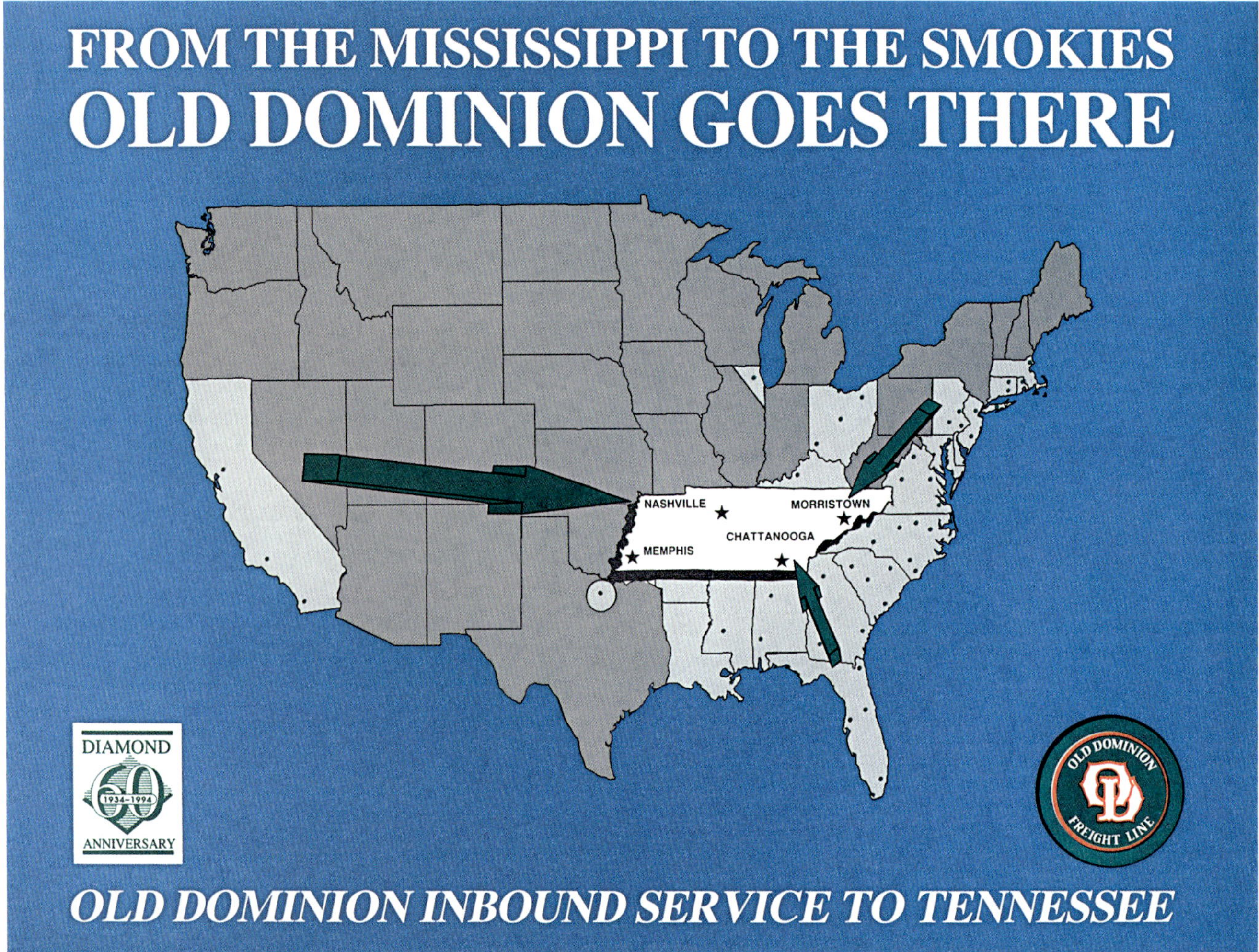

Old Dominion strove to become a strong player in regional markets and advertised within each region to show the company's strength.

We met with our top management immediately to see if we could commit to adopt their service if we bought them.

The team said, "Yes, we will commit to their transit times if we buy this company."

It was this commitment to strategy that flowed into every subsequent acquisition.

We went in there armed with a commitment from management that, if we were to buy it, we would adopt their transit times and keep trying to run their freight like they ran it, and that would be part of the fulfillment of the strategy that we had agreed to. And so, at 4 o'clock that afternoon, we called back to headquarters and said, "Okay, we're going to take this thing over next Friday."

After that Thursday meeting, Joel McCarty and I went to Charlotte to reach agreement, prepare the documents, and close this acquisition in a record three days.[55]

Goggin Truck Line was another Southeast regional player that was able to provide Old Dominion with several more service centers that helped the company expand geographically.[56] The acquisition allowed Old Dominion to improve direct service coverage, reducing agency and interline relationships, and to improve transit times on about 750 traffic lanes. "Out of a dozen or so acquisitions in our history, this is by far the largest," David said about the Goggin purchase, noting that Goggin had $58 million in revenues in 1997, and that Old

Dominion would acquire 380 tractors and 1,238 trailers in the deal.[57]

Not long thereafter, Old Dominion heard about a small Tennessee carrier called Skyline Transportation that was available, and in early 1999, Old Dominion acquired selected assets of Skyline's LTL operations, rounding out the trio of acquisitions that the company began investigating in 1998, and allowing Old Dominion to become a stronger regional player in the Southeast.[58]

In all, between 1995 and 2008, Old Dominion successfully completed 11 acquisitions.

Closing Out the Century

Old Dominion's dedicated focus on customer service allowed the company to succeed even when the industry as a whole faltered. The 1990s saw the introduction of many policies that would guide the company going forward. According to Rick Keeler, retired senior vice president of pricing and strategic development:

> *The customer has to perceive a value in your company. That value can be seen directly in terms of transit service. It can be in terms of the ability to respond quickly to their needs, to respond to them adequately and quickly on claims, and to be their partner in their business. One of the things that we began in 1997 was continuous improvement of all those areas, so that as we experienced tough times, we could try to avoid playing the pricing game. ... Most of the time, because of that value, because of the relationship that our salespeople have with the customers, we positioned ourselves as premier, both in terms of service and quality, and it was worth something to most of those customers.*
>
> *Our salespeople had to sell it back to the customer, and our sales management team did a great job working with the sales reps, and I think it was pretty successful.... It was successful for the employees, and most importantly, the customers had a sustainable price and quality that they could live with.*[59]

Old Dominion began 1999 with the goal of improving transit and customer service so the company could grow revenues between 10 percent and 12 percent, with improved revenue and a lower operating ratio. The company began achieving that goal by continuing to focus on improving service and quality, and the results paid off.

The company met its goals—and also enjoyed some added bonuses on the customer service side. "Our transit service has improved by 2.4 percent from last year while tightening the service standards on over 1,000 lanes," David reported near the end of 1999. "The consistency of our transit time performance has improved 25 percent. Complaints received from external as well as internal customers regarding how their problems have been handled have nearly disappeared."[60]

As a result, Old Dominion's sales growth throughout the first nine months of 1999 reached 11.1 percent, with an operating ratio that improved from 93.8 percent in 1998 to 93.3 percent in September 1999. "Last year's performance, plus our performance this year, has allowed us to continue better-than-average pay increases," David told Old Dominion family members.[61]

As the 20th century came to a close, the company's revenue topped $426 million, but Wall Street firms did not follow the company, which many analysts found unusual.[62]

"The stock is thinly traded," the *Charlotte Observer* reported. "Still, its poor [share] performance puzzles the few investment experts who follow it. By all standard measures, the share price is low: near book value, three times cash flow, and with a price/earnings ratio below eight."[63]

However, at the time Old Dominion was not concerned about stock prices. "We just run our truckline, do the best job we can, and believe that this will result in increased value to our shareholders," Earl explained.[64]

In 2003, David and Earl Congdon posed with the restored 1946 Ford straight truck presented to Earl in celebration of Old Dominion's 50th anniversary.

CHAPTER NINE

DRIVING INTO THE MILLENNIUM

2000–2005

If a customer needs something fixed, we'll fix it. ... We're a support for the field, and if we have to get down in the trenches to help fix things, we do it. We're willing to do it in the daytime, in the nighttime, early in the morning, and I think that's what makes us different than other carriers.

—Marty Freeman,
Old Dominion senior vice president of sales[1]

OLD DOMINION RODE INTO THE millennium by marking an important milestone—Earl Congdon's 50th year with the company. After starting with Old Dominion as a 19-year-old in 1950, Earl had been a major reason for the company's successes over his 50-year career with Old Dominion, and he continued to serve as the company's chairman and CEO, with his son David serving as Old Dominion's president and chief operating officer.[2]

As Old Dominion looked back at its past, the company also continued to make new innovations and started the millennium in a fitting way—by building its largest facility to date, a 247-door break-bulk service center in Morristown, Tennessee, that spanned 40 paved acres.[3]

The three acquisitions that Old Dominion completed near the end of 1999 created a challenge at the company's existing Morristown terminal, which necessitated the opening of a new facility. As David Congdon recalled:

> *We were operating out of a 46-door terminal, and when we did the Goggin acquisition, that really pushed us over the edge in terms of not being able to handle the freight. So we kept Goggin's Knoxville terminal, which was just 40 miles down the road; Knoxville became our break-bulk for freight going toward the west, and Morristown became our break-bulk for freight going toward the east, and we were shuttling trailers in between the two. ... When we opened the new Morristown, Tennessee, service center, that revolutionized our ability to move freight more smoothly between the whole Northeast, all of Virginia, North Carolina, South Carolina, and all of our Western states from the Northeast to the Gulf Coast region, from the Southeast—Florida, Georgia, Alabama, South Carolina—going to our Midwest markets. We started becoming more profitable, and we were able to improve our service product dramatically.*[4]

By the time Old Dominion opened its new Morristown site, the company could claim 103 locations, 6,600 employees, and more than 11,000 pieces of equipment, and with David securely at the wheel, the company was well equipped to take on the next decade and continue to grow.[5] In 2000, Old Dominion began selling "full-service coverage" in 22 states. Although the option was expensive

Old Dominion's Morristown, Tennessee, service center offered the company 40 paved acres to accommodate many of the company's trucks and a 247-door facility for loading and unloading.

Old Dominion's state-of-the-art 162,000-square-foot corporate office in Thomasville, North Carolina, is considered the company's nerve center and central location to this day.

and initially cut into the company's profitability, Old Dominion felt it necessary, since many customers gave their business only to carriers with complete state coverage. "If a carrier doesn't have full-state coverage, it doesn't get the business," Earl explained.[6]

Another innovation that Old Dominion adopted as the company entered the millennium was Speed Service, which offered to trim delivery time off of the company's normal service times for a slightly higher charge.[7] Old Dominion still offers Speed Service, "which features guaranteed delivery and offers exclusive use of an Old Dominion truck," noted Marty Freeman, Old Dominion senior vice president of sales, who oversees the program.[8] The Speed Service department was separated into two distinct offerings. "Speed Service Guaranteed offers deliveries within our normal transit times guaranteed, or our freight charges are free," David announced in 1999.

Speed Service on Demand, a separate venture, offered "time-specific deliveries at the customer's request, or our freight charges are free," David noted.[9]

Old Dominion ended 2000 with record revenues of more than $475 million.[10] However, income slowed toward the end of the year due to harsh winter weather across the entire route system.[11] As the company looked ahead, it also considered a new home base for its growing staff.

A New Home

By 2001, Old Dominion was running out of space at its 60,000-square-foot location in High Point.[12] "We have been in our general headquarters building in High Point for nearly 21 years and have outgrown it," Earl told staffers in 2000.[13] The company chose to move the headquarters to a 162,000-square-foot facility, a former Bassett showroom in Thomasville, North Carolina, just a few miles from the previous location.[14] The new office was equipped with a real-time shipment tracking center, "considered by many analysts to be the best in the industry," noted an article in the *Winston-Salem Journal*.[15]

Some analysts attributed the company's move in part to its focus on technology. "A major reason Old Dominion needs more room is to accommodate its growing information technology division," stated a *Triad Business News* article.[16]

David, in his quest to take the company into the 21st century, may have been a leader in showing concern for the environment. "I've been on a paper-eliminating rampage for years," David said in 2001. "Continuing to build modern information channels with our customers is important."[17]

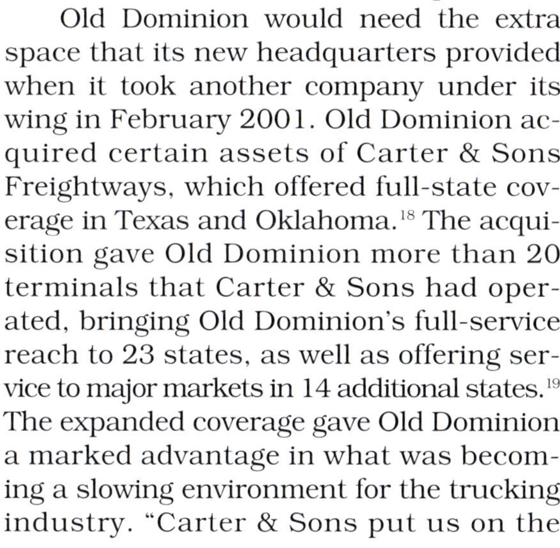

Old Dominion would need the extra space that its new headquarters provided when it took another company under its wing in February 2001. Old Dominion acquired certain assets of Carter & Sons Freightways, which offered full-state coverage in Texas and Oklahoma.[18] The acquisition gave Old Dominion more than 20 terminals that Carter & Sons had operated, bringing Old Dominion's full-service reach to 23 states, as well as offering service to major markets in 14 additional states.[19] The expanded coverage gave Old Dominion a marked advantage in what was becoming a slowing environment for the trucking industry. "Carter & Sons put us on the map with regional business that we didn't have in the Gulf Coast region surrounding Dallas," David said.[20]

When Old Dominion bought Carter & Sons, the country was just entering a recessionary period fueled by unemployment across the country, and other carriers were struggling to find their footing.[21] Old Dominion's acquisition would help catapult the company to the top of the industry despite the struggling economy. David noted:

> *All the carriers were crying the blues. And we were able to then sell between our whole network, but primarily the Southeast and the Northeast, to and from full-state coverage in Texas and Oklahoma. That was a big splash for us, and it was our second major regional move to overlay regional on top of interregional service. And we adopted their lanes, their transit times, their operating methodology, so we announced it on a Tuesday, took them over on Friday, took their freight in our network, and converted them into Old Dominion systems Monday morning. That's been our methodology. We do acquisitions like no other LTL carrier has done before, and I think we've been the most successful.*[22]

When Old Dominion expanded its Greensboro, North Carolina, terminal into a major interregional hub in 2002, the company further increased its freight-handling capacity.

With even more of its company's trucks covering the roads thanks to the Carter acquisition, Old Dominion needed even more space where trailers could be loaded and unloaded, and where maintenance could be conducted. Old Dominion focused on expanding its Greensboro, North Carolina, terminal into a major interregional hub with 234 doors by 2002.[23]

"That was another very important real estate expansion that improved our service in the East and the South lanes," David later said.[24]

A Competitor Succumbs

As Old Dominion expanded its network throughout 2001 and 2002, its competitors did not fare quite as well. On Labor Day 2002, Consolidated Freightways announced it was closing its doors.[25] Not only would this mark a significant event in Old Dominion's competitive strategy, but it would change the way that other trucking companies priced their services. According to David:

> *That was a pretty monumental event for our industry. Prior to their demise, and maybe for as much as a couple of years prior to their demise, they were desperate, but they were losing market share because their service levels were deteriorating, and they were throwing out tremendous discounts in order to get freight, and they were causing, I think, the rest of the industry to have to reduce rates to maintain market share.*
>
> *As I recall, pricing was not good from the fourth quarter of 2001 through the first half of 2002*

How September 11, 2001, Changed the Trucking Industry

No one can forget the tragedy that occurred on September 11, 2001, with the horrific loss of nearly 3,000 lives leading to a gripping fear of terrorism that spread across the country and spanned borders into other nations. Understandably, the government responded by tightening security everywhere. No longer was it a simple matter to cross into Canada or board an airplane. The changes were evident to everyone in the transportation industry.

Not only did Old Dominion face issues at the country's borders following the September 11th tragedy, but the company also had a difficult time even getting donated goods into New York.[1] Old Dominion had offered to haul them for free to help survivors

because of the anchor that they had on price levels and their prominence in the marketplace. They were cutting prices. That was causing Roadway to cut prices, Yellow to cut prices, ABF to cut prices. All the national carriers or anyone that had national lanes were really cutting rates. [Losing Consolidated Freightways] was a game changer for the industry. We calculated that we inherited about $60 million of long-haul business. Partially because of the new long-haul business, but more so because the anchor came off of pricing, the pricing industry-wide rose dramatically in the quarter following their demise. For the entire next year, pricing levels were up, quarter over quarter, in the 6 percent to 9 percent range. With that opportunity and the bankruptcy sale, we purchased a number of their facilities. ... I think we became the largest purchaser of Consolidated Freightways facilities.[26]

Greg Gantt, chief operating officer, served as vice president of the central region in the 1990s. He recalled the benefits Old Dominion gained from acquiring Consolidated Freightways facilities:

We didn't have enough terminal capacity before; we didn't have big enough facilities. ... We bought a couple of big facilities from Consolidated Freightways after they went out of business: Indianapolis, Indiana; Harrisburg, Pennsylvania; and Columbus, Ohio. That new infrastructure really helped set the stage and gave us something to work with, where we could efficiently move our freight through the system. All the geographic expansion that

Opposite and above: David Congdon spoke at a Red Cross event following the September 11 tragedy. Old Dominion raised $50,000 to assist the victims, families, and firefighters affected by the attacks.

and volunteers.[2] As part of its Our Donation For Love program, the company raised $50,000 for the American Red Cross following the tragedy.[3]

Old Dominion faced a slowdown in freight hauling immediately following the tragedy and saw additional effects grow as time passed.[4] The company upgraded security procedures following September 11, which included issuing photo ID badges to all employees, questioning anyone without a badge, and careful monitoring to ensure that all gates and trailers remained locked.[5]

The Old Dominion family atmosphere permeates everything that the company does and is present in its offices and terminals. Pictured left to right: Bobby Beeson, Chuck Pearson, L. B. Clayton, Diane Robbins, Kim Freeman, Helen Knight, Willie Paige, and Vinnie Gross.

we did over the years, giving us the additional coverage, covering the markets that we served with our own Old Dominion green-and-white trucks and Old Dominion people, that really helped our structure and gave us the ability to take those next steps to improve our service.[27]

As Old Dominion continued to gain market share by adding Consolidated Freightways' former customers, the company also faced ever-changing government mandates that would soon require it to spend an additional $2,000 to $5,000 on each new truck it purchased, for cleaner, more environmentally friendly engines. Environmental Protection Agency changes meant that trucks had to improve their emissions, and Old Dominion and other trucking companies would absorb the cost of those improvements through higher equipment costs.

As Joel McCarty, Old Dominion's senior vice president and general counsel, explained:

When Consolidated Freightways went out of business, we bought a lot of those properties at auction ... at very good prices. These properties proved to be advantageous because they helped to enhance our infrastructure and gain the capacity to grow in areas where we needed the growth.

HUSBAND AND WIFE DRIVER TEAMS

BACK IN THE 1930S, WHEN OLD DOMINION PUT its first truck on the road, drivers who passed by Lillian Congdon behind the wheel of an Old Dominion truck most certainly did a double take. Female drivers were nearly unheard of then, and husband and wife driver teams were even less common. However, by the early 21st century, it was not uncommon to see a couple hop out of a truck's cab in unison and make their way into a truck stop to enjoy a meal together. That's because husband and wife truck driving teams have become more pervasive as time passed, and Old Dominion happily embraced the trend.

Old Dominion encourages spouses or other family members to create truck driving teams and trains them at the company's driving school.[1] The unique arrangement allows husbands and wives to work together, alternating shifts behind the wheel.

According to a 2008 market behavior report, 12 percent of truck owner-operators drove as a team, and just over half of those were married to their driving partners.[2] Of Old Dominion's 234 driving teams in 2000, 30 percent to 40 percent were husband and wife teams who could earn more than $100,000 a year.[3]

The arrangements have many benefits. Truck drivers were able to be with their spouses more often, and they could see the country together. Old Dominion gained an edge because teams spent less time stopping to eat or sleep, since one took the wheel while the other rested. The trucks are equipped with sleeping berths, and many also had small refrigerators and stoves.[4]

Wanda Barnett, who worked for Old Dominion as part of a driving team with her husband James, told a reporter in 2000 that she enjoyed seeing the country with her husband, and that trucking was an industry that remained wide open for women.[5] "It's not like the old image of trucking," Barnett told the *Knoxville News-Sentinel*. "The truck stops are really nice."

By 1994, of the 140 driver teams at Old Dominion, 40 of them were married couples like Susan and Randy Eanes, pictured here.

Thanks to Old Dominion's strong, efficient footing, the company was not as negatively impacted by the additional expense as a smaller carrier would have been, making the company's growth and strategic acquisitions more of an asset than ever before.

Success Leads to Fleet Improvements

In 2002, Old Dominion experienced market share gains, with net income rising 55 percent to $18 million, compared to 2001 levels.[28] By then, Old Dominion employed more than 7,000 people and operated 117 service centers.[29] The company knew that its strong standing reflected its strength, and responded by making available an additional 3 million shares of stock, which, if sold, would potentially generate $68.67 million in revenue to reduce its debt, buy equipment, and expand its reach further.[30] If all of the stock sold, the company's executive management team would go from owning 67 percent of the stock to 44 percent.[31]

Following the completed stock sale, David Congdon announced that the company had approximately 600 outside shareholders, and that the stock sale assisted in financing capital expenditures for 2003. In addition, the sale helped Old Dominion strengthen its profile among investment analysts. "We now have five investment analysts writing about us," David announced following the stock sale.[32]

The strategy paid off. In the 12 months ending May 30, 2003, Old Dominion's stock soared 177.8 percent, and the next month, the stock split 3-for-2.[33] Old Dominion celebrated the success with its largest order ever, purchasing $48 million worth of tractors and trailers to update its fleet.[34]

Industry analysts were surprised at Old Dominion's achievements in light of the conditions in 2003, including the lingering effects of a recession, lower freight volumes, and high insurance and fuel costs. Charles Diehl, president of the North Carolina Trucking Association, was taken aback at Old Dominion's success considering the financial environment at the time, noting, "To succeed the way things have been the last couple of years is impressive. To excel is amazing."[35]

According to Chip Overbey, senior vice president of marketing, pricing, and strategic development:

> *Our national account customers, you know, the FORTUNE® 500 and up of the world, they would ask, "Hey, what makes y'all different?"*
>
> *And I'm going to tell you, one of the things I always told them was this: "I believe what makes us different is the management group we've got here. We all work very well together, and we've been together a long time, so we trust each other. ... We believe in the brand, we believe in building the brand, and we believe we can accomplish anything we set our minds to."*[36]

By 2003, Old Dominion was one of only eight LTL truck lines remaining in business from the list of the 60 largest LTL lines published in 1980—the rest had been bankrupt or sold, and all but one were unionized. Old Dominion attributed its longevity to several factors, one of which has been the company's decision to remain union-free. "It's the cornerstone of our existence and company policy and leadership for my dad, myself, and my family," David told *Business North Carolina* magazine. "I believe if we had been a union company, we would not be here today."[37]

As David explained, "Why are we performing better than almost all of our competitors? There is no single answer to this question. It is the result of a combination of many ingredients, the first and foremost being the Old Dominion family and team spirit that forms the foundation for all we do."[38]

That family atmosphere was evident when the *Business North Carolina* reporter walked past Earl's office during David's 2003 interview and saw a stack of birthday cards waiting on his desk. David revealed that Earl took the time to send each employee a birthday card, despite the fact that the company had thousands of staffers by that point.[39]

Between the time David took over as president in 1997 and 2003, Old Dominion had doubled the size of the company. Old Dominion had also focused on diversification, with the percentage of customers in the South decreasing from 47.7 percent in 1997

Opposite: Old Dominion trucks faced stricter emissions standards in 2004, making it paramount that all trucks were thoroughly brought up to date in one of the company's service centers. Pictured here is a 2004 Freightliner FLD-120.

FREIGHTLINER
LE·3575

to 37.5 percent in 2003. That meant regional recessions posed less of a risk for the company as a whole.[40] "The South has been so anemic that if we hadn't taken the steps we have, we could have been in the shape of some of our competitors," David noted in 2003, proving that Old Dominion's expansion into the North and West had been a smart strategy.[41]

Road to Economic Recovery

Old Dominion came out of the 2001 recessionary period not only intact, but with a profit. The company had shown itself capable of thriving even during economic downturns. As the economy began to improve, Old Dominion had a chance to flourish. By 2004, Old Dominion's business had picked up so well that the company was eager to get more trucks on the road.[42] "Our business is booming pretty much in all our regions," David told the *Winston-Salem Journal* in June 2004. "I'm not sure we could handle it being much better considering we're stretched for drivers right now."[43]

The company's success meant new challenges for drivers, since by 2004, 83 percent of Old Dominion's shipments occurred in three days or less, with many customers demanding quick deliveries.[44] In 2004, the number of hours that drivers could work changed, marking the first major adjustment in that area since the 1930s.[45] Based on the new rule, the Federal Motor Carrier Safety Administration announced that effective January 4, 2004, all truck drivers must take off at least 10 consecutive hours before driving in interstate commerce unless they are able to rest in a sleeper berth, and that no driver could be on the road after being on duty for 14 consecutive hours. During any 14-hour consecutive on-duty period, drivers might drive up to 11 hours without a rest.[46]

The hours-of-service regulation was not the only government decree Old Dominion had to adopt in 2004. That year, the Environmental Protection Agency had adopted new emission standards for diesel engine trucks. "Anything manufactured since 2004 had to meet more stringent emissions, 2007 had to meet another criteria, 2010 had to meet another hurdle, and every one of those years, we're seeing degradation in the engine life and much-increased cost in the equipment, too," noted Ed Richardson, Old Dominion vice president of equipment and maintenance.[47]

Aside from the new government mandates, Old Dominion instituted changes of its own. The company launched its own new third party services group, Old Dominion Business Solutions, "which offers customers several logistics services other than just standard LTL freight delivery such as transportation management, fleet management, and TMS software applications," noted Marty Freeman, Old Dominion senior vice president of sales. "We can actually provide outsourced warehouse and driver labor to them. We can lease them trucks and paint their names on the side of the trailers where it looks transparent to their customers while Old Dominion Business Solutions is managing the transportation of the fleet."[48]

All of the new innovations went hand in hand with Old Dominion's long-standing philosophy that the customer is key. Old Dominion was finding that one of its most important strengths was having such solid customer relationships that the company could anticipate a customer's needs and meet those needs before being asked.

Expanding Into New Markets

Old Dominion started off 2005 in an auspicious fashion as CEO Earl Congdon was inducted into the North Carolina Transportation Hall of Fame.[49] Prior inductees included flight innovators Orville and Wilbur Wright. With 56 years as an Old Dominion employee, Earl's contributions to the industry were widely recognized by Old Dominion employees and the trucking industry at large. Thanks to all of the company's improvements and additional territory gained through expansion, Old Dominion celebrated a billion-dollar year in 2005, with revenues of $1.06 billion and annual earnings of $53.5 million.[50]

Following in Earl's tradition of expanding through acquisition, Old Dominion made a strategic purchase in 2005 when it acquired Wichita Southeast Kansas Transit (WSKT), a trucking company which produced $68 million in revenues in 2004. Old Dominion planned to consolidate 33 of that company's 43 service centers and routes into existing Old Dominion operations.[51] David did not consider the agreement just another routine acquisition. He recognized the purchase would be paramount to the company's future:

> *That acquisition had a great strategic purpose. It opened new geography, gave us service centers where we could combine them and get synergies, and it overlaid approximately $45 million of regional business on top of approximately $50 million of regional business we already had. Doubled our regional presence. And it gave us new territory and new customers that they had on a regional basis that we could sell on a long-haul basis. It gave our current long-haul customers regional service that we didn't have before, so cross selling it all is just a business benefit. In fact, I think, looking back, the WSKT acquisition could be one of the most important in the history of the company.*[52]

In 2011, Old Dominion's marketing efforts highlighted the company's continued strong focus on customer service.

CHAPTER TEN

Old Dominion Freight Line Today

2006 and Beyond

The whole company has just grown tremendously. ... We've become No. 1, and it's been an accomplishment, quite an accomplishment.

—Joel McCarty,
senior vice president, general counsel, and secretary[1]

Old Dominion opened 2006 by acquiring the assets of UW Freight Line, a Utah-based LTL carrier, enabling Old Dominion to launch full-state coverage in four additional states, bringing full coverage to a total of 37 states.[2] At the time, Earl Congdon described the transaction as "representative of our continuing ability to expand our market share through accretive acquisitions in addition to our primary organic growth strategies."[3]

The UW acquisition differed from previous transactions because the business had been operating several small terminals that employed two drivers with no manager, which was unlike Old Dominion's normal operating procedure. The situation was initially a challenge because the smaller terminals didn't possess the technology required for tracking the freight in the manner that Old Dominion had established. "But after a while—it didn't take us too long—we figured out how to get these guys hooked up with the handheld computers, how to manage the dispatch for both men, and how to handle paperwork," David said.[4]

The UW acquisition allowed Old Dominion to open 16 new service centers in just the first quarter of 2006.[5] In July 2006, Old Dominion added three more service centers—a 16-door facility in Delaware, a 38-door distribution center in Texas, and a 16-door service center in Louisiana.[6]

Old Dominion enjoyed several distinctions in 2006, including being named among the "100 Best Companies in the United States" by investment research firm DeMarche Associates,[7] and one of the nation's "100 Fastest-Growing Small Companies" by *BusinessWeek*.[8] The next year, Old Dominion ranked 20th on *Transport Topics*' list of 100 largest for-hire carriers.[9]

"I tell you what, those types of awards and recognition sure do make you proud," David said. "As I look at that, I really have to give credit for all of our success to the power of the team, the kind of culture we have in our company, and how proud everyone is of our company and our service product. The whole team won that award."[10]

At the end of 2006, Old Dominion announced that it had a record year, with $1.3 billion in sales and $72.6 million in net income for the year. Earl attributed a significant part of that growth to booming business at service centers that had been opened for one year or longer.[11]

Drivers can review shipments, transit times, and delivery schedules directly from the road using Old Dominion's customized software, and customers can closely track their shipments online.

Improving Technology as Old Dominion Grows

Between 2000 and 2007, Old Dominion spent about $80 million on handheld computers for delivery personnel, dockyard management systems, radio frequency identification (RFID) tracking systems, and other technological upgrades.[12] Old Dominion also continued making acquisitions. In 2007, Old Dominion purchased certain assets of Priority Freight Lines, a Washington state–based company with a four-state market that had the advantage of allowing Old Dominion to offer full-state coverage in its 38th state.[13] The acquisition meshed well with the company's UW business to offer expanded regional service in the Northwest.

"Priority served Washington and gave us some additional coverage in Washington and Oregon, out to Spokane, Washington, and also Boise, Idaho," David said. "They connected the UW territory to the Pacific Northwest territory. It also brought us some regional business, and it gave us the ability to sell between California and Arizona on the south end of the I-5 corridor to the Northwest."[14]

In addition, the Priority acquisition gave Old Dominion a gateway to Vancouver for the company's western Canada operations. "Today, when you look at our growth by region, the Pacific Northwest is the fastest-growing region in our company," David noted. "The Priority acquisition helped in this growth."[15]

Later in 2007, Old Dominion bought Colorado-based Bullocks Express Transportation, Inc., offering additional coverage in the West.[16] "Bullocks was not performing very well, and the owners had reached the decision that it was time for them to get out of the business," David said. "Their lane was from Denver, Colorado, through New Mexico to Dallas, Texas. And so, we were able to just take their roughly $10 million of revenue and put it into our network. ... We didn't buy any tractors or trailers from them. We basically bought their book of business."[17]

The company did not slow down throughout the remainder of 2007, building a $20 million, 250-door terminal in Dallas, as well as laying out plans to add 60 to 70 service centers over a three-to-five-year period.[18] To aid in the massive expansion, Old Dominion created a logistics department to handle its warehouse management, allowing customers to ship through Old Dominion and manage and store products anywhere in the country.[19]

Going International as Management Shifts

In March 2007, Old Dominion took the big step of launching services into China, partnering with Chinese company Cargo Services Far East Ltd. to offer shipping services to American companies that do business with China.[20] Initially, Old Dominion did not target any specific industries in China. However, Greg Plemmons, vice president of Old Dominion Global, told a *Business Journal* reporter at the time that he expected China's "booming furniture and textile companies to be among the first beneficiaries."[21]

In 2008, Old Dominion looked to move into Europe as well.[22] Old Dominion had initially performed international freight runs for its existing LTL customers on a case by case basis, but the company later discovered that the global business could be significantly expanded in a way that David had not anticipated:

> *Through Greg Plemmons' leadership, we established relationships around the world that allowed us to move shipments between the United States and anywhere across the globe. Previously, we did this on a shotgun basis, as a value add to our existing LTL customers. We weren't building much business with this approach, and Greg came to us with a strategy. He said, "I think it's time to put a rifle on this thing. Pick a lane."*
>
> *So we picked China, and he started shopping, looking for potential partners. It took almost two years to establish a relationship with Cargo Services, a Chinese company, where we could offer a door-to-door sell with end-to-end visibility. If, for example, our customer in the US is sourcing from someplace in China, or almost anywhere in the world for that matter, we can arrange shipments, either full container, LTL, or air. We could manage the shipments through the overseas port, into the US port, and all the way to the customer's door in the United States.*
>
> *We later introduced Pacific Promise, a guaranteed, expedited solution that offers transit times that*

By 2011, Old Dominion covered all of North America, with complete coverage across the entire United States and direct service to Canada, Mexico, and China.

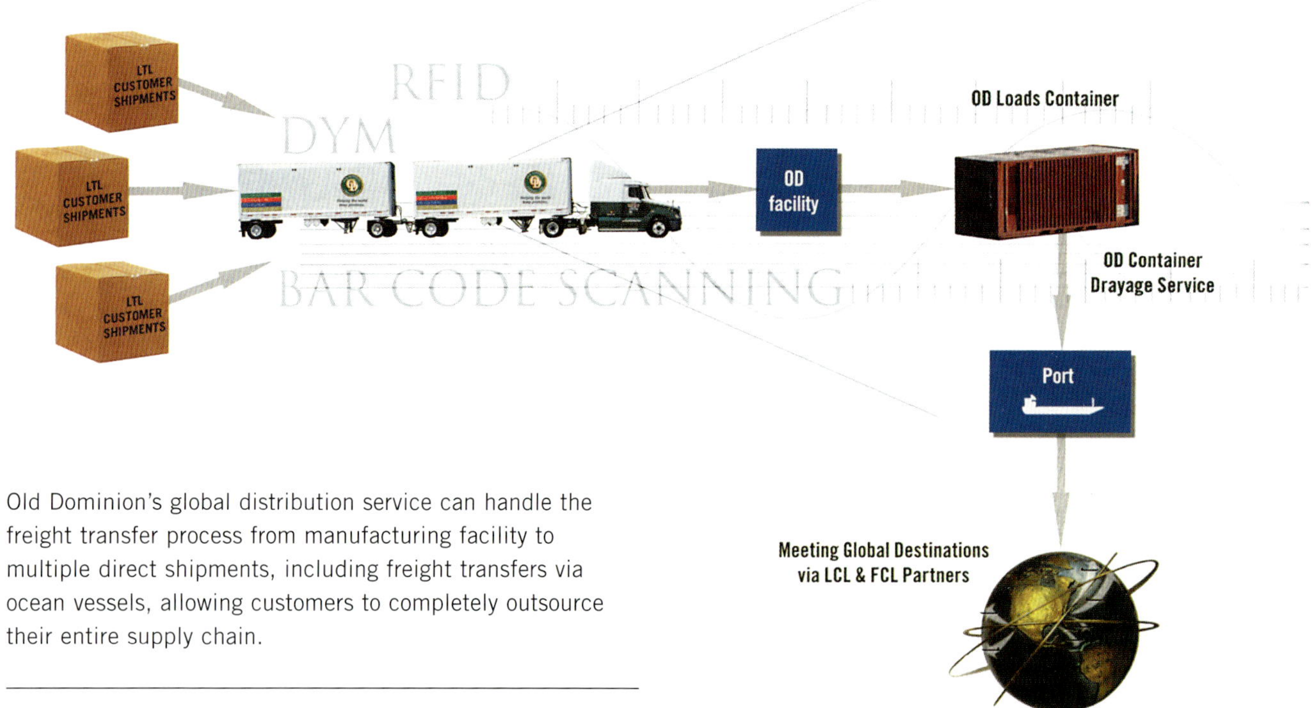

Old Dominion's global distribution service can handle the freight transfer process from manufacturing facility to multiple direct shipments, including freight transfers via ocean vessels, allowing customers to completely outsource their entire supply chain.

are much faster than traditional LCL service and at prices that are up to 75 percent less expensive than air freight. For example, through Pacific Promise we are able to offer transit times from Asia of 20 days to the US East Coast, where traditional shipping options would be over 30 days.

Marrying these import/export services with our network in North America allows us to offer a unique suite of services. Imagine a container load of sold merchandise being imported into the United States. In the past, the container would likely have moved into a US distribution center, where it would be placed in inventory, then shipped back out via LTL or truckload. Our import for distribution model gives the customer the ability to bypass their distribution center by having Old Dominion manage the full container through the US port, then into one of our service centers utilizing the Old Dominion drayage division. Once there, we would break out the shipments, label them if necessary, and deliver the shipments directly to our customer's final destination. The same concept can work in reverse with consolidation for export.[23]

By 2011, Old Dominion's global business represented approximately 6 percent of overall revenue, but approximately 15 percent of the company's net income. According to David, "Today, we move shipments between the United States and about 40 to 50 different countries in any given month."

Old Dominion's explosive growth was due to many factors, but Plemmons gave much of the credit to Old Dominion's strength in management, as well as to careful analysis:

It's a lot of things, honestly, but it starts with a commitment from the top, from Earl and from David and, prior to his passing, certainly John Yowell's commitment to what we're trying to accomplish. Today, that can-do team spirit continues to excel through the work of Greg Gantt, Marty Freeman, Chip Overbey, Joel McCarty, and Wes Frye, among many others. I think there's a recognition from the very top that while Old Dominion still has a lot of growing to do within the lower 48, at some point we'll reach a level of maturity where we'll need to rely on international markets, too, to sustain the kind of growth that our shareholders expect. Secondly, we plan carefully. It's not happenstance that we grow at 10 percent. That was our projection. We laid out a plan to reach those levels.[24]

As Old Dominion expanded with a global perspective, the company also experienced a shift in leadership. After serving in an executive capacity with Old Dominion for 58 years, Earl made some strategic decisions. Effective January 1, 2008, David became president and CEO of Old Dominion, while Earl was appointed executive chairman of the board of directors, and John Yowell, who sadly passed away in 2010, became executive vice president and chief operating officer.[25]

"I am extremely pleased with the board's actions, which will allow me the opportunity to transition from my daily responsibilities as CEO to concentrate on strategic planning, acquisitions, and other significant matters that affect the company," Earl said in 2008 when the transition was announced. "I am totally confident in both David and John's abilities to continue to lead our company in their new positions."[26]

Economic Woes

Old Dominion established full coverage for its 39th state in 2008 after purchasing selected assets of Montana-based Bob's Pickup & Delivery.[27] But by the end of that year, the company saw a noticeable shift happening not just at Old Dominion or in the trucking industry, but across the country as the economy began to suffer.

"In the fall of 2008, we saw tonnage falling off," David said. And the numbers backed up management's observation—the company's earnings declined in 2008 to $68.7 million, a drop of 4.4 percent compared with 2007.[28]

By 2009, the majority of the world was mired in a severe recession. The United States in particular faced a mortgage crisis and crushing unemployment rates. Old Dominion was not immune to the difficult financial climate. "It was the toughest year I've ever seen in 32 years of freight, as far as pricing goes," said Marty Freeman, Old Dominion's senior vice president of sales.[29]

Old Dominion's executives realized that they would have to make dramatic changes to keep up with the falling economy, but they also recognized when they had to hold their ground. Several of Old Dominion's major competitors lowered their prices below the actual cost of moving freight, but Old Dominion chose not to compete on price, deciding that the company would maintain prices, relying instead on its reputation for providing excellent service.[30]

Although Old Dominion initially lost some customers, many of them returned within a month, noting that they could not risk shoddy service, even if it meant paying more.[31] "One thing I can say about our strategy is that we questioned it day in and day out at our staff meetings," David said. "We kept asking, 'Are we doing the right thing?' And we kept coming back and saying, 'Yes, we are,' because we have been building service value. We've been building our service reputation. We've been investing so much in the service reputation that we did not want to see our service deteriorate, and we believed wholeheartedly that we could sell the value at a higher price."[32]

In making the decision not to lower prices, Old Dominion turned to Chief Financial Officer Wes Frye for guidance. When Frye provided the company with his forecast analysis, executives realized it would not make financial sense to make drastic price reductions. According to David:

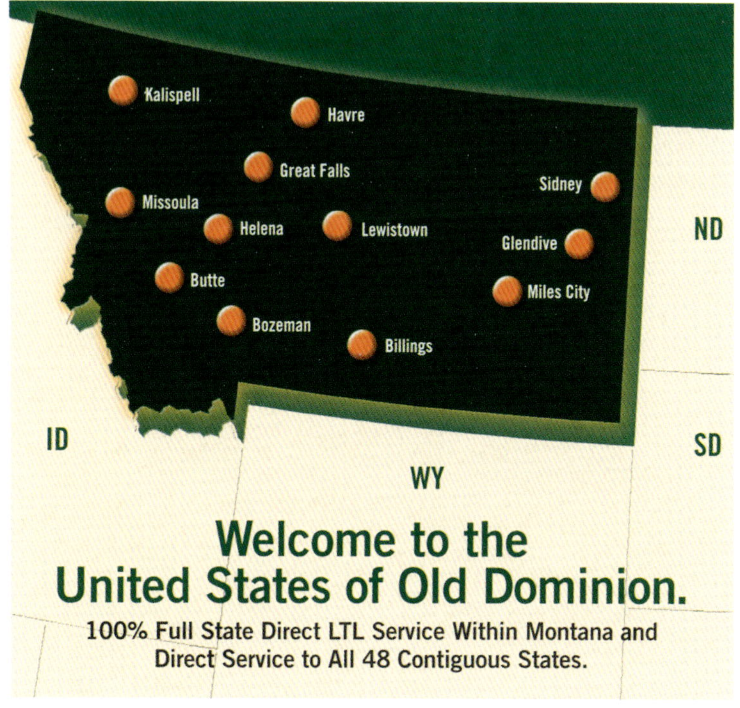

In 2008, after adding Montana to its list of states offering full-state direct LTL service, and, importantly, complete national coverage, Old Dominion was able to offer direct service to all 48 contiguous states.

The Heart of the Company Passes Away

John Yowell was a beloved member of the Old Dominion family for 27 years, until he passed away unexpectedly on December 30, 2010. It was an extremely difficult loss for the company as a whole, and for the Congdon family especially.

He joined Old Dominion in 1983 at the urging of his father-in-law Earl Congdon. Yowell was running the IT department at another company at the time and initially turned down Earl's offer to join Old Dominion—but he did agree to come by the office and look at the company's computerized costing model with Bill Carpenter, then Old Dominion's executive vice president, and Earl.[1]

"At the time, we were really small," Yowell recalled in a 2010 interview. "And there was one CRT [computer monitor] in the middle of the office, and Earl sat down to show me the costing model, and he was just kind of sitting there, and I realized he didn't know how to turn it on. So I reached over and I turned on the computer for him, and he just looked up at Bill and he told him, 'See? I told you he was pretty sharp.' "[2]

Earl soon offered Yowell a chance to run the IT department at Old Dominion. Although he was initially reluctant because he didn't want to be known as "the son-in-law," he eventually took the position. "To be honest with you, it's probably the best decision I ever made," Yowell admitted. "I love my job."[3]

Yowell eventually rose through the ranks to executive vice president and chief operating officer. Every employee valued his thoughtful input and strong values. Yowell's strong values will continue to guide the company for decades to come. "John Yowell was just a man of tremendous integrity, and I think he taught everybody a lot from that standpoint with his integrity and his standards of how he wanted people to be treated," recalled Greg Gantt, who took over as chief operating officer after

John Yowell's kindness and compassion touched countless people. In 2011, the John Yowell Old Dominion Family Spirit Award was created in his memory.

Yowell's passing. "He set the bar for all of us from that standpoint."[4]

Employees appreciated not only his strategic insight, but also the personal touch he applied, making it his mission to ensure that every staffer felt like part of the Old Dominion family. "One of our employees has a voicemail from John on her five-year anniversary," recalled Mike Venegoni, president of Vault Logistics. "It's about three years old, and she still has it on her phone, and she plays it back, where he called and said he couldn't be in the meeting to recognize her five-year anniversary, but he congratulated her and told her she was a valuable employee. She still saves that. She played it back yesterday."[5]

Yowell was always concerned with the well-being of his Old Dominion family members, as well as the rest of the community at large. Earl Congdon noted:

> *He was the closest thing that we had in the company to a chaplain, and that's going to be a big hole to fill. He was the type of fellow who, if he heard that an employee had a problem—maybe they've got a sick child or they've lost one—he'd be the first one on the telephone to find out how we at the company could help. Or he'd be the first one to get a call from an employee who was in trouble and wanted to know if there was something the company could do to help out. We'll all be working a little harder to fill that role. ... Every time John Yowell would end up with a prayer for a meal, he would always end it with, "God, help us to help others."*
>
> *And he was doing things in the community that we didn't know about. For example, when our priest was eulogizing him during the funeral, he said that he got this call from John Yowell, and John told him, "If there's any young person who is missing out on a church activity because of money, that can't be allowed. I want to know about it."*[6]

John Yowell served on the board of directors for Open Door Ministries for 12 years, and, as a volunteer, he was renowned for his kindness.[7] Within months of Yowell's passing, the John Yowell Old Dominion Family Spirit Award was established in his honor.[8]

In addition to his Old Dominion family, Yowell left behind his wife, Audrey Congdon, and his children Seth and Megan Yowell, along with a large extended family. Everyone whose life he touched will always fondly remember his generosity and dynamic personality.

We knew that for every single percentage point of price reduction, we would need 4 percent to 5 percent more tonnage to offset that price reduction to end up with the same earnings per share. Assuming we were able to gain that tonnage to have the same earnings, but if we increased revenue at a lower price, our operating ratio would have gone up.

We would have needed 8 percent to 10 percent more tonnage to keep the operating ratio where we wanted it to be. We would be shooting ourselves in the foot if we started chopping rates without getting significantly more tonnage. It didn't make sense to cut rates for more tonnage in a recessionary tonnage environment. With those thoughts in mind, we stuck to our guns to produce the best service product we've ever had and try to be profitable.[33]

Although some in the industry scratched their heads at Old Dominion's refusal to lower prices during the recession, other analysts recognized that the company was doing exactly the right thing to allow it to stay on top. "The discounting made no sense," noted Old Dominion board member and freight industry veteran Leo Suggs. "In many cases, it was obvious that [other companies] were discounting to the point that they didn't even cover their variable

Old Dominion asked employees to sign a pledge promising to strive toward continuing the company's dedication to helping the world keep promises.

SAFETY AS A PRIORITY

OLD DOMINION HAS ONE OF THE LOWEST ACCIDENT frequency ratios in the industry, in large part due to the company's consistent focus on safety.[1] For a trucking company, safety is key, and Old Dominion has maintained a strict policy designed to protect the well-being of its employees and the motoring public. "The key has always been awareness, keeping employees in the company aware of our safety statistics," noted Brian Stoddard, Old Dominion's vice president of safety and personnel. "When I first came into the safety department, our accidents were about 12.5 per million miles, and it's below four now."[2]

By 2007, Old Dominion had fitted each of the company's tractors with a lane departure warning system, which alerted the driver if the truck was leaving its lane without the turn signal being deployed. "With safety remaining a top priority for our company, we are confident the decision to install this technology will prove to be an effective means of preventing accidents," Stoddard said.[3]

The most important change for drivers in terms of safety and efficiency over the years was the development of onboard computer systems. "Instead of just having a manual fuel pump, there's actually technology in the operation of the engine and the operation of the truck that controls engine speed and road speed for the vehicle," said Sam Faucette, Old Dominion's director of

costs, let alone make any profit. ... I think the Old Dominion management team is not only experienced, but they're very wise, and they made the right decision. Consequently, during that period of time, while they were not thrilled with the reduced profits, they were in a category all by themselves in terms of profitability. Their focus on things like reducing freight claims and continuing to improve service, certainly proved to be the right things to do."[34]

Some who kept a keen eye on the trucking industry as a whole were inspired by what they considered to be Old Dominion's strong belief in valuing its services. "Whenever you have a recession, a lot of companies say that they're going to remain disciplined on pricing and other elements of their strategy, and you often see companies violate the spirit of that," said Thom Albrecht, a transportation industry analyst with BB&T Capital Markets. "What was more impressive and surprising was that [Old Dominion] was able to maintain that in the face of the worst recession since World War II."[35]

To help employees weather the recession, Old Dominion reassigned some drivers to work on the docks so that when the work picked up again, the drivers would be available immediately.[36] "In a union free environment, we have options with our drivers," said Mike Wood, vice president of the Midwest Region. "They can run line-haul, work as a city driver, work on the dock, or perform yard switching. This gives us great flexibility to service our customers."[37]

That creativity in staffing allowed Old Dominion to maintain its family feel, even as business slowed. "Old Dominion did not cut any wages, or benefits, while everybody else in the industry did," said Matt Nowell, an account specialist with Old Dominion, and David's son-in-law. "I think that's a testament to our senior management that they've kept the family spirit Earl Congdon Sr. and Lillian instilled in this company when they started."[38]

And as part of that family atmosphere that existed for years within the company, Old Dominion employees followed management's lead with the company's policies during the recession.

It became clear that as other carriers cut prices to gain market share, they experienced lapses in quality. Since Old Dominion didn't follow that trend, its customers benefited as the company directed its efforts to consistently improving its service and reliability. "All of the parts and pieces that make up this company buckled down to do what was right for the customer and what is central to our brand promise,"

safety compliance, training, and recruiting. "We can monitor performance with much more detail as far as how the truck is operating."[4]

However, the engine computer alone lacked a way to monitor the specific fuel economy of individual drivers throughout the course of their working hours. Old Dominion does not usually assign the same driver to the same truck at all times. Instead, the company "slip seats," meaning that one driver may drive three different trucks during the course of the same week.[5]

Therefore, with Old Dominion's adoption of the electronic onboard recorder (EOBR), manufactured by PeopleNet, the company is now able to monitor driver performance measures and vehicle performance, as well as actual hours of service. Drivers log in and out of the computer during their shifts, and if a problem is observed, the line-haul manager addresses it directly with the employee.[6] "It's a good tool for everyone," Faucette said. "The drivers like it. Their buy-in is no more paper. It gives them an actual readout, time-wise, of how much they can continue to work each day because their clock counts backwards from the time they stop."[7]

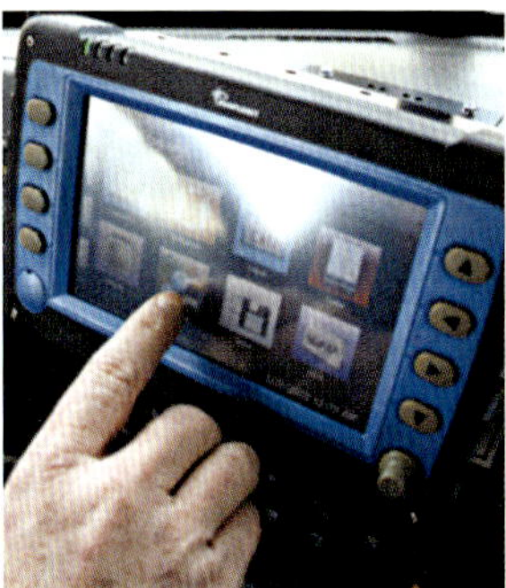

Between Old Dominion's PeopleNet system, its dockyard management system, its onboard computers, and its safety-monitoring capabilities, the company remains at the forefront of freight technology.

said David Carter, Old Dominion director of marketing. "Old Dominion intensified the focus on training and customer service, all of the aspects that everybody in the industry talks about but doesn't really deliver against. It made a big, big, difference. ... I think the underlying, most important element that helped us succeed during this recession was the strength of our team and our people."[39]

New Strides in 2009

Old Dominion did not let the weak economy impact its plans to offer additional features in 2009, and the company rolled out its guaranteed Security Divider Service that year, offering compartmentalized freight security.[40] Delicate or security sensitive freight would be loaded in the front of the trailer. The Old Dominion driver then places a divider that separates it so no one else can touch the freight, and the entire area is secured with a lock.[41] In addition, Old Dominion began offering its "White Glove Service," which means that Old Dominion will work with an agent, and together they will pick up the item a customer orders, take it inside of the delivery location, unpackage it, assemble it, and leave with the packing debris.[42] For instance, Old Dominion performs this service for medical tables and chairs, dental chairs, exercise equipment, and televisions.

In 2009, as the struggling economy slowly began to stabilize, Old Dominion celebrated its 75th anniversary. That November, David Congdon rang the NASDAQ stock market's closing bell.[43] "It was extremely exciting," David said. "We had a great group of customers there, and some members of our finance department who deal directly with NASDAQ. We celebrated afterward and had a nice dinner with our customers."

The projection screen in Times Square featured the Old Dominion executives on the floor of the NASDAQ and showed an Old Dominion tractor-trailer coming around the bend. "They showed pictures of all of us inside, all of our people who were there enjoying this with us," David said. "I had my family there, my wife, my daughter, and my son-in-law. We just had a great time and we're looking forward to doing it again."[44]

Unfortunately, the shortfalls in the US economy affected the company's numbers as the decade ended. In 2009, revenues dropped to $1.3 billion, down from $1.5 billion in 2008, with earnings declining 49.2 percent to $34.9 million.[45] Despite the setback, Old Dominion still led the industry as the only public LTL carrier to remain profitable in 2009.[46]

Rolling Into a New Decade

Trucking analysts considered 2010 to be "a year of rebuilding for LTL carriers," the *Journal of Commerce* reported. Old Dominion was uniquely positioned to gain a large section of that growing market share, since the company had not suffered as much as its competition during the down period.[47]

The key category which differentiated Old Dominion from other freight companies during that period—and continues to set the company apart—has been customer service,

Left: In November 2009, as the company celebrated its 75th anniversary, David Congdon rang the closing bell with family, staff, and customers at NASDAQ. *(Photo © 2009, The NASDAQ OMX Group, Inc.)*

Opposite: As part of the company's marketing strategy, Old Dominion advertises its long history of stability and growth in the tumultuous transportation industry.

In these days of transportation turmoil, Old Dominion is still keeping promises.

As the transportation landscape changes on an almost daily basis, we'd like to remind you that Old Dominion is stable, strong and keeping promises for customers every day, just like we have for 75 years.

Stability

We have a 75-year history of solid growth, strong financial performance, a highly experienced executive management group and a proudly union-free workforce. We are one company, with one vision for the future, with no operational or integration issues. We are poised for growth.

Coverage

Old Dominion has complete nationwide coverage, seamless service to Mexico with satellite tracking capabilities and direct service to Canada. We also offer extensive global service to Puerto Rico, the Caribbean and all major markets in China.

Capacity

We now service all 48 contiguous states with 206 service centers, 5,170 tractors and 20,011 trailers, which are all supported by state-of-the-art operational technology. And with plans to add even more in the future, we're ready now to handle all your shipping needs.

Don't leave your shipping to fate. Call OD today.

800.235.5569 | Call us today to speak to a service center representative or visit us on the web.
TrustOD.com

OD • DOMESTIC | OD • EXPEDITED | OD • GLOBAL | OD • TECHNOLOGY

Helping the world keep promises.™

DRIVER TECHNOLOGY

OLD DOMINION'S COMMITMENT TO USING THE most advanced driver technology has helped the company succeed in the industry. "I think we're light-years beyond our competitors as far as technology is concerned," said Chris Harrell, who specializes in Old Dominion's PeopleNet onboard computer system and is David Congdon's son-in-law. "I'm sure our customers have more visibility with us than they do with any other company."[1]

Old Dominion's drivers use handheld computers that track where the drivers and shipments are at all times. This allows customers to go online to track their shipments, determine when they will be delivered, and find out who signed for them postdelivery.[2]

Old Dominion rolled out its PeopleNet system to company drivers in 2010. It uses GPS technology and allows Old Dominion to log transactions and closely monitor shipments and deliveries. "It saves us fuel, it tells us how our drivers are driving the trucks, it gives us fuel mileage, and it also tells us exactly where our drivers are at any given time," explained Terry Hutchins, Old Dominion's vice president of field services.[3]

PeopleNet represents an approximately $10 million investment for Old Dominion, but will save the company money in the long run. "We believe it'll pay off in a year in just fuel alone," said Ken Erdner, Old Dominion's vice president of technology and information systems. "When you look at the drivers being able to drive more efficiently based on these computers helping them out and the training we're giving them, if we can save three-tenths of a mile per gallon, it pays off in a year."

The system can also show Old Dominion whether a driver is off his route, and even provide information on the truck's internal operations. "In just the first couple of months, we've caught three or four engines that were about to blow up because the oil pressure was going down," Erdner said. "The system automatically sent emails out for repairs to make sure that they got done, and we've been able to save those engines, which would have cost $20,000 to $25,000 apiece to fix."[4]

If Old Dominion saves one-tenth of a mile per gallon company-wide, it will equate to roughly $2.9 million. However, PeopleNet has advan-

Freeman said. "It's obvious from our financials in 2009 that we were the best operating LTL company out there, and the reason for that is because we gave the best customer service."[48]

By 2010, Old Dominion maintained a record of 98.7 percent on-time delivery, which the company had achieved by consistently emphasizing proper training.[49] Maintenance has also remained a strong focus for Old Dominion, with maintenance parts alone costing the company more than $1 million a month by 2010, not including labor and outside repairs.[50] The equipment most often replaced at Old Dominion were the sleeper team operation trucks, which are traded out approximately every four years or 1 million miles, whichever comes first.[51] "The sleeper team unit usually has two people working side by side 24 hours a day driving the truck, so those trucks wear out faster," explained Old Dominion's vice president of maintenance Ed Richardson.[52]

To ensure high standards for its maintenance employees, Old Dominion employed two full-time technician trainers. As of 2010, Old Dominion became home to the only Automotive Service Excellence (ASE)-certified trucking training program in existence.[53] Old Dominion completed a 15-month-long process to qualify for the certification, offered by the National Automotive Technicians Education Foundation.[54]

Old Dominion also remained committed to reducing its environmental impact, investing $30,000 per truck, as compared to 2003 prices, in upgrading

Old Dominion drivers are trained in using the most current technology in the industry to ensure freight deliveries are made on time. Drivers can review shipments, transit times, and schedules directly from the road using Old Dominion's customized software.

tages besides the financial aspect. "One of the biggest returns on investment, really, is driver safety," Harrell explained. "It's hard to quantify, but it's a very important part of working for Old Dominion. We're all about safety, and it's going to allow our drivers to have a better quality of life. It is part of the safety measures which we instill in all our drivers."[5]

to clean diesel engines.[55] New emissions regulations in 2010 had such a dramatic impact on the company's pollution levels that Old Dominion discovered its trucks had dirtier air going into the trucks than the air that came out of the exhaust.[56]

By 2010, Old Dominion consumed 70 million gallons of diesel fuel annually, according to Mark Penley, Old Dominion's fuel manager, whose mother Karen is David's sister and Earl's daughter. Mark began working for Old Dominion when he was a teenager, and came aboard full-time after college.[57]

Buying that much fuel has proven useful to Old Dominion in regards to fuel pricing. "We're starting to feel that we have more negotiating power than we thought we've had in the past, and we're taking advantage of that," Penley explained. "We're really looking at our sourcing models. Out of our 216 service centers, we have about 45 where we actually purchase fuel in large quantities to store and dispense on-site."[58]

Error-Free Work

Back in the 1980s, Earl Congdon pioneered the company's commitment to "Error-Free Work." Old Dominion has never been closer to achieving that goal. Back in the 1980s, Old Dominion had an approximate 25 percent error rate on invoices when freight bill entry was performed in the field. However, in 2010, when all billing entries were handled in Old Dominion's Morristown

Old Dominion coordinates every aspect of its Speed Service, which offers customers customized air freight delivery to anywhere in the continental United States.

and Thomasville locations, the error ratio has dropped to eight-tenths of 1 percent.[59]

An independent study performed by an outside firm revealed that Old Dominion had the most correctly billed and rated invoices in the industry.[60] Although Old Dominion outsources the mailing of its invoices, the company does not outsource the job internationally. "We're an American company, and I'm not going to take the business overseas," explained Dave Heaton, Old Dominion vice president of corporate services.[61]

During the 1990s, Old Dominion's cargo claim ratio ranged from 1.5 percent to 2.0 percent of revenue, but by 2010, the rate had fallen to 0.47 percent. "The lowest in the industry," noted Ernie Benge, Old Dominion's director of claims.[62]

Many factors have contributed to Old Dominion's ability to achieve such low claims rates, including the company's dedication to maintenance. "Our fleet—we will put it up against any in the industry as far as a safe, good, well-maintained operation out there," Richardson said.[63]

Old Dominion also helped reduce claims rates with an increased emphasis on training for dockworkers, drivers, and supervisors. Other simple but important steps the company took to increase safety and reduce claims was to retrofit all of its trailers with E-track ratchet straps in the trailers, as well as loading decks, to keep the cargo secure.[64] Joann McMillan, a longtime member of Old Dominion's claims department, credited the improved claims rate to "a combination of the right people, a lot of training, and a concerted effort at every level, from the drivers, to the dock, to the people who do the other functions, and it finally jelled. I can't say any one section of the company is responsible for it. It's just a concerted pulling together."[65]

The low claims rate proved an important selling tool that, coupled with the company's firm dedication to service, helped keep long-term customers on board. According to Doug Ball, who retired as Old Dominion's director of claims prevention in 2009, "You could see the results of your work and that was really a great feeling. I think that's one of the many reasons for the customer loyalty that Old Dominion enjoys today, because if we did have a problem, we'd work on solving it."[66]

Old Dominion's Unique Success

Old Dominion has long differentiated itself from its competitors. A financial analyst who covers the transportation industry, Ed Wolfe of Wolfe Trahan & Co. recognized the importance of Old Dominion's unique business model. As Wolfe explained in 2010:

> *I'm generally negative on the fundamentals of the LTL sector, but I think Old Dominion is a company specifically doing something that no one else is.*
>
> *It's a really funny story, but a couple of years ago, I downgraded the entire group at one point—I don't remember exactly when this was—all to underperform or sell. David called me up, and he said, "I understand your view on the industry, but what I don't understand is how you can lump Old Dominion in with the rest of the that group when we are clearly the performance leader."*
>
> *That comment stuck in the back of my craw, and today, it's absolutely true. I had always viewed that the LTLs move as a group, but if you actually look over year-to-date, Old Dominion's stock is up 20 percent, and the rest of the group is down 20 percent. He's been right. Old Dominion has been able to differentiate itself.*[67]

When calling on new accounts, Old Dominion has been fairly easy to sell over the past several years thanks to its distinctive position in the industry. Sales specialist Karen Dillman, a 22-year employee of Old Dominion, considered the company's reputation a major selling point with customers. "I tell them that we've been in business 76 years, and we sell our value over price, focusing on all the things we have to offer the customer," she said.[68]

As Chief Operating Officer Greg Gantt explained:

> *I think our salespeople truly believe in our system. They believe in what we're doing. You know, they sell with confidence, and, gosh, that's HUGE.*
>
> *We get feedback from customers all the time. They'll send us an email and say, "Hey, your driver did this or that and helped us with this delivery, that delivery, or with this pickup. Your customer service is so helpful, and it's a pleasure to call Old Dominion. I can always count on you."*
>
> *We get a lot of feedback on that from time to time, and, again, I think, to me, that reinforces what we're trying to train our people to do. There's value in good customer service. There's value in driver service. How you do your job makes a difference, and determines the selection customers make in which carrier to use.*
>
> *It's working. The real value is getting people to buy into what we're doing, and if everybody is sold on the fact that they play a key role in this value proposition, then the rest of it is easy.*[69]

With more than 450 stores and five distribution centers, Sports Authority relies on Old Dominion to offer consistent service as the company's exclusive LTL carrier. According to Mark Albright, the vice president of corporate logistics with Sports Authority, "I look back over 30 years, and I look at Old Dominion, and I remember them when they were a small, regional LTL company based out of the Southeast. … Even though they've gotten a lot bigger, I don't think they've lost that. They still treat every one of their customers as if Old Dominion was a small company, and you're the most important thing they've got to work on."[70]

That spirit of dedicated customer service is directly related to the close-knit working environment that has always been one of Old Dominion's greatest strengths. According to Wes Frye, senior vice president of finance and chief financial officer:

> *We have a team here who knows their business, and we work extremely well together, and we've made the investments in resources, not only in IT but in people, experienced people. That just allows us to do a better job of monitoring our costs and monitoring our margins and assimilating what type of pricing that we need in order to dictate what's profitable, and that's all pretty much a result of providing best-in-class service. You can't do any of that unless you are providing the service that is better than anyone else in terms of transit times and cargo claims and customer service*

generally, so I think it's a combined effort of people working closely and making sure we're all harmonious in terms of what we're doing and what our objectives are.[71]

As Senior Vice President of Sales Marty Freeman explained, "Everything we've done here is teamwork, and there are a lot of people who have been responsible for the sales here. It's like a football team to me. If you want to be the best, you've got to have the best players, and that's what our sales directors are out doing. They're building the skills of the players we have, and they're looking for improvements every year."[72]

Promises

In 2010, Old Dominion also continued to gain momentum in its branding effort. On the heels of a new company positioning launch known as "Helping the World Keep Promises,™" as well as the celebration of the company's 75th anniversary in 2009, Old Dominion grew its brand presence. All internal studies showed that the Promises positioning was gaining traction with the shipping public as people were looking for a company, a brand, and a service solution they could count on during a time of economic uncertainty. The Promises positioning delivered on all counts and was well received in all communication channels, from print, to digital, to national television spots. Even industry analysts began to comment on the strength of the Old Dominion brand.

Promises worked because it was not a clever gimmick, but rather because it truly reflected who and what the people of Old Dominion were all about. The branding effort was congruent with the personality and accurately represented the employees' desire to fulfill the commitments of service they have made. The Old Dominion brand is about family and delivering on promises made, promises the Old Dominion family has made to each other, promises the Old Dominion family has made to its customers, and promises Old Dominion's customers have made to their customers. Old Dominion was no longer just a trucking and logistics company, but rather it was becoming known as the brand that was "Helping the World Keep Promises.™"

Vault Logistics™

From the drivers, to the customer service reps, to the company's management, Old Dominion firmly supports its customer base, launching new services focused directly on customer requests.[73] To that end, in August 2011, Old Dominion launched its new Vault Logistics service. "The market today is really demanding that we offer a broader array of services," explained Old Dominion's President of Vault Logistics Mike Venegoni. "Our customers are demanding it. So we want to be able to bring supply chain solutions to our clients that compliment the LTL services and global services that we already offer."[74]

Vault represents a third-party logistics (3PL) division that allows customers to benefit from Old Dominion's broad-ranging expertise. Old Dominion can offer customized supply chain solutions that can help customers overcome their unique challenges, all while controlling costs and increasing efficiency.

"Our promise to the market is 'We help your business grow.' It's not to come in and save a few pennies on this load or that shipment," Venegoni explained. "It's saying to our customers, 'What can we do overall to align with your strategies and your goals as a company to help you accomplish the most efficient supply chain?' "[75]

Vault helps streamline customer operations, saving time and money by offering full supply chain management with a single point of contact.[76] According to Venegoni:

If they're spending millions a year on freight, we can audit those figures and make sure they're accurate. We can save customers money. Vendor inventory management helps take days off an

In August 2011, Old Dominion launched its new Vault Logistics service, a third-party logistics (3PL) division that offers customized supply chain solutions that can help customers overcome their unique challenges, all while controlling costs and increasing efficiency.

Old Dominion has long maintained a commitment to having the best trucks on the road, with a strong focus on maintenance, safety, and controlling environmental emissions.

inventory out of the supply chain, and the value of one day of inventory can be significant. That's where you start getting into first-year cash flow contributions to profit and losses for your customer in the range of millions of dollars. Order accuracy is important, keeping the line flowing, and then having our people dedicated onsite is part of a package deal that helps cut down their expenses. ... These can contribute to significant multiyear dollar savings.[77]

Old Dominion Truck Leasing

Old Dominion Truck Leasing, privately held by the Congdon family and run by Jack, John, and Jeff Congdon, owned about 1,200 pieces of equipment, including tractors, trailers, and straight trucks, and employed 110 people as of 2010.[78] Leases usually spanned between three and six years, depending on the miles the company intended to travel in the truck.[79]

When the leased trucks require maintenance, they go to one of Old Dominion Truck Leasing's nine locations. If the truck breaks down and isn't near one of those locations, it can be serviced in one of the National Truck Leasing system's locations, since Old Dominion is an affiliate. According to Jack, "We have more locations than Ryder National Lease does, and we pledge to each other that we will take care of these other customers of National Truck Leasing's trucks that are in our territory as if they were our own. It works quite well."[80]

In addition to leasing equipment to other businesses, Old Dominion Leasing services other companies' trucks via maintenance contracts. "They own them, we just maintain them at these locations," Jack said. "On the other hand, we'll do maintenance for people not under contract. We do that for two reasons—one is it may develop into a contract or perhaps develop into a lease by doing that."[81]

Old Dominion Leasing finances leases even if another company owns the trucks. The company typically finances larger groups of equipment in the 40 to 50 unit range.[82] Old Dominion Truck Leasing also provides additional services. Within its Dominion Dedicated Logistics branch, the company can provide trucking companies with drivers, whether or not the company is leasing its trucks from Old Dominion Leasing.[83]

The Old Dominion Family

Old Dominion may no longer be totally family-owned, but it will always have a family feel.[84] Karen Dillman offered this example of Old Dominion's commitment to preserving its family atmosphere:

I've been here for 22 years, and I've had a lot of job offers with other carriers, and some of them have even offered me more money, but I realize the grass sometimes isn't greener on the other side. This company is the best company I've ever worked for because it's so family-oriented.

We used to have a gentleman who had some bad health problems, probably would have been 15 years ago. He was just emptying our trash cans. He would ride the bus up here. He would empty trash cans, hang around for two or three hours, sit in the break room and talk to the drivers as they came in and out. Then he'd go home. Well, we had a manager one time who wanted to get rid of him, and Earl told the manager that the man had a job here as long as he made it to work. He said, "Do not ever send him home. If he wants to come up here for an hour a day, I don't care what it is, he's got a job as long as he's breathing."

This guy was probably 70. Earl knew the guy didn't have a lot of money, that he'd put his life into

A Timeline of Technology Innovations at Old Dominion

Prior to 1980, Old Dominion used a completely paper-based system for its freight management and customer contact was by telephone.

1960s–1970s

- First used computers for general business applications.

1980

- Old Dominion installed computers at its headquarters and began installing computers on a limited basis in its service centers.

1983

- John Yowell joined Old Dominion as director of information management systems. He led the company's efforts to move beyond a paper-based organizational model to a fully integrated, computerized system.

1984–1985

- Computers were installed in every Old Dominion service center. Dedicated data lines connect every terminal to Old Dominion's High Point, North Carolina, headquarters, creating a private computer network spanning the company's entire service area.
- Old Dominion developed the key applications for its new information management system in-house, with the first application being a basic message-switching program. It later went on to develop freight tracking and customer notification systems; freight billing and rating; over, short, or damage claims; line-haul dispatching, and creating manifests detailing trailer contents.

1986

- With computerized systems in place throughout Old Dominion's service network, the company was capable of providing near real-time shipment status, and customers could be notified via phone or fax.

1988

- Old Dominion began implementing an electronic data interchange system that provided participating customers with shipment status updates and invoicing.

1990–1992

- The company continued to develop proprietary automated systems to optimize shipping routes and provide customers with up-to-date shipping notifications.

the company and had worked here for years. Earl just wanted to give him a place to go.[85]

The close ties between employees at Old Dominion is due in large part to the Congdons, who have opened their doors and expanded their definition of family to include the entire company. "I can remember back when things were a little tough, and we would be here all week long in Martinsville, we'd go down to High Point and work the weekends, and Earl would be out there on the dock, plus David, his sister Karen, working freight," said Wayne Goldston,

1992

- Old Dominion developed its first handheld computer application designed for use by pickup and delivery drivers. Handheld computers were first used in the field at the company's Atlanta, Georgia, facility. The handheld computers originally featured embedded wireless radio communication systems. Unfortunately, due to hardware malfunctions and issues with data communications coverage, Old Dominion was forced to stop using handheld computers until those problems could be resolved.

1994–1995

- Old Dominion began implementing its first application to plan and optimize inbound delivery routes.

1996

- Ken Erdner joined Old Dominion as manager of the company's computer department. Under his leadership, Old Dominion developed many of the company's technology innovations.
- New computerized dockyard management systems, developed in-house, allowed Old Dominion to reduce paperwork, increasing the speed of its freight-tracking abilities while providing enhanced accountability for individual dockworkers. With the new system, Old Dominion was able to monitor freight movement across all of its service centers more accurately than ever before.
- Old Dominion developed and implemented a complete customer notification system for scheduling appointments.

1997

- The first Old Dominion website was launched, allowing customers to research the company and track shipment status online.

1999–2008

- Old Dominion launched an improved handheld computer system for use by all pickup and delivery drivers.
- Radio frequency identification (RFID) tags were installed in all Old Dominion tractors, trailers, and converter dollies. Tag readers at the entrance gates to all Old Dominion facilities automatically tracked all arrivals and departures of shipments and equipment.
- The company launched ODFL4me.com, providing customers with enhanced online tools to directly manage their accounts.
- ODFL continued improving and refining its computerized customer support and tracking systems, including software designed to cut line-haul dispatch times.

2008 and beyond

- Old Dominion installed PeopleNet onboard communication systems on all of its tractors. PeopleNet allowed Old Dominion to fully integrate its freight-tracking capabilities while increasing productivity and reducing its environmental impact by decreasing waste and inefficiencies.

manager of Old Dominion's Martinsville, Virginia, distribution center. "My dad died in 1991, and David was a pallbearer at his funeral. When a president of a company will give up his time to be a pallbearer at my father's funeral, that's something to be said about him. They're like family."[86]

Congdon family members who join the company have found that employees treat them with warm regard as if they've always known them. "I always knew it was a well-run company, it was a good company that was in good standing, but I didn't realize how supportive every single employee

By 2011, Old Dominion's Truck Tour visited 51 cities across the United States since its inception three years earlier. The tour featured an interactive museum and allowed customers, employees, and prospects to learn about the company's long history.

really is and how much every employee I ran into loved the company and would do anything to make sure it's properly run, which is very impressive," said Megan Yowell, John Yowell's daughter and Earl's granddaughter. She joined Old Dominion in 2010 as a sales rep.[87]

Staff members aren't alone in seeing the Old Dominion family connection in everything the company does. Industry analysts described the same traits when considering Old Dominion's success. According to John Larkin, managing director of the Transportation Research Group at analyst firm Stifel Nicolaus:

> *The company is, in our view, the best less-than-truckload carrier out there. The management team is excellent. They've been together a long time, and even as the company has grown, they've found a way to make everyone feel as though they're still part of a family business where everyone is important. If you take the time to sponsor barbecues at terminals, and senior management actually shows up at those things and speaks to the employees who are out there making it happen every day, that seems to go a long way towards making everybody feel like they're working for a great company that's run by terrific people who really are looking out for everyone's interests.*[88]

Working closely with the board of directors, David and Earl, as the company's CEO and board chairman, respectively, have led the company to increase its growth even as Old Dominion's competitors have faltered. They demonstrate their keen understanding of the industry at every quarterly analyst call. "I think it's so wonderful to hear Earl Congdon on the phone once a quarter," said analyst Ed Wolfe. "I look forward to it. He's such a dean of the industry, and to hear his deep and friendly Southern drawl on the calls just makes me very happy every quarter. ... That's what's really different about this company, having a father and son on a call."[89]

Perhaps part of Old Dominion's tremendous growth is due to the fact that the company never tried to rush its expansion during the early days. Harwood Cochrane, a close friend of the Congdon family and founder of Overnite Transportation, now a subsidiary of UPS, said he always referred to Earl as a late bloomer.[90] "But when he bloomed, he certainly did bloom," Cochrane noted. "I mean, I don't mind telling you the company amazes me."[91]

Earl, whose parents founded the company more than 75 years ago, described his son David as "the best LTL company president in this country today, and how could I ask for more?"[92]

Reflecting on the company he joined full-time when he was just a teenager, Earl considered building the Old Dominion family the most important factor in making the company such a long-term success, "In creating this Old Dominion family, I'm so proud of our drivers and warehouse workers, our mechanics, all of our employees, who have had such faith in our management."[93]

The Road Ahead

As the world continues to recover from the worst recession in many decades, Old Dominion has remained on track for double-digit earnings growth in 2011. Old Dominion has spread across the globe, with freight service available throughout all of North America, as well as China and points around the world, ensuring the company is in the best position to help its customers succeed despite a fragile economic climate.

Revenues have consistently beat company and analyst forecasts, with second quarter sales in 2011 jumping to $480 million, up more than 30 percent from the previous year, even beating Old Dominion's previous record high of $417 million. With both shipments and tonnage on the increase in 2011, that ambitious growth is expected to continue.[94]

The company has traveled so far since it was first founded in 1934. From the small freight-hauling operation Earl Sr. and his wife Lillian launched from their home with a single truck, Old Dominion Freight Line has grown to employ more than 12,000 people, with nearly 6,000 tractors, 22,000 trailers, and 216 service centers nationwide. Old Dominion vehicles crisscross the country, traveling more than 400 million miles a year by 2011.

Old Dominion has built its reputation on keeping promises, and that is one tradition the company will continue to hold sacred, no matter what challenges the company might face on the road ahead.

Notes to Sources

CHAPTER ONE

1. Earl Congdon, *History of Old Dominion Freight Line, Financial Information*, unpublished manuscript, 28 June 2010, 4.
2. Earl Congdon, "A Conversation With Earl Congdon," Old Dominion Freight Line 2009 Annual Report, 8.
3. Earl Congdon, *History of Old Dominion Freight Line, Financial Information*, 2–3.
4. Ibid., 3–4.
5. *History of Old Dominion Freight Line, Financial Information*, 3.
6. Earl Congdon, interview by Jeffrey L. Rodengen, digital recording, 12 July 2010, Write Stuff Enterprises, LLC.
7. William Bien, "Woman Heads Freight Line," *Richmond News Leader*, 19 July 1954, 21.
8. Ibid.
9. Earl Congdon, *History of Old Dominion Freight Line, Financial Information*, 4.
10. "A Conversation With Earl Congdon."
11. "Woman Heads Freight Line."
12. *History of Old Dominion Freight Line, Financial Information*, 5.
13. Ibid.
14. "Woman Heads Freight Line."
15. *History of Old Dominion Freight Line, Financial Information*, 5.
16. "Woman Heads Freight Line."
17. *History of Old Dominion Freight Line, Financial Information*, 6.
18. "Woman Heads Freight Line."
19. Thomas Gale Moore, "Trucking Deregulation," The Concise Encyclopedia of Economics website, Library of Economics and Liberty, www.econlib.org/library/Enc1/TruckingDeregulation.html.
20. "A Conversation With Earl Congdon."
21. Ibid.
22. Earl Congdon, interview by Jeffrey L. Rodengen, digital recording, 13 September 2010, Write Stuff Enterprises, LLC.
23. "A Conversation With Earl Congdon."
24. Ibid.
25. Ibid.
26. *History of Old Dominion Freight Line, Financial Information*, 6.
27. Ibid.
28. Ibid.
29. "A Conversation With Earl Congdon."
30. *History of Old Dominion Freight Line, Financial Information*, 17.
31. Ibid., 6–7.
32. "Woman Heads Freight Line."
33. "A Conversation With Earl Congdon."
34. "Woman Heads Freight Line."
35. *History of Old Dominion Freight Line, Financial Information*, 7.
36. Ibid., 8.
37. Ibid., 8.
38. "A Conversation With Earl Congdon."
39. *History of Old Dominion Freight Line, Financial Information*, 9.
40. "A Conversation With Earl Congdon."
41. *History of Old Dominion Freight Line, Financial Information*, 21.
42. Ibid., 9.
43. *History of Old Dominion Freight Line, Financial Information*, 11.
44. Ibid., 22.
45. C. M. Mark, letter to Lillian Congdon, 28 July 1939.
46. *History of Old Dominion Freight Line, Financial Information*, 23–24.
47. Ibid., 20.

CHAPTER ONE SIDEBAR: The Fascinating Background of Lillian Congdon Crowder

1. Susan Ware, *Holding Their Own: American Women in the 1930s*, (Boston: Twayne, 1982), excerpted at www.novelguide.com/a/discover/adec_0001_0004_0/adec_0001_0004_0_01237.html/.
2. William Bien, "Woman Heads Freight Line," *Richmond News Leader*, 19 July 1954, 21.
3. Ibid.
4. Earl Congdon, interview by Jeffrey L. Rodengen, digital recording, 12 July 2010, Write Stuff Enterprises, LLC.

CHAPTER ONE SIDEBAR: The Impact of the Motor Carrier Act

1. Thomas Gale Moore, "Trucking Deregulation," The Concise Encyclopedia of Economics, Library of Economics and Liberty website, www.econlib.org/library/Enc1/TruckingDeregulation.html.
2. Ibid.

CHAPTER TWO

1. Earl Congdon, *A Conversation With Earl Congdon*, Foundation of Success series, DVD.
2. Earl Congdon, *History of Old Dominion Freight Line, Financial Information*, unpublished manuscript, 28 June 2010, 8.
3. Ibid.
4. "The Good War and Those Who Refused to Fight It," PBS website, http://www.pbs.org/itvs/thegoodwar/timeline_01.html.
5. *History of Old Dominion Freight Line, Financial Information*, 24–25.
6. "A Conversation With Earl Congdon."
7. Ibid.
8. Ibid.
9. Eric Arnesen, *Encyclopedia of US Labor and Working-Class History*, (New York: Taylor & Francis Group, 2007), Vol. 1, 605.
10. "Teamsters Union," Encyclopedia Britannica website, http://www.britannica.com/EBchecked/topic/585238/Teamsters–Union.
11. *Encyclopedia of US Labor and Working-Class History*, 606.
12. *History of Old Dominion Freight Line, Financial Information*, 27.
13. Ibid., 12, 27.
14. *History of Old Dominion Freight Line, Financial Information*, 27.
15. Ibid.,12 and 29.
16. *A Conversation With Earl Congdon.*
17. Ibid.
18. Ibid.
19. *History of Old Dominion Freight Line, Financial Information*, 29.
20. Ibid.,12.
21. Ibid., 29.
22. Ibid.
23. Ibid., 27.
24. Ibid.
25. Ibid.
26. Ibid., 28.
27. Ibid., 12–13.
28. Ibid., 29.
29. *A Conversation With Earl Congdon.*
30. *History of Old Dominion Freight Line, Financial Information*, 28.
31. *A Conversation With Earl Congdon.*
32. Ibid.
33. *History of Old Dominion Freight Line, Financial Information*, 28–29.
34. Ibid., 29.
35. William Bien, "Woman Heads Freight Line," *Richmond News Leader*, 19 July 1954, 21.
36. *History of Old Dominion Freight Line, Financial Information*, 40–41.
37. Ibid., 30.
38. Ibid., 35.
39. Annual Report to the Interstate Commerce Commission, Old Dominion Freight Line corporate archives, 31 December 1944.
40. *History of Old Dominion Freight Line, Financial Information*, 36.
41. Annual Report to the Interstate Commerce Commission.
42. *History of Old Dominion Freight Line, Financial Information*, 36.
43. "What Things Cost in 1944," Television History—The First 75 Years website, http://www.tvhistory.tv/1944%20QF.htm.
44. "World War II Timeline: 1945," World War II History website, http://www.worldwariihistory.info/1945.html.
45. *History of Old Dominion Freight Line, Financial Information*, 38.
46. Ibid., 37.
47. Ibid., 37.
48. Earl Congdon, *History of Old Dominion Freight Line, Financial Information*, 38.
49. David E. Brown and Shepherd W. McKinley, *North Carolina: New Directions for an Old Land, An Illustrated History*, (Sun Valley, California: American Historical Press, 2006), 234.
50. *History of Old Dominion Freight Line, Financial Information*, 38.
51. Ibid., 38–39.
52. Ibid., 39.
53. Ibid.
54. Earl Congdon, interview by Jeffrey L. Rodengen, digital recording, 13 September 2010, Write Stuff Enterprises, LLC.
55. *History of Old Dominion Freight Line, Financial Information*, 35.
56. Ibid., 35–36.
57. Ibid., 41–42.
58. Ibid., 42–43.
59. Ibid., 42–43.
60. *A Conversation With Earl Congdon.*
61. Ibid.
62. Ibid.
63. *History of Old Dominion Freight Line, Financial Information*, 44.
64. Annual Report to the Interstate Commerce Commission, Old Dominion Freight Line corporate archives, 31 December 1948.
65. *History of Old Dominion Freight Line, Financial Information*, 45.
66. Earl Congdon, interview by Jeffrey L. Rodengen, digital recording, 12 July 2010, Write Stuff Enterprises, LLC.
67. *History of Old Dominion Freight Line, Financial Information*, 45.
68. Ibid., 46–47.
69. Ibid., 47.
70. Earl Congdon, *History of Old Dominion Freight Line, Financial Information*, 47.
71. Ibid., 48.
72. Ibid., 46.
73. Earl Congdon interview, 13 September 2010.
74. Ibid.

75. *History of Old Dominion Freight Line, Financial Information*, 53.
76. Earl Congdon interview, 13 September 2010.
77. *History of Old Dominion Freight Line, Financial Information*, 49.
78. *History of Old Dominion Freight Line, Financial Information*, 50; Annual Report to the Interstate Commerce Commission, Old Dominion Freight Line corporate archives, 31 December 1949.
79. *History of Old Dominion Freight Line, Financial Information*, 48.
80. Ibid, 50.

CHAPTER TWO SIDEBAR: Old Dominion's Early Branding Efforts

1. Earl Congdon, *History of Old Dominion Freight Line, Financial Information*, unpublished manuscript, 28 June 2010, 39.
2. Ibid.

CHAPTER TWO SIDEBAR: The Name "Old Dominion"

1. "The Commonwealth of Virginia," Netstate website, www.netstate.com/states/intro/va_intro.htm.
2. Ibid.

CHAPTER THREE

1. Earl Congdon, *A Conversation With Earl Congdon*, Foundation of Success series, DVD.
2. Earl Congdon, interview by Jeffrey L. Rodengen, digital recording, 12 July 2010, Write Stuff Enterprises, LLC; Earl Congdon, *History of Old Dominion Freight Line, Financial Information*, unpublished manuscript, 28 June 2010, 53.
3. Earl Congdon interview, 12 July 2010.
4. Ibid.
5. *History of Old Dominion Freight Line, Financial Information*, 54.
6. Ibid., 53–54.
7. Earl Congdon interview, 12 July 2010.
8. *History of Old Dominion Freight Line, Financial Information*, 54.
9. Earl Congdon interview, 12 July 2010.
10. Earl Congdon interview, 12 July 2010.
11. Ibid.
12. *International Trail*, Vol. 38, No. 3, 1968, 1.
13. *A Conversation With Earl Congdon.*
14. *History of Old Dominion Freight Line, Financial Information*, 54.
15. Ibid.
16. Earl Congdon, interview by Jeffrey L. Rodengen, digital recording, 13 July 2010, Write Stuff Enterprises, LLC.
17. Earl Congdon interview, 13 July 2010.
18. *History of Old Dominion Freight Line, Financial Information*, 55.
19. Ibid.
20. Ibid., 55–56.
21. Ibid.
22. Earl Congdon interview, 13 September 2010.
23. Ibid.
24. *History of Old Dominion Freight Line, Financial Information*, 56.
25. Ibid.
26. Ibid.
27. *A Conversation With Earl Congdon.*
28. Ibid.
29. *History of Old Dominion Freight Line, Financial Information*, 56.
30. Earl Congdon interview, 13 September 2010.
31. *History of Old Dominion Freight Line, Financial Information*, 57.
32. Ibid., 57.
33. Ibid., 59.
34. Ibid., 61.
35. Ibid., 62.
36. Ibid.
37. Ibid.
38. Ibid.
39. Ibid.
40. Ibid., 62–63.
41. Ibid., 63.
42. Ibid.
43. Ibid.
44. Ibid., 65.
45. Ibid., 61.
46. Ibid.
47. Ibid.
48. William Bien, "Woman Heads Freight Line," *Richmond News Leader*, 19 July 1954, 21.
49. Ibid.
50. *A Conversation With Earl Congdon.*
51. Ibid.
52. Ibid.
53. *History of Old Dominion Freight Line, Financial Information*, 67.
54. Ibid.
55. *International Trail*, 2.
56. Earl Congdon interview, 12 July 2010.
57. Ibid.
58. Ibid.
59. Ibid.
60. *History of Old Dominion Freight Line, Financial Information*, 67.
61. Earl Congdon interview, 12 July 2010.
62. *History of Old Dominion Freight Line, Financial Information*, 67.

CHAPTER THREE SIDEBAR: What Did Old Dominion Haul?

1. Earl Congdon, *History of Old Dominion Freight Line, Financial Information*, unpublished manuscript, 28 June 2010, 60.
2. Earl Congdon, interview by Jeffrey L. Rodengen, digital recording, 13 September 2010, Write Stuff Enterprises, LLC.
3. Ibid.
4. *History of Old Dominion Freight Line, Financial Information*, 60.

CHAPTER THREE SIDEBAR: Interline Trucking in the 1950s

1. Earl Congdon, *History of Old Dominion Freight Line, Financial Information*, unpublished manuscript, 28 June 2010, 59.

2. Earl Congdon, *History of Old Dominion Freight Line, Financial Information*, 59.
3. Ibid.

CHAPTER FOUR

1. Ray Hubbard, "Personality Profile: Earl Congdon of High Point," *High Point Enterprise*, 24 August 1969, 5.
2. Earl Congdon, *History of Old Dominion Freight Line, Financial Information*, unpublished manuscript, 28 June 2010, 70.
3. *History of Old Dominion Freight Line, Financial Information*, 70.
4. Earl Congdon, interview by Jeffrey L. Rodengen, digital recording,12 July 2010, Write Stuff Enterprises, LLC.
5. Earl Congdon, interview by Jeffrey L. Rodengen, digital recording, 13 September 2010, Write Stuff Enterprises, LLC.
6. *History of Old Dominion Freight Line, Financial Information*, 70.
7. Ibid., 71.
8. Ibid.
9. *History of Old Dominion Freight Line, Financial Information*, 71.
10. Earl Congdon interview, 13 September 2010.
11. Ibid.
12. Ibid.
13. Ibid.
14. *History of Old Dominion Freight Line, Financial Information*, 72.
15. Bob Hoover, interview by Jeffrey L. Rodengen, digital recording, 30 August 2011, Write Stuff Enterprises, LLC.
16. Earl Congdon interview, 13 September 2010.
17. Ibid.
18. *History of Old Dominion Freight Line, Financial Information*, 74.
19. Ibid., 75.
20. Earl Congdon interview, 13 September 2010.
21. Earl Congdon interview, 12 July 2010.
22. Ibid.
23. Earl Congdon interview, 13 September 2010.
24. *History of Old Dominion Freight Line, Financial Information*, 76.
25. "SBI Agents Arriving Here to Watch Trucker Strike," *High Point Enterprise*, 3 December 1959, Section C.
26. Earl Congdon interview, 13 September 2010.
27. *History of Old Dominion Freight Line, Financial Information*, 79.
28. Bob Hoover interview.
29. "SBI Agents Arriving Here to Watch Trucker Strike."
30. Earl Congdon interview, 13 September 2010.
31. "History of Violence at Strikebound Truck Line," undated newspaper article, Old Dominion Freight Line corporate archives.
32. Earl Congdon interview, 13 September 2010.
33. Ibid.
34. "Violence in Strike Everyone's Concern," *High Point Enterprise*, 30 December 1959.
35. Bob Hoover interview.
36. "Bundle on the Floor, Teamster Trademark," *High Point Enterprise*, 19 March 1960.
37. *History of Old Dominion Freight Line, Financial Information*, 80.
38. J. W. P. Mooney, "At Bottoms-Fiske, Strike Still Goes On after Year," *High Point Enterprise*, undated article, Old Dominion Freight Line corporate archives.
39. Earl Congdon interview, 13 September 2010.
40. "Bottoms-Fiske Strike Ends," *High Point Enterprise*, 1 March 1961, Section B.
41. *History of Old Dominion Freight Line, Financial Information*, 81.
42. Bottoms-Fiske Truck Lines, Report on Audit, prepared by A.M. Pullen & Co., CPA, 31 December 1960.
43. Ibid.
44. Joe Brown, "Business Notes," *High Point Enterprise*, undated article, Old Dominion Freight Line corporate archives.
45. Ibid.
46. Ibid.
47. Ibid.
48. Earl Congdon, interview by Jeffrey L. Rodengen, digital recording, 3 November 2010, Write Stuff Enterprises, LLC.
49. Ibid.
50. Ibid.
51. Earl Congdon interview, 13 September 2010.
52. Joann McMillan, interview by Jeffrey L. Rodengen, digital recording, 13 July, 2010, Write Stuff Enterprises, LLC.
53. "Report on Examination for the Year Ended December 31, 1962," Leach, Calkins & Scott, CPA, Old Dominion Freight Line corporate archives.
54. *History of Old Dominion Freight Line, Financial Information*, 83.
55. Ibid., 1.
56. *History of Old Dominion Freight Line, Financial Information*, 82.
57. "10,000 Miles of Trouble-Free Service," advertisement in *Fleet Owner*, June 1963.
58. Jack Congdon interview by Jeffrey L. Rodengen, digital recording, 22 September 2010, Write Stuff Enterprises, LLC.
59. Ibid.
60. Ibid.
61. Ibid.
62. *History of Old Dominion Freight Line, Financial Information*, 83–84.
63. "Report on Examination for the Year Ended December 31, 1964," Leach, Calkins & Scott, CPA, Old Dominion Freight Line corporate archives.
64. Report on Earl E. Congdon, Sadler & Associates, 11 February 1965, Old Dominion Freight Line corporate archives.
65. Ibid.

66. "Report on Examination of Financial Statements for the Year Ended December 31, 1966," Leach, Calkins & Scott, CPA, Old Dominion Freight Line corporate archives.
67. H. W. Marshall, letter to Earl Congdon, 3 April 1967.
68. "Old Dominion Freight Line Report on Survey," 20 February 1967, Old Dominion Freight Line corporate archives.
69. Ibid.
70. "Report on Examination of Financial Statements and Supplemental Data for the Year Ended December 31, 1969," Old Dominion Freight Line corporate archives; Old Dominion Freight Line Financial Statement, Old Dominion Freight Line corporate archives, 31 December 1968.
71. Earl Congdon interview, 13 September 2010.
72. *History of Old Dominion Freight Line, Financial Information*, 84.
73. Ibid., 85.
74. Ibid.
75. *History of Old Dominion Freight Line, Financial Information*, 87.
76. Earl Congdon interview, 13 September 2010.
77. *History of Old Dominion Freight Line, Financial Information*, 87.
78. Ibid., 86.
79. Ibid.
80. Ibid., 87.
81. Ibid.
82. Ibid., 85.
83. "Personality Profile: Earl Congdon of High Point."
84. Press Release, August 10, 1969, Old Dominion Freight Line corporate archives.
85. Earl Congdon interview, 13 September 2010.
86. "Report on Examination of Financial Statements and Supplemental Data, for the Year Ended December 31, 1969," Leach, Calkins & Scott, CPA, Old Dominion Freight Line corporate archives.

CHAPTER FOUR SIDEBAR: What is LTL Trucking?

1. "LTL Market Penetration," *Old Dominion Family*, August-September-October 1980, 9.
2. "Less Than Truckload Shipping," Wikipedia website, http://en.wikipedia.org/wiki/Less_than_truckload_shipping.

CHAPTER FIVE

1. David Congdon, interview by Jeffrey L. Rodengen, digital recording, 12 July 2010, Write Stuff Enterprises, LLC.
2. "Acquisition of Stock of Trucking Companies with Operating Authority," Old Dominion Freight Line corporate archives.
3. Earl Congdon, *History of Old Dominion Freight Line, Financial Information*, unpublished manuscript, 28 June 2010, 92.
4. *The Pacemaker*, Old Dominion Freight Line internal publication, October 1978, 2.
5. *History of Old Dominion Freight Line, Financial Information*, 87.
6. Earl Congdon, interview by Jeffrey L. Rodengen, digital recording, 12 July 2010, Write Stuff Enterprises, LLC.
7. *History of Old Dominion Freight Line, Financial Information*, 88.
8. *History of Old Dominion Freight Line, Financial Information*, 89.
9. Earl Congdon interview, 12 July 2010.
10. *History of Old Dominion Freight Line, Financial Information*, 88.
11. Earl Congdon, interview by Jeffrey L. Rodengen, digital recording, 3 November 2010, Write Stuff Enterprises, LLC.
12. "Congdon is New Prexy of Group," *High Point Enterprise*, 21 September 1971, B1.
13. Holt McPherson, "Good Afternoon," *High Point Enterprise*, 28 September 1971, 4A.
14. David Congdon interview.
15. Ibid.
16. Ibid.
17. Ibid.
18. Ibid.
19 Earl Congdon interview, 3 November 2010.
20. Ibid.
21. Ibid.
22. *History of Old Dominion Freight Line, Financial Information*, 89.
23. Fourth Floor Conference Posters, 7 December 1995, Old Dominion Freight Line corporate archives.
24. *History of Old Dominion Freight Line, Financial Information*, 89.
25. Earl Congdon, interview by Jeffrey L. Rodengen, digital recording, 13 September 2010, Write Stuff Enterprises, LLC.
26. *History of Old Dominion Freight Line, Financial Information*, 89.
27. Ibid., 90.
28. Earl Congdon, letter to Henry Marshall, 20 November 1974.
29. Earl Congdon, letter to Henry Marshall, 20 June 1974.
30. Old Dominion Freight Line Financial Statement, Old Dominion Freight Line corporate archives, 31 December 1974, 2.
31. Old Dominion Freight Line Financial Statement, corporate archives, Old Dominion Freight Line corporate archives, 31 December 1975, 2.
32. Ernie Benge, interview by Jeffrey L. Rodengen, digital recording, 13 July 2010, Write Stuff Enterprises, LLC.
33. Earl Congdon, letter to members of the Executive Profit Sharing Program, Old Dominion Freight Line corporate archives, 21 July 1975.
34. Old Dominion Freight Line Financial Statement, Old Dominion Freight Line corporate archives, 30 November 1976.

35. *History of Old Dominion Freight Line, Financial Information*, 90.
36. Earl Congdon interview, 12 July 2010.
37. *History of Old Dominion Freight Line, Financial Information*, 91.
38. Ibid., 91–92.
39. Ibid., 99.
40. Ibid., 100.
41. Ibid., 100.
42. "Acquisition of Stock of Trucking Companies With Operating Authority," 3.
43. Earl Congdon interview, 13 September 2010.
44. Earl Congdon interview, 12 July 2010.
45. Ibid.
46. Earl Congdon interview, 13 September 2010.
47. Ibid.
48. Earl Congdon interview, 12 July 2010.
49. David Congdon interview.
50. Ibid.
51. Ibid.
52. Ibid.
53. Ibid.
54. Ibid.
55. *History of Old Dominion Freight Line, Financial Information*, 93.
56. "Acquisition of Stock of Trucking Companies With Operating Authority," 16.
57. *History of Old Dominion Freight Line, Financial Information*, 93–94.
58. Earl Congdon interview, 13 September 2010.
59. "Acquisition of Stock of Trucking Companies with Operating Authority," 19.
60. *History of Old Dominion Freight Line, Financial Information*, 93; Earl Congdon interview, 12 July 2010.
61. *History of Old Dominion Freight Line, Financial Information*, 93.
62. "Where the Missing Truck Freight is Going," *BusinessWeek*, 24 December 1979.
63. Ibid.
64. Annual Report to the Interstate Commerce Commission, Old Dominion Freight Line corporate archives, 31 December 1979, 11.

CHAPTER FIVE SIDEBAR: Making It Work

1. Brian Stoddard, interview by Jeffrey L. Rodengen, digital recording, 14 July 2010, Write Stuff Enterprises, LLC.
2. Ernie Benge, interview by Jeffrey L. Rodengen, digital recording, 13 July 2010, Write Stuff Enterprises, LLC.

CHAPTER FIVE SIDEBAR: Keeping Pace with Vehicle Maintenance

1. *The Pacemaker*, Old Dominion Freight Line internal publication, 1977, 2.
2. *The Pacemaker*, Old Dominion Freight Line internal publication, undated clipping, 2.
3. Ibid.
4. Ibid.
5. Ibid.

CHAPTER SIX

1. Buddy McBride, interview by Jeffrey L. Rodengen, digital recording, 13 July 2010, Write Stuff Enterprises, LLC.
2. Earl Congdon, interview by Jeffrey L. Rodengen, digital recording, 13 September 2010, Write Stuff Enterprises, LLC.
3. Earl Congdon, *History of Old Dominion Freight Line, Financial Information*, unpublished manuscript, 28 June 2010, 95.
4. Ibid.
5. Ibid., 95–96.
6. "Motor Carrier Act of 1980," Reference.com website, http://www.reference.com/browse/Motor_Carrier_Act_of_1980.
7. Ibid.
8. Earl Congdon, interview by Jeffrey L. Rodengen, digital recording, 12 July 2010, Write Stuff Enterprises, LLC.
9. Ibid.
10. Ibid.
11. Earl Congdon, Speech to the Triangle Traffic Club in Durham, North Carolina, on 4 September 1980, printed in *Old Dominion Family*, August-September-October 1980, 8.
12. Earl Congdon, "Deregulation Speech," Rowan Traffic and Transportation Club, Salisbury, North Carolina, 10 April 1980.
13. "Kennedy Joins Carter in the Rose Garden," *Ironwood Daily Globe*, 1 July 1980.
14. "Trucking Industry Faces Huge Losses This Year," *Winchester Star*, 23 October 1980, 25.
15. Thomas Corsi, Curtis M. Grimm, and Jane Feitler, "The Impact of Deregulation on LTL Motor Carriers: Size, Structure, and Organization," *Transportation Journal*, Winter 1992.
16. Earl Congdon interview, 13 September 2010.
17. Ibid.
18. *History of Old Dominion Freight Line, Financial Information*, 98.
19. Earl Congdon interview, 12 July 2010.
20. *History of Old Dominion Freight Line, Financial Information*, 100.
21. Earl Congdon interview, 12 July 2010.
22. Jim Galligan, "ATA Special," *Commercial Car Journal*, undated clipping.
23. Mike Wood, interview by Jeffrey L. Rodengen, digital recording, 13 July 2010, Write Stuff Enterprises, LLC.
24. John Yowell, interview by Jeffrey L. Rodengen, digital

recording, 12 July 2010, Write Stuff Enterprises, LLC.
25. Earl Congdon, "Message from the President," *Old Dominion Family*, August 1980, 1.
26. *History of Old Dominion Freight Line, Financial Information*, 98.
27. Earl Congdon, "Message from the President," *Old Dominion Family*, April 1980, 1.
28. Earl Congdon, "Message from the President," *Old Dominion Family*, June 1980, 1.
29. Annual Report to the Interstate Commerce Commission, Old Dominion Freight Line corporate archives, 31 December 1980.
30. Ibid.
31. Earl Congdon, interview by Jeffrey L. Rodengen, digital recording, 13 July 2010, Write Stuff Enterprises, LLC.
32. Earl Congdon, "Message from the President," *Old Dominion Family*, August-September-October 1980, 1.
33. Earl Congdon, letter to all employees, Old Dominion Freight Line corporate archives, 22 December 1981.
34. *History of Old Dominion Freight Line, Financial Information*, 98.
35. Ibid.
36. Earl Congdon, "Message from the President," *Old Dominion Family*, Winter 1981, 1.
37. Ibid.
38. David Congdon, interview by Jeffrey L. Rodengen, digital recording, 13 July 2010, Write Stuff Enterprises, LLC.
39. Earl Congdon, "Message from the President," *Old Dominion Family*, Spring 1982, 1.
40. James T. Gregerson, letter to Earl Congdon, 5 January 1982.
41. Earl Congdon, "Message from the President," *Old Dominion Family*, Summer 1982, 1.
42. David Penley, interoffice correspondence with Earl Congdon, Old Dominion Freight Line corporate archives, 5 June 1981.
43. "Message from the President," Summer 1982, 1.
44. Charlie Lehman, "Old Dominion on 'Exciting' Roll," *High Point Enterprise*, 18 September 1983, B1.
45. "Message from the President," Summer 1982, 1.
46. Ibid.
47. Ibid.
48. *History of Old Dominion Freight Line, Financial Information*, 101.
49. "Old Dominion on 'Exciting' Roll."
50. Ibid.
51. Earl Congdon, "Message from the President," *Old Dominion Family*, Winter 1983–1984, 1.
52. "Old Dominion on 'Exciting' Roll."
53. Thomas J. Donohue, letter to American Trucking Association members, 15 October 1984; Gaylord Shaw, "Old Dominion Freight Line," *Business North Carolina*, June 1984, 37.
54. "Old Dominion Executives Take to the Road," *Old Dominion Family*, Winter 1983–1984, 1.
55. "Old Dominion Freight Line."
56. Ibid.
57. "Old Dominion Executives Take to the Road," Winter 1983–1984, 1.
58. Ibid.
59. Earl Congdon, "Message From the President," *Old Dominion Family*, Spring-Summer 1984, 1.
60. Earl Congdon interview, 12 July 2010.
61. Ibid.
62. Earl Congdon, "Message from the President," *Old Dominion Family*, Fall 1984, 1.
63. Earl Congdon interview, 12 July 2010.
64. Ibid.
65. Jim Gregerson, letter to Earl Congdon and Bill Carpenter, 10 May 1984.
66. Earl Congdon interview, 12 July 2010.
67. Ibid.
68. Charles Lehman, "Old Dominion Cuts Staff Following Profit Drop," *High Point Enterprise*, 21 June 1985.
69. Ibid.
70. Ibid.
71. *History of Old Dominion Freight Line, Financial Information*, 96.
72. Lynn Daniel, "Rapid Transport Restructuring Study," report to Earl Congdon, John Ebeling, and Doug Slate, 8 November 1985.
73. Earl Congdon, *History of Old Dominion Freight Line, Financial Information*, 96.
74. *History of Old Dominion Freight Line, Financial Information*, 96.
75. Earl Congdon interview, 12 July 2010.
76. Ibid.
77. Ibid.
78. Ibid.
79. Ibid.
80. John Yowell interview, 12 July, 2010.
81. Ibid.
82. Earl Congdon, interview by Jeffrey L. Rodengen, digital recording, 3 November 2010, Write Stuff Enterprises, LLC.
83. Ibid.
84. Ibid.
85. Earl Congdon interview, 12 July 2010.
86. Ibid.
87. Ibid.
88. Ibid.
89. David Congdon interview, 12 July 2010.
90. Earl Congdon interview, 12 July 2010.
91. Ibid.
92. Buddy McBride interview.
93. Earl Congdon interview, 12 July 2010.
94. Ibid.
95. Buddy McBride interview.

96. Earl Congdon interview, 12 July 2010.
97. Ibid.
98. David Congdon interview.
99. Earl Congdon interview, 12 July 2010.
100. Buddy McBride interview.
101. Earl Congdon interview, 12 July 2010.
102. Buddy McBride interview.
103. David Congdon interview.
104. Ibid.
105. "Total Quality Management," American Society for Quality website, http://asq.org/learn-about-quality/total-quality-management/overview/overview.html.
106. David Congdon interview.
107. Ibid.

CHAPTER SIX SIDEBAR: Operating in the Wake of the Energy Crisis

1. "Fuel?? Fuel Mileage!," *Old Dominion Family*, February 1981, 7.
2. Ibid.
3. Ibid.
4. Ibid.
5. Ibid.

CHAPTER SIX SIDEBAR: Keeping Tire Expenses in Check

1. "Our Tire Program—A Combined Effort," *Old Dominion Family*, August 1980, 1.
2. Ibid.
3. Ibid.
4. Ibid.
5. Ibid.

CHAPTER SEVEN

1. John Yowell, interview by Jeffrey L. Rodengen, digital recording, 12 July 2010, Write Stuff Enterprises, LLC.
2. Earl Congdon, "Message From Our Chairman," *Old Dominion Family*, Spring 1988, 1.
3. Earl Congdon, interview by Jeffrey L. Rodengen, digital recording, 3 November 2010, Write Stuff Enterprises, LLC.
4. John Ebeling, "The President's Comments," *Old Dominion Family*, Spring 1989, 1.
5. Ibid.
6. Earl Congdon interview, 3 November 2010.
7. David Congdon, interview by Jeffrey L. Rodengen, digital recording, 12 July 2010, Write Stuff Enterprises, LLC.
8. Ibid.
9. Ibid.
10. Ibid.
11. Ibid.
12. Nicholas Brown, "High Point Trucking Firm Looks to Future," *Greensboro News & Record*, 7 August 1989.
13. Ibid.
14. Patricia Cavanaugh, "Tough End to a Tough Decade," *Transport Topics*, 13 August 1990, 25.
15. Earl Congdon, "Message From Our Chairman," *Old Dominion Family*, Summer 1989, 1.
16. Barbara Rudolph and Bernard Baumohl, "No Joyride in 1989," *TIME*, 9 January 1989.
17. Timothy Curry and Lynn Shibut, "The Cost of the Savings and Loan Crisis: Truth and Consequences," FDIC website, http://www.fdic.gov/bank/analytical/banking/2000dec/brv13n2_2.pdf.
18. John Ebeling, "The President's Comments," *Old Dominion Family*, Spring 1990, 1.
19. Ibid.
20. Ibid., 2.
21. Ibid.
22. Earl Congdon interview, 3 November 2010 .
23. Ibid.
24. "Old Dominion Freight Line, A History of Excellence," brochure, Old Dominion Freight Line corporate archives, 3.
25. Earl Congdon, "Family Article," *Old Dominion Family*, Winter 1991, 1.
26. Earl Congdon, "Family Article," *Old Dominion Family*, Summer 1991, 1.
27. Earl Congdon, interview by Jeffrey L. Rodengen, digital recording, 12 July 2010, Write Stuff Enterprises, LLC.
28. Ibid.
29. Old Dominion Freight Line, Common Stock, 24 October 1991, 11.
30. Earl Congdon interview, 3 November 2010.
31. David Congdon interview.
32. Earl Congdon interview, 3 November 2010.
33. David Congdon interview.
34. Ibid.
35. "2,000,000,000 Shares, Old Dominion Freight Line Inc. Common Stock," stock offering document, Alex. Brown & Sons, 24 October 1991, 1.
36. Jack Scism, "Non-Union Shop Credited for Success," *Greensboro News & Record*, 24 November 1991, E1.
37. Ibid.
38. Pearce W. Hammond, "North Carolina Fleet Reaps Rewards from Successful Business Strategies," *Southern Motor Cargo*, December 1993, 10.
39. "Steering Wheels," *Business North Carolina*, August 2003, 40.
40. John Ebeling, "President's Comments," *Old Dominion Family*, Spring 1992, 1.
41. Joel McCarty, interview by Jeffrey L. Rodengen, digital recording, 13 July 2010, Write Stuff Enterprises, LLC.
42. Earl Congdon interview, 3 November 2010.
43. "Old Dominion Freight Line, Inc. Announces Record 1991

Earnings From Continuing Operations of 90 Cents Per Share," Business Wire, 24 February 1992.
44. John Ebeling, "President's Comments," *Old Dominion Family*, Spring 1992, 1.
45. Ibid.
46. "Forbes Ranks Old Dominion Freight Line Among 200 Best Small Companies in America," Business Wire, 9 November 1992.
47. "North Carolina Fleet Reaps Rewards From Successful Business Strategies," 10.
48. Karl F. Kunkel, "Old Dominion Survives Deregulation," *Triad Business News*, 13–19 July 1992, 5–6.
49. Ibid.
50. Ibid.
51. "North Carolina Fleet Reaps Rewards From Successful Business Strategies," 10.
52. Ibid.
53. Earl Congdon, "Family Article," *Old Dominion Family*, Spring 1993, 1.
54. David Congdon interview.
55. Earl Congdon, "Family Article," *Old Dominion Family*, Spring 1993, 1.
56. Deena C. Knight, "The Road Less Traveled," *Business Life*, October 1993, 14.
57. "North Carolina Fleet Reaps Rewards From Successful Business Strategies," 13.
58. David Congdon interview.
59. Old Dominion Freight Line 1993 Annual Report, 2.
60. Ibid., 3.
61. "North Carolina Fleet Reaps Rewards From Successful Business Strategies," 15.
62. Earl Congdon, "In Memoriam," *Old Dominion Family*, Winter 1993.
63. Ibid.
64. Ibid.

CHAPTER SEVEN SIDEBAR: Error-Free Work

1. Earl Congdon, "Message From Our Chairman," *Old Dominion Family*, Spring 1988, 1.
2. "EFW = $2,5000,000 in Profits in 1988," *Old Dominion Family*, Spring 1988, 2.
3. Ibid.
4. Ibid.
5. Ernie Benge, interview by Jeffrey L. Rodengen, digital recording, 13 July 2010, Write Stuff Enterprises, LLC.

CHAPTER SEVEN SIDEBAR: Old Dominion's Truck Driver Training School

1. Brian Stoddard, interview by Jeffrey L. Rodengen, digital recording, 14 July 2010, Write Stuff Enterprises, LLC.
2. Ibid.
3. Ibid.
4. "Old Dominion Starts Truck Driver Training School for Dock Employees," *Old Dominion Family*, Winter 1988, 20.
5. Brian Stoddard interview.
6. Ibid.
7. Ibid.

CHAPTER EIGHT

1. Greg Gantt, interview by Jeffrey L. Rodengen, digital recording, 2 August 2011, Write Stuff Enterprises, LLC.
2. Kevin McKenzie, "Shippers Find Nonunion, Other Alternatives During Truck Strike," *Commercial Appeal*, 17 April 1994, 1C.
3. "Revenue Up, Income Down at Old Dominion Freight," *News & Record*, 22 April 1994, B7.
4. John Ebeling, "A New Era," *Old Dominion Family*, Summer 1994, 1.
5. Earl Congdon, "Message From Our Chairman," *Old Dominion Family*, Winter 1994, 1.
6. "Employee Survey 1993," *Family Newsline*, 18 March 1994, 2.
7. Ibid.
8. Ibid.
9. "Improvements Focused on Claims, P&D, Dock & Line-Haul Efficiency," *Family Newsline*, July 1994, 1.
10. "Old Dominion Freight Line Reports 21.2 Percent Earnings Per Share Growth to $1.20 Per Share for 1994; Fourth Quarter EPS Triples," Business Wire, 26 January 1995.
11. Earl Congdon, "Growth in 1995 Leads to A Better Year in 1996," *Family Newsline*, December 1995, 1.
12. Earl Congdon, "Message From Our Chairman," *Old Dominion Family*, Winter 1994, 1.
13. Chris Isidore, "2 Trucking Firms Buck the System with Streamlined Rate Structures," *Journal of Commerce*, 29 March 1995, 3B.
14. Ibid.
15. John Ebeling, "A Word From Management," *Family Newsline*, February 1995; Earl Congdon, interview by Jeffrey L. Rodengen, digital recording, 13 September 2010, Write Stuff Enterprises, LLC.
16. Rick Keeler, "Western Area Expansion," *Family Newsline*, October 1995, 1.
17. Ibid.
18. Ibid.
19. John Ebeling, "Positioning Old Dominion to be a Major Player in the Future," *Family Newsline*, August 1995, 1.
20. Ibid.
21. Jennifer Fron, "Hard-Hit Truck Lines Expect Lower Income," *Denver Post*, 17 October 1995, C03.
22. Ibid.

23. Chris Isidore, "Old Dominion Sees 2nd Quarter Results Down Significantly," *Journal of Commerce*, 5 June 1995, 2B.
24. *Old Dominion Freight Line Inc. GuideBook 1996*, (North Carolina: Old Dominion Freight Line, 1996), 5.
25. Old Dominion Freight Line 1995 Annual Report, 1.
26. Earl Congdon, "Growth in 1995 Leads to A Better Year in 1996," *Family Newsline*, December 1995, 1.
27. Greg Gantt, "Old Dominion Expanding into 1996," *Family Newsline*, March 1996, 1.
28. Chris Isidore, "Nonunion Truckers Move onto Bumpy Road," *Journal of Commerce*, 5 January 1996, 1A.
29. Chris Isidore, "Rising Diesel Prices Hit Carriers, 18 Shippers," *Journal of Commerce*, September 1996, 1B.
30. John Ebeling, "Driving Into the 21st Century," *Family Newsline*, June 1996, 1.
31. John Ebeling, "Plans for Growth Continue," *Family Newsline*, June 1997, 1.
32. David Congdon, interview by Jeffrey L. Rodengen, digital recording, 12 July 2010, Write Stuff Enterprises, LLC.
33. L. B. Clayton, interview by Jeffrey L. Rodengen, digital recording, 13 July 2010, Write Stuff Enterprises, LLC.
34. David Congdon, interview by Jeffrey L. Rodengen, digital recording, 16 September 2010, Write Stuff Enterprises, LLC.
35. John Larkin, interview by Jeffrey L. Rodengen, digital recording, 14 September 2010, Write Stuff Enterprises, LLC.
36. Ibid.
37. David Congdon interview.
38. Chip Overbey, interview by Jeffrey L. Rodengen, digital recording, 10 August 2011, Write Stuff Enterprises, LLC.
39. David Congdon interview.
40. Ibid.
41. Rick Keeler, interview by Jeffrey L. Rodengen, digital recording, 15 August 2011, Write Stuff Enterprises, LLC.
42. Chip Overbey, interview by Jeffrey L. Rodengen, digital recording, 25 February 2011, Write Stuff Enterprises, LLC.
43. Terry Hutchins, interview by Jeffrey L. Rodengen, digital recording, 14 July 2010, Write Stuff Enterprises, LLC.
44. Ibid.
45. David Congdon interview.
46. Ibid.
47. Terry Hutchins interview.
48. "The Quest for Transportation's Best," *Distribution*, August 1997.
49. David Congdon interview.
50. Ibid.
51. John Downey, "Dominion Over New Territory," *Triad Business News*, 11 July 1997, 1.
52. *Old Dominion Freight Line Inc. GuideBook 1998*, (North Carolina: Old Dominion Freight Line, 1998), 5.
53. Daniel P. Bearth, "Old Dominion to Buy Assets of Goggin TL," *Transport Topics*, 10 August 1998, 61.
54. David Congdon interview.
55. Ibid.
56. David Congdon interview.
57. David Congdon, "Goggin Asset Acquisition," *Family Newsline*, Fall 1998, 1.
58. Ibid.
59. Rick Keeler interview.
60. David Congdon, "Our Accomplishments," *Family Newsline*, Fall 1999, 1.
61. Ibid.
62. Ted Reed, "Truck Line Looking Good," *Charlotte Observer*, undated newspaper clipping.
63. Ibid.
64. Ibid.
65. Ibid.

CHAPTER EIGHT SIDEBAR: Maintaining Driver Relationships

1. David Congdon, interview by Jeffrey L. Rodengen, digital recording, 12 July 2010, Write Stuff Enterprises, LLC.
2. Ibid.
3. Cornell Brenson, interview by Jeffrey L. Rodengen, digital recording, 15 September 2010, Write Stuff Enterprises, LLC.
4. Cornell Brenson interview.
5. Ibid.
6. Richard Craver, "Truck Driver Going Strong After 51 Years," *High Point Enterprise*," undated newspaper clipping.
7. Cornell Brenson interview.
8. Ibid.
9. Ibid.
10. "Truck Driver Going Strong After 51 Years," 1A.

CHAPTER EIGHT SIDEBAR: Integrating Acquisitions

1. Mike Wood, interview by Jeffrey L. Rodengen, digital recording, 13 July 2010, Write Stuff Enterprises, LLC.
2. Bill Cranfill, interview by Jeffrey L. Rodengen, digital recording, 14 July 2010, Write Stuff Enterprises, LLC.
3. Leo Suggs, interview by Jeffrey L. Rodengen, digital recording, 17 September 2010, Write Stuff Enterprises, LLC.
4. David Congdon, interview by Jeffrey L. Rodengen, digital recording, 12 July 2010, Write Stuff Enterprises, LLC.
5. David Congdon, interview by Jeffrey L. Rodengen, digital recording, 16 September 2010, Write Stuff Enterprises, LLC.
6. Ibid.

CHAPTER NINE

1. Marty Freeman, interview by Jeffrey L. Rodengen, digital

recording, 13 July 2010, Write Stuff Enterprises, LLC.
2. David Congdon, "Our Accomplishments," *Family Newsline*, Fall 1999, 1.
3. Greg Gantt, "Morristown Up & Rolling," *Family Newsline*, Spring 2000, 1.
4. David Congdon, interview by Jeffrey L. Rodengen, digital recording, 16 September 2010, Write Stuff Enterprises, LLC.
5. David Congdon, "A Banner Year Beckons Us," *Family Newsline*, Spring 2000, 1.
6. Earl Congdon, "Strengthening Our Position for the New Economy and the New Year," *Family Newsline*, Winter 2000, 1.
7. Marty Freeman interview.
8. Ibid.
9. "Our Accomplishments," 1.
10. Sam A. Hieb, "Keep on Trucking," *Triad Business News*, 15 June 2001, 14.
11. "Old Dominion Freight Line Expects Fourth Quarter Earnings of $0.28 to $0.32 Per Share, Cites Unusually Harsh Winter Weather and Slowing Economy," Business Wire, 11 January 2001.
12. Mark Binker, "Old Dominion Moving Offices to Thomasville; The Trucking Company Will Buy the Former Bassett Showroom," *Greensboro News & Record*, 15 November 2000, A1.
13. "Strengthening Our Position for the New Economy and the New Year," 1.
14. "Keep on Trucking," 14.
15. Richard Craver, "Carrying on Innovation And Astute Leadership Are Keeping Old Dominion Moving Through Perilous Times," *Winston-Salem Journal*, 7 September 2003, D1.
16. "Keep on Trucking," 14.
17. Ibid.
18. Ibid.
19. Jon Denton, "Old Dominion Buys Carter & Sons Freightways," *Daily Oklahoman*, 16 February 2001.
20. David Congdon interview, 16 September 2010.
21. "It's Official: 2001 Recession Only Lasted Eight Months," *USA Today*, 17 July 2003.
22. David Congdon interview, 16 September 2010.
23. "Keep on Trucking," 14.
24. David Congdon interview, 16 September 2010.
25. Ibid.
26. David Congdon interview, 16 September 2010.
27. Greg Gantt, interview by Jeffrey L. Rodengen, digital recording, 2 August 2011, Write Stuff Enterprises, LLC.
28. "Old Dominion Freight Posts Fourth-Quarter Income Gains," *Winston-Salem Journal*, 21 January 2003, D1.
29. David Congdon, "2002 Performance," *Family Newsline*, Spring 2003, 3.
30. Richard Craver, "Old Dominion Revs Up Stock Offering," *High Point Enterprise*, 11 October 2002, 7C.
31. Ibid.
32. "2002 Performance," 3.
33. Edward Martin, "Steering Wheels," *Business North Carolina*, August 2003, 40.
34. Ibid.
35. Ibid.
36. Chip Overbey, interview by Jeffrey L. Rodengen, digital recording, 2 August 2011, Write Stuff Enterprises, LLC.
37. "Steering Wheels," 47.
38. "2002 Performance," 3.
39. "Steering Wheels," 47.
40. Ibid., 48.
41. "Carrying on Innovation And Astute Leadership Are Keeping Old Dominion Moving Through Perilous Times," D1.
42. Richard Craver, "Road to Recovery: Economic Rebound Is Putting Load on Trucking Companies," *Winston-Salem Journal*, 25 June 2004, D1.
43. Ibid.
44. Amy Dominello, "Officials: Freight Will Drive Economy; Leaders Say the Triad is an Ideal Place for Regional Hubs and Distribution Centers," *Greensboro News & Record*, 16 December 2004, B1.
45. Sam Faucette, interview by Jeffrey L. Rodengen, digital recording, 13 September 2010, Write Stuff Enterprises, LLC.
46. "FMCSA Issues Final Rule on Drivers Hours of Service," Wisconsin Movers Association website, http://www.wismovers.org/Final_rule_HOS.htm.
47. Ed Richardson, interview by Jeffrey L. Rodengen, digital recording, 14 July 2010, Write Stuff Enterprises, LLC.
48. Marty Freeman interview.
49. Jeanne Sturiale, "Business Milestones," *Winston-Salem Journal*, 27 March 2005, B8.
50. "Old Dominion 4Q and 2006 Earnings Come in Strong with a Favorable Tax Rate and Fewer Claims," Associated Press, 1 February 2007.
51. "Old Dominion Trucking Line to Buy Wichita Southeast," *Winston-Salem Journal*, 5 January 2005, D1.
52. David Congdon interview, 16 September 2010.

CHAPTER NINE SIDEBAR: How September 11, 2001, Changed the Trucking Industry

1. John Yowell, interview by Jeffrey L. Rodengen, digital recording, 12 July 2010, Write Stuff Enterprises, LLC.
2. David Congdon, speech to American Red Cross, 18 October 2001.
3. Ibid.

4. David Congdon, interview by Jeffrey L. Rodengen, digital recording, 16 September 2010, Write Stuff Enterprises, LLC.
5. Stan Choe and Ted Reed, "Employers Respond to Alert; Workers Told to Look at Need for Travel," *Charlotte Observer*, 19 March 2003, 1D.

CHAPTER NINE SIDEBAR: Husband and Wife Driver Teams

1. Stan DeLozier, "Trucking Teamwork; Freight Lines Favor Husband-Wife Duos," *Knoxville News-Sentinel*, 18 February 2000, B1.
2. "Team Players," Overdrive Online website, http://www.overdriveonline.com/team-players.
3. "Trucking Teamwork; Freight Lines Favor Husband-Wife Duos," *Knoxville News-Sentinel*, 18 February 2000, B1.
4. Ibid.
5. Ibid.
6. Ibid.

CHAPTER TEN

1. Joel McCarty, interview by Jeffrey L. Rodengen, digital recording, 13 July 2010, Write Stuff Enterprises, LLC.
2. "Old Dominion Freight Line Signs Definitive Agreement to Purchase UW Freight Line," Business Wire, 17 January 2006.
3. Ibid.
4. David Congdon, interview by Jeffrey L. Rodengen, digital recording, 16 September 2010, Write Stuff Enterprises, LLC.
5. Trang Ho, "Old Dominion Opens 16 New Centers in Q1," *Investor's Business Daily*, 23 May 2006, B08.
6. "Old Dominion Opens More Service Centers," *Business Journal*, 25 July 2006.
7. "Old Dominion Named As One of 100 Best," *Business Journal*, 14 August 2006.
8. "Old Dominion Named One of Nation's Fastest-Growing Companies," *Business Journal*, 31 May 2006.
9. "Triad Companies Among the Nation's Largest," *Business Journal*, 20 September 2007.
10. David Congdon interview, 16 September 2010.
11. "Old Dominion Sees Double-Digit Profit Gains," *Business Journal*, 1 February 2007.
12. "Old Dominion Freight Line Eyes Growth Through Acquisitions and Expanding Segments," Associated Press, 27 June 2007.
13. "Old Dominion Freight Line Signs Definitive Agreement to Purchase Assets of Priority Freight Lines," Business Wire, 17 April 2007.
14. David Congdon interview, 16 September 2010.
15. Ibid.
16. "Old Dominion to Buy Colorado Freight Carrier," *Business Journal*, 11 December 2007.
17. David Congdon interview, 16 September 2010.
18. "Old Dominion Builds New Dallas Terminal," *Business Journal*, 24 April 2007.
19. Laura Youngs, "Old Dominion to Expand Through Logistics, Service Centers," *Business Journal*, 19 November 2007.
20. Michelle Cater Rash, "Old Dominion to Start Service Into China Next Month," *Business Journal*, 19 March 2007.
21. Michelle Cater Rash, "Old Dominion to Start Service into China Next Month," *Business Journal*, 19 March 2007.
22. Laura Youngs, "Going Global: David Congdon," *Business Journal*, 7 January 2008.
23. David Congdon interview, 16 September 2010.
24. Greg Plemmons, interview by Jeffrey L. Rodengen, digital recording, 16 September 2010, Write Stuff Enterprises, LLC.
25. "Old Dominion Freight Line Names David Congdon President and Chief Executive Officer Effective January 1, 2008," Business Wire, 5 November 2007.
26. Ibid.
27. "Old Dominion Freight Line Signs Definitive Agreement to Purchase Montana-based Bob's Pickup & Delivery," Business Wire, 11 February 2008.
28. "Old Dominion Profits Fall 30 Percent in Q4," *Business Journal*, 29 January 2009.
29. Marty Freeman, interview by Jeffrey L. Rodengen, digital recording, 13 July 2010, Write Stuff Enterprises, LLC.
30. Ibid.
31. William B. Cassidy, "LTL Carriers Rebuild," *Journal of Commerce*, 15 March 2010.
32. David Congdon interview, 16 September 2010.
33. Ibid.
34. Leo Suggs, interview by Jeffrey L. Rodengen, digital recording, 17 September 2010, Write Stuff Enterprises, LLC.
35. Thom Albrecht, interview by Jeffrey L. Rodengen, digital recording, 17 September 2010, Write Stuff Enterprises, LLC.
36. Mike Wood, interview by Jeffrey L. Rodengen, digital recording, 13 July 2010, Write Stuff Enterprises, LLC.
37. Ibid.
38. Matt Nowell, interview by Jeffrey L. Rodengen, digital recording, 23 September 2010, Write Stuff Enterprises, LLC.
39. David Carter, interview by Jeffrey L. Rodengen, digital recording, 16 February 2011, Write Stuff Enterprises, LLC.
40. Marty Freeman interview.
41. Ibid.

42. Ibid.
43. "Old Dominion Freight Line, Inc. President and CEO to Ring the NASDAQ Stock Market Closing Bell," Globe Newswire, 16 November 2009.
44. David Congdon interview, 16 September 2010.
45. Old Dominion Freight Line 2009 Annual Report, 8.
46. Ibid, 2.
47. William B. Cassidy, "LTL Carriers Rebuild," *Journal of Commerce*, 15 March 2010.
48. Marty Freeman interview.
49. Ibid.
50. Ed Richardson, interview by Jeffrey L. Rodengen, digital recording, 14 July 2010, Write Stuff Enterprises, LLC.
51. Ibid.
52. Ibid.
53. Ibid.
54. "Old Dominion Recognized as ASE Certified Training Provider," PR Newswire, 31 March 2010.
55. Ed Richardson, interview by Jeffrey L. Rodengen, digital recording, 14 July 2010, Write Stuff Enterprises, LLC.
56. Ed Richardson interview.
57. Mark Penley interview.
58. Ibid.
59. Dave Heaton, interview by Jeffrey L. Rodengen, digital recording, 13 July 2010, Write Stuff Enterprises, LLC.
60. Ibid.
61. Ibid.
62. Ernie Benge, interview by Jeffrey L. Rodengen, digital recording, 13 July 2010, Write Stuff Enterprises, LLC.
63. Ed Richardson interview.
64. Terry Hutchins, interview by Jeffrey L. Rodengen, digital recording, 14 July 2010, Write Stuff Enterprises, LLC.
65. Joann McMillan, interview by Jeffrey L. Rodengen, digital recording, 13 July 2010, Write Stuff Enterprises, LLC.
66. Doug Ball, interview by Jeffrey L. Rodengen, digital recording, 1 October 2010, Write Stuff Enterprises, LLC.
67. Ed Wolfe, interview by Jeffrey L. Rodengen, digital recording, 17 September 2010, Write Stuff Enterprises, LLC.
68. Karen Dillman, interview by Jeffrey L. Rodengen, digital recording, 14 September 2010, Write Stuff Enterprises, LLC.
69. Greg Gantt, interview by Jeffrey L. Rodengen, digital recording, 2 August 2011, Write Stuff Enterprises, LLC.
70. Mark Albright, interview by Jeffrey L. Rodengen, digital recording, 14 September 2010, Write Stuff Enterprises, LLC.
71. Wes Frye, interview by Jeffrey L. Rodengen, digital recording, 12 August 2011, Write Stuff Enterprises, LLC.
72. Marty Freeman, interview by Jeffrey L. Rodengen, digital recording, 2 August 2011, Write Stuff Enterprises, LLC.
73. Terry Hutchins, interview by Jeffrey L. Rodengen, digital recording, 14 July 2010, Write Stuff Enterprises, LLC.
74. Mike Venegoni, interview by Jeffrey L. Rodengen, digital recording, 16 February 2011, Write Stuff Enterprises, LLC.
75. Ibid.
76. Ibid.
77. Ibid.
78. Jack Congdon, interview by Jeffrey L. Rodengen, digital recording, 22 September 2010, Write Stuff Enterprises, LLC.
79. Ibid.
80. Ibid.
81. Ibid.
82. Ibid.
83. Ibid.
84. Karen Dillman interview.
85. Ibid.
86. Wayne Goldston, interview by Jeffrey L. Rodengen, digital recording, 16 September 2010, Write Stuff Enterprises, LLC.
87. Megan Yowell, interview by Jeffrey L. Rodengen, digital recording, 1 October 2010, Write Stuff Enterprises, LLC.
88. John Larkin, interview by Jeffrey L. Rodengen, digital recording, 14 September 2010, Write Stuff Enterprises, LLC.
89. Ed Wolfe interview.
90. Harwood Cochrane, interview by Jeffrey L. Rodengen, digital recording, 22 September 2010, Write Stuff Enterprises, LLC.
91. Ibid.
92. Earl Congdon, *A Conversation With Earl Congdon*, Foundation of Success series, DVD.
93. Ibid.
94. "Logistics Company Heading For Double-Digit Earnings Growth," *Forbes* website, http://www.forbes.com/sites/zacks/2011/08/26/logistics-company-heading-for-double-digit-earnings-growth.

CHAPTER TEN SIDEBAR: The Heart of the Company Passes Away

1. John Yowell, interview by Jeffrey L. Rodengen, digital recording, 12 July 2010, Write Stuff Enterprises, LLC.
2. Ibid.
3. Ibid.
4. Greg Gantt, interview by Jeffrey L. Rodengen, digital recording, 2 August 2011, Write Stuff Enterprises, LLC.
5. Mike Venegoni, interview by Jeffrey L. Rodengen, digital recording, 16 February 2011, Write Stuff Enterprises, LLC.
6. Earl Congdon, interview by Jeffrey L. Rodengen, digital recording, 13 January 2011, Write Stuff Enterprises, LLC.
7. "Volunteers Open Doors for Thousands," *High Point Enterprise* website,

http://www.hpe.com/view/full_story/12906806/article-Volunteers-open-doors-for-thousands-?instance=column_maryBogest.
8. David Carter, interview by Jeffrey L. Rodengen, digital recording, 16 February 2011, Write Stuff Enterprises, LLC.

CHAPTER TEN SIDEBAR: Safety as a Priority

1. Ernie Benge, interview by Jeffrey L. Rodengen, digital recording, 13 July 2010, Write Stuff Enterprises, LLC.
2. Brian Stoddard, interview by Jeffrey L. Rodengen, digital recording, 14 July 2010, Write Stuff Enterprises, LLC.
3. "Old Dominion Makes Iteris Lane Departure Warning Technology Standard Equipment on National Truck Fleet," Business Wire, 9 August 2006.
4. Sam Faucette, interview by Jeffrey L. Rodengen, digital recording, 13 September 2010, Write Stuff Enterprises, LLC.
5. Ibid.
6. Ibid.
7. Ibid.

CHAPTER TEN SIDEBAR: Driver Technology

1. Chris Harrell, interview by Jeffrey L. Rodengen, digital recording, 20 September 2010, Write Stuff Enterprises, LLC.
2. Terry Hutchins, interview by Jeffrey L. Rodengen, digital recording, 14 July 2010, Write Stuff Enterprises, LLC.
3. Ibid.
4. Ken Erdner, interview by Jeffrey L. Rodengen, digital recording, 14 September 2010, Write Stuff Enterprises, LLC.
5. Chris Harrell interview.

INDEX

Page numbers in italics refer to photographs and illustrations.

P

Q

R

S

OLD DOMINION
FREIGHT LINE